LUCKY ME

LUCKY ME

My Life with—and without—
My Mom, Shirley MacLaine

SACHI PARKER
FREDERICK STROPPEL

GOTHAM BOOKS

GOTHAM BOOKS
Published by Penguin Group (USA) Inc.
375 Hudson Street, New York, New York 10014, U.S.A.
Penguin Group (Canada), 90 Eglinton Avenue East, Suite 700, Toronto, Ontario M4P
2Y3, Canada (a division of Pearson Penguin Canada Inc.); Penguin Books Ltd, 80 Strand,
London WC2R 0RL, England; Penguin Ireland, 25 St Stephen's Green, Dublin 2,
Ireland (a division of Penguin Books Ltd); Penguin Group (Australia), 707 Collins Street,
Melbourne, Victoria 3008, Australia (a division of Pearson Australia Group Pty Ltd);
Penguin Books India Pvt Ltd, 11 Community Centre, Panchsheel Park, New Delhi–110
017, India; Penguin Group (NZ), 67 Apollo Drive, Rosedale, Auckland 0632, New
Zealand (a division of Pearson New Zealand Ltd); Penguin Books (South Africa),
Rosebank Office Park, 181 Jan Smuts Avenue, Parktown North 2193, South Africa;
Penguin China, B7 Jiaming Center, 27 East Third Ring Road North, Chaoyang District,
Beijing 100020, China

Penguin Books Ltd, Registered Offices: 80 Strand, London WC2R 0RL, England

Published by Gotham Books, a member of Penguin Group (USA) Inc.

First printing, February 2013
1   3   5   7   9   10   8   6   4   2

LIBRARY OF CONGRESS CATALOGING-IN-PUBLICATION DATA
has been applied for.

ISBN 978-1-592-40788-0

Printed in the United States of America
Set in Bembo
Designed by Spring Hoteling
Insert photographs on pages 2–3 copyright © Look magazine; middle photograph on
page 5 copyright © Getty Images/CBS Photo Archive; middle photograph on page 7
and top photograph on page 8 copyright © Getty Images/Ron Galella Ltd.; all other
photos courtesy of the author.

While the author has made every effort to provide accurate telephone numbers, Internet
addresses, and other contact information at the time of publication, neither the publisher
nor the author assumes any responsibility for errors, or for changes that occur after
publication. Further, the publisher does not have any control over and does not assume
any responsibility for author or third-party websites or their content.

This is a work of nonfiction. However, the names and identifying characteristics of
certain individuals have been changed to protect their privacy, and dialogue has been
reconstructed to the best of the author's recollection.

Penguin is committed to publishing works of quality and integrity.
In that spirit, we are proud to offer this book to our readers;
however, the story, the experiences, and the words
are the author's alone.

To Arin and Frankie

CONTENTS

Pangloss sometimes said to Candide, "There is a concatenation of events in this best of all possible worlds: for if you had not been kicked out of a magnificent castle for love of Miss Cunégonde: if you had not been put into the Inquisition: if you had not walked over America: if you had not stabbéd the Baron: if you had not lost all your sheep from the fine country of El Dorado: then you would not be here eating preserved citrons and pistachio-nuts."

—Voltaire, *Candide*

LUCKY ME

PROLOGUE

M om, is there something going on that I don't know about?"

We were driving back to Malibu. It was a spring afternoon, and we were cruising along the 405, heading up from San Diego. The year was 1982.

Mom had been quiet as usual, deep in her own thoughts. She would point out a scenic highlight here and there: "Isn't that beautiful," she'd say, sighing, with the matter-of-fact serenity of someone who had seen the world several times over and knows all its secrets.

I was thinking, too. There was something on my mind. Something concerning her and Dad. It had been in the back of my head for a long time, much longer than I ever knew, and now suddenly it had rushed forward with startling urgency.

Why I was thinking about the subject at this particular moment, I couldn't say. My life had just come to another one of its dead-end moments: a relationship gone bad, a possible future cut short, everything in turnaround. The new love of my life had turned out to be a disappointment. In fact, he had turned out to be something of a sociopath.

And Mom had driven down the coast to rescue me.

That hadn't been the original plan: I'd invited her down to San Diego ostensibly for the purpose of sharing the exciting news about my engagement to this marvelous man. Privately, however, I knew he wasn't so marvelous. In fact, I knew I was making a big mistake, and I didn't have the strength to walk away from it without help.

Mom, who could spot a bullshit situation a mile away, was just the hero I needed. She stepped into the motel room, sized up my unsavory fiancé in an instant, and said, "Let's get the hell out of here."

So we were on our way back home. It was a two-hour drive up the coast to Malibu, which gave me ample time to ponder the often ridiculously bad decisions I had made in my sputtering romantic life. Over the years, I seemed to have developed this pronounced habit of seeking out, or being sought by, men of a distinctly ugly character. These were not merely the stereotypical selfish boors you saw in sit-coms and beer commercials; no, they were profoundly deceptive, manipulative, and immoral men who would drag me headlong into a series of emotionally damaging, physically compromising relationships. Why was this always happening to me? What had plunged me into this "smart woman, foolish choices" cycle of masochism?

Maybe it was all this dwelling on the dark complexity of relationships that brought me around to my big question: "Mom, is there something going on that I don't know about?"

She looked over at me with a quizzical look, an indulgent smile. "What do you mean?"

"I mean, between you and Dad."

She frowned slightly. The subject didn't appeal to her. It wasn't that she didn't want to talk about Dad; she just couldn't see how he mattered in any present equation.

"Nothing's going on. We're fine."

"I don't mean right now. I mean . . . Well, you know, he's in Japan, and you're here, and you never see each other . . ." They had been living apart for almost thirty years now, on opposite sides of the ocean.

And that was fine with Mom. "It's an excellent arrangement. I recommend it for any marriage." Now, I don't want to suggest that Mom had any hostile feelings toward Dad. She loved him, more than anyone or anything, but she didn't need him by her side every day. Once or twice a year was more than enough.

"No, but . . . I feel like there's something going on, something that you and Dad haven't told me, and it's something really important."

"There's nothing important," she said in a distant voice. Followed by a silence. This meant that there *was* something.

"But I can feel it. It's something really big."

"You're imagining it. You have an overactive imagination, you know that."

I took a deep breath. I was taking a risk now. "I don't believe you."

She didn't answer for a moment. I couldn't read her face—I wasn't sure if she was going to let it drop entirely, or if she was measuring a particularly devastating reply.

Finally she spoke: "I'll tell you when we get home."

So we continued up the San Diego Freeway in silence. Now it

was confirmed—there was *something*—but I would have to wait another two hours for the big reveal. She had a great knack for showmanship.

The suspense was exquisite. What could it be? Would this be one of those life-changing revelations that finally puts the whole world into focus for me? Or would it be a total anticlimax?—"I couldn't deal with your father's snoring." Or, most likely, would she come up with some deft evasion at the last minute?

There was no way to tell with Mom. Something unknowable lurked at her very center. She was constantly coming out with books and magazine interviews promising insights into her inner self, and there were, to be sure, plenty of candid, sometimes shocking details. Oh, she always delivered. Still, like any accomplished magician or striptease artist, the more she revealed, the more she concealed. Just when you thought you had her in your sights, you blinked and she was gone.

So the fact that she might tell me something truly revelatory left me feeling a little uneasy. Did I really want to know this? Was I ready? Should I just have let sleeping dogs lie?

We finally arrived in Malibu, and went up the front walk in silence. Above us loomed the porch-balcony where Mom had had her first encounter with extraterrestrials. According to her, there was a knock on the balcony door, she opened it, and there they were. They didn't stay for long; they were just passing by.

She never told me what they looked like, or what kind of spaceship they had, or how they had come to learn perfect English. Only that, because she was an Enlightened One, the aliens had chosen her as a conduit to relay their messages to the rest of the world.

I never doubted that this had happened. I saw no reason not to believe that there might be life forms on other planets; and if they ever did come to Earth, why wouldn't they look up Mom right off the bat? She was just the type an extraterrestrial would have cozied up to.

Once inside the house, Mom went straight to her study without a word. She opened a closet door; inside, on the floor, was an old brown safe. "What's that?" I asked, but she didn't answer. She was intent on milking every last bit of drama out of this.

She hunched down over the safe and very carefully worked the dial, twisting it back and forth like a professional safecracker. She kept looking back over her shoulder to make sure I wasn't taking note of the combination.

Finally there was a click, and the safe fell open.

Inside was a rectangular tin box, the kind in which you might find cookies at Christmas. Mom held this box in her outstretched arms, as if she were bearing a sacred relic on a pillow. With a nod, she bade me follow her into the bedroom.

She pointed to the bed. I sat down, and she placed the cookie box beside me. She slowly lifted the lid.

Inside the box was a stack of old, yellowed telegrams—some, I saw, dating as far back as 1956.

"Read," she said. "This will explain everything. . . ."

Chapter 1

Humble Beginnings

A *karesansui* is a style of Japanese Zen garden, developed by Buddhist monks. It's a dry or rock garden; there are no flowers, just sand and moss. Traditionally there are fifteen stones in this garden, and they are so carefully arranged that, at any given point in the garden, you can see only fourteen of them. You can never see the fifteenth stone. But you know it's there.

I moved to Japan when I was two years old.

This should be an undisputed fact—it definitely happened. I was there—but through some curious quirk of misinformation (which, oddly, my mom never corrected, and over the years has often encouraged), most sites on the Internet contend that I was six years old when I moved.

This age confusion arose perhaps because my mother shot the film *My Geisha* in Japan in 1962, when I was six, and it may have been assumed that she became so enamored of the country that she left me behind, to soak up the benefits of its extraordinary culture.

But I was already there. I'd arrived in 1959. There's a picture of me stepping off the airplane at Tokyo Airport, and I'm unmistakably a child of two. So that should settle the question.

I went to Japan to live with my father, Steve Parker. He was a businessman-entrepreneur, and he had his operations in Tokyo.

Mom stayed behind in Los Angeles because, well, she was busy. She'd just been nominated for an Academy Award for her performance in *Some Came Running*, and she was getting ready to do Billy Wilder's *The Apartment* with Jack Lemmon. In the meantime she would work on *Can-Can*, the Cole Porter musical, with Frank Sinatra and Maurice Chevalier. It was not a great film, but it had its diversions. Perhaps its most memorable moment came when Soviet premier Nikita Khrushchev visited the set during filming. Mom got to dance the can-can for him, tossing the back of her skirt in his face. He found the spectacle immoral. "Humanity's face is more beautiful than her backside," he stodgily philosophized. I doubt he was singling out my mother in particular, because, at age twenty-four, she looked fabulous from any angle.

In any case, she had a lot on her plate—she was fast becoming a celebrity of the first order—so it was naturally inconceivable that she would give it all up and move to Tokyo with Dad and me. That much I got. But why would she so easily give *me* up? That was more of a mystery. Especially in that prefeminist age, when mothers were supposed to cling to their children with the ferocity of lionesses.

Was I a particularly unmanageable child? I don't think so. On the contrary, we seemed to get on very well together. There was a picture shoot done for *Life* magazine, which showed the two of us, me and Mom, in numerous cavorting and playful poses, including the famous cover shot of us wearing strings of pearls on top of our heads and puffing up our cheeks like blowfish. We were two peas in a pod, a couple of show business hams. The text had Mom expatiating at length on the joys of motherhood: nothing could have prepared her for the sense of fulfillment, the deep well of emotion, and so on and so forth.

Given her parental pride, it was all the more puzzling that she would just have let me go. Obviously, she had great faith in my father's child-rearing abilities, but still, there must have been another reason.

Well, the untold secret story—at least until my mother's Hollywood memoir *My Lucky Stars* was published in 1995—is that I *had* to be taken out of the country, as a safety precaution. Because my freedom—perhaps my life—was in danger.

In those days, Mom was an honorary member of the legendary Rat Pack crew: Sinatra and Dean Martin (her *Some Came Running* costars), Sammy Davis Jr., Peter Lawford—the whole gang. She palled around with them in Las Vegas, and they considered her something of a mascot (as opposed to the women they kept around for decorative and/or amorous purposes). She would perform with them, party with them, and yet somehow retain her popular image as an innocent pixie. It was a great setup—she could enjoy all the fun of the boys' club without being harmed by the negative associations of their freewheeling booze-and-broads lifestyle.

Nevertheless, there was a downside to all this roistering merriment. At some point Mr. Sinatra apparently fell afoul of the Mob—he had crossed somebody somewhere, on a business deal or a singing engagement, or maybe he'd insulted a big shot's wife at a ringside table—and the word was out that payback was coming. One of the rumors circulating was that Shirley MacLaine's daughter was in jeopardy of being kidnapped.

Me—kidnapped! To avert this possibility, I was shipped off to Japan for safekeeping. Mom hated to let me go, but she had to, for my sake. It was a great sacrifice on her part, and in some ways she never recovered. At least that was her version.

I was a little skeptical about this story. After all, the Mob knew where Japan was, if they really wanted to find me. And why Frank Sinatra would have cared whether I was kidnapped was never clear to me. In light of his supercool ring-a-ding-ding philosophy, I can't imagine my abduction would have taken much of a toll on his psyche.

In any event, the threat gradually passed, everything got smoothed over—soon Frank Sinatra was brokering deals between Sam Giancana and JFK, and all was right with the world—but nobody ever thought to bring me back. I lived in Japan for the next ten years, spending only my summers and holidays with Mom in L.A.

MOM and Dad met in New York City in 1952. She says when he walked into the bar on West Forty-Fifth Street, where she and her fellow chorus members from *Me and Juliet* were hanging out, she was immediately taken with his handsome swagger and his charm. He wasn't tall—five nine—so she made the interesting decision to take off her high heels, so she wouldn't be taller than he was. I don't think I've ever seen Mom give ground to anyone. For Steve Parker, though, she willingly made herself smaller.

They chatted, had a few drinks, and he proposed to her that very night. She didn't accept until the next day. Their lives were so hectic, however, that they didn't get around to tying the knot until 1954. They got married between the matinee and the evening performance of *The Pajama Game*, in which she was appearing on Broadway. Norman Vincent Peale officiated at the ceremony.

Mom credited Dad with being the most powerful influence on her life. He was a mentor to her, a motivator, a truth-teller, and a sharer of dreams. He encouraged her ambitions and guided her on her search for self-knowledge.

Perhaps his most significant and lasting contribution was a book he brought to her on the set of *The Trouble with Harry*, her first film. The book was called *A Dweller on Two Planets*. It was written back in the 1880s, by Frederick S. Oliver, and was apparently the forerunner to all those books dealing with New Age mysticism. Oliver claimed to be channeling, through the process of visions and "automatic writing," the words of an ancient spirit named Phylo the Tibetan. Phylo had lived in the city of Atlantis, centuries before, and he had many stories to tell about the advanced Atlantean culture and its parallels to modern life.

The book, written in florid biblical prose, deals with karma and reincarnation, both subjects that would become central to my mother's philosophy. Indeed, she traced her interest in spirituality to *A Dweller on Two Planets*. Why Dad had chosen to give her that particular book was not especially evident, but Mom said he was always an expert at reading people. He could sense what they would respond to; that's what made him such a good businessman.

Soon after this, Mom and Dad moved to Hollywood, but when her career started to take off, so did Dad. He didn't appreciate being known as "Mr. Shirley MacLaine," and he had business back in Japan, so they decided to live apart.

Their separateness, and their understanding that they would have an "open marriage," did not diminish in any sense Mom's love for my father. I would say she loved him as deeply as anyone in her life. Dad was her true soul mate, even though they lived in different countries for almost their entire marriage.

. . .

MY first real memory is of flying across the Pacific Ocean. I can't say for certain if I'm remembering that very first trip or a subsequent flight, because I did shuttle back and forth several times to visit my mom in L.A. (probably stealing into town under cover of dark, so that those darn kidnappers wouldn't notice).

The experience of the flight itself is still very vivid to me. The airline was Northwest Orient, it was a propeller plane, and it took about three days in all. We would make stopovers to refuel on several Pacific islands—Wake, Guam. I remember walking the beach at Wake Island, enjoying the warm ocean breeze, marveling at the exotic seashells, and feeling that I had entered some heavenly realm. There was no sign at all of the horrific toll the war had exacted on these blood-soaked sands just fifteen years earlier.

Then back on the plane. In those days there were beds on the plane, bunk-style, for long flights. They strapped you in with seat belts when you went to sleep. This was also before they had movies on airplanes—which was before they had individual TV screens, which was before they phased everything out so that we're back where we started—so you had to provide your own entertainment.

In my case, that meant singing. I would sing for everybody on the plane. It sounds obnoxious now—if a young child started singing and dancing up the aisles nowadays, you'd have more than one passenger deploying the escape chute. Back in the 1950s, though, it must have seemed charming and wholesome, and emblematic of the best in American youth.

There was no one to stop me from performing, anyway. I was flying alone. Without guardians or chaperones. I'm told I was as brave and stalwart a little traveler as you could wish for. Still, there must have been times when I felt lonely and scared, because I remember one of the stewardesses sitting beside me, cradling me in her arms, and rocking me gently for what may have been hours. It wasn't the last time a complete stranger reached out to rescue me when my own family was nowhere in sight.

I remember finally landing in Japan, my dad waiting on the tarmac for me, in a sharp business suit, with his rakish Clark Gable mustache, looking for all the world like a movie star. No exaggeration—Dad really had that kind of worldly glamour. He was extremely charming, very warm, and a man's man, fond of handshaking and backslapping. And the more he drank (which he did, quite a lot), the more charming he got. Life was a big party for him—and I had just been invited to join it.

I ran up to him now and jumped with delight into his strong arms. I was home! Home in a place where I didn't know a word of the language. Except for my own name, of course. Sachiko.

You might wonder, why did I have a Japanese name if I wasn't actually born in Japan or even of Japanese heritage? Actually, my full name is Stephanie Sachiko Parker. Stephanie is the female version of Steve, my dad's name. And Sachiko . . . Well, Dad had a story about that, which he told me as we drove to his house.

He had been stationed in Japan after the war. Just outside Hiroshima. And there was a little girl who used to hang around right outside the barracks.

She was about two years old, and she was always playing in this empty lot, all by herself. Her clothes were torn and raggedy, she had snot running from her nose, hair all tangled . . . She looked totally uncared-for.

So I asked around, found out she didn't have any family. Both her parents had died from radiation poisoning. From the bomb.

Poor little kid was all alone. So I took her into the barracks, and the boys and I sort of adopted her. She was a little cutie; we all were in love with her. So much so, that it got to the point where I decided to adopt her for real. She was going to be my own daughter. I had all the paperwork going, should have been a cinch . . .

Then she started getting sick, too. Same radiation poisoning. Poor kid. After a while . . . she died . . .

He took a long beat, measuring the silence.

Finally: *Her name was Sachiko.*

When we got home to our house in the Shibuya section of Tokyo, there was a surprise there waiting for me. Her name was Miki.

Miki was Dad's Japanese "friend." His live-in friend, to be precise. She'd been with my dad for many years already, they had become very comfortable together, and she welcomed my addition to the family unit with all the effusive warmth of a reticulated python. The first moment I walked through the door, she fixed me with a cold, silent glare, equal parts jealousy and icy contempt.

Miki and Dad had met many years before, at a teahouse. Teahouses are places in Japan where businessmen go to relax, and be entertained by the geishas. They're not really brothels, as Westerners might imagine. Everything is very proper and civilized. The geishas are treated with the utmost respect. If by chance a spark of interest is struck between two consenting parties, there might be a discreet trip up the staircase, but what went on up there was strictly the business of the participants involved.

The geishas' primary function at a teahouse is to provide companionship, attentiveness, and entertainment. They sing, they dance, they serve drinks, they keep the conversation moving. They're always from very good families, and highly educated—they can usually speak three or four languages. A geisha is classy, sophisticated, and very elegant.

Miki wasn't a geisha. She was a maid. She started working at the teahouse when she was a little girl. Indeed, when Dad first met Miki, she was only twelve years old. This was before the war, when my grandfather, whom I never met, had his shipping business in Japan, and Dad was in his twenties, enjoying the life of a dashing overseas adventurer. Dad became friendly with the young Miki, and then, as she matured, he became friendlier. I don't know when they became lovers, but when Dad moved back to Japan after the war, Miki was waiting for him, and they took up where they'd left off.

Where they'd left off did not include me in the least. The disparity between Dad and Miki's lifestyle and mine was pretty stark. They were always off to fancy restaurants, off to the theater, off to Dad's yacht, off to Dad's private island, off to Hawaii, Italy—just having a hell of a time for themselves.

Mom, it should be noted, knew about Miki. As I said, she and Dad had an open marriage, and were perfectly accepting of each other's affairs. However, Mom believed that that was all it was—an affair, one of my father's little dalliances. She didn't suspect that Miki was, for all intents and purposes, Dad's other wife. The one he had all the fun with.

While Dad and Miki were out playing, I wasn't completely neglected. I had a governess, Eguchi-san, who looked after me and instilled in me all the virtues of Japanese womanhood: meekness, humility, subservience.

Eguchi-san was not an attractive woman, by any means. As I recall her, she looked sort of like a toad—or rather, to give her the eminence she deserved, a bullfrog. She was short, dumpy, hunched, and round-shouldered, and her wrinkled, bumpy face was perfectly consonant with the rest of her amphibious aspect. She was also very old. At least she seemed very old to me.

"Remember, Sachiko-san," she would say, with the wisdom

of the ages rattling around in her creaky voice, "the stake that sticks out will get hammered down." She was fond of these ancient Japanese maxims that encapsulated the whole of life experience in a few well-chosen words.

"A frog in a well knows nothing of the sea."

"If you chase two hares, you will never catch one."

"Never, never gossip about people, or their shadows will follow you forever."

I adored her. She wasn't in any sense warm or cuddly. An extremely traditional and strict governess, she considered all rules sacrosanct and not to be transgressed. This gave me a very deep and precious sense of security. I knew where I stood with her. She never kissed me, never hugged me, but she didn't have to. I knew she loved me.

And I knew she hated Miki. She never said as much, but I could tell. Eguchi-san similarly sensed my unspoken enmity toward Miki, and that cemented a very powerful bond between us.

The trouble was, Eguchi-san was there only during the day, between nine and six. At night, when Dad and Miki were out nightclubbing, I had to fend for myself.

How does a lonely little American girl entertain herself in an empty Tokyo house? Well, I ate lemons. There were always plenty of lemons in the refrigerator, and every night I would eat one, or two. There was something about the pretty yellow color and the lemony smell and the sour taste that was utterly comforting to me. So I ate lemon after lemon after lemon. Years later, whenever I went to the dentist, he would ask me why I had no enamel left on my teeth.

I don't remember what else I did to amuse myself, but I got through the evenings somehow. These weren't unhappy times for me, necessarily, because I didn't know anything else, and I did have some company: our dog, Taiho, a magnificent Akita husky named for a champion sumo wrestler. I adored him, and cuddled with him every night—we needed each other.

I loved Japan, I truly did. I wouldn't have traded my childhood there for anyplace else in the world. It's a land of breathtaking wonder, and quiet serenity. The majesty of the mountains to the north. The spare simplicity of a rock garden. The opulent bursts of cherry blossoms in the spring.

My own home was a magical melding of East and West. The house was ranch-style, and most of the rooms were Westernized. In the living room, there was a raised tatami platform, which I would turn into a stage. I would happily perform for guests, singing and dancing and soaking up their applause. There was also a traditional Japanese bath; my dad loved to soak in it, and I would always have to bring him a sake or scotch to accompany his relaxation.

The backyard of the house was my special place, a dreamlike little world that filled me with enchantment. Each stone and bush, in its size and placement, had meaning. There was a koi pond, stocked with the beautiful expensive fish; some of the koi were almost a hundred years old. A stream flowed down a gentle incline, and in a corner of the yard was a beautiful stone fountain, cut from a boulder, with a bamboo trough feeding the water into the basin, which would fill up and spill over into the stream.

The centerpiece of the yard was a spectacular cherry blossom tree. I would climb that tree up to one particular branch, high above, and sit there for hours and hours, lost in my own world. The stream would be running just below me, and the pond was to my side, where I could look down and see the fish. I don't know what I thought about when I was up there all those hours. I was just there. The tree was my friend. I would talk to it. It was something I could count on.

Eguchi-san took me often to the museums in Tokyo. She was a great lover of the arts, and wanted to introduce me to every aspect of Japanese culture. She would take me anywhere, at any time, in search of an exhibit or a presentation. She taught me how to paint, how to dress, how to arrange flowers. Every moment of life was informed by art. "This is your culture, Sachiko-san," she would say, ignoring the fact that it wasn't my culture at all. "It is who you are."

At the museum, there were watercolors and sumi ink paintings from various periods, some hundreds of years old. We stopped before a landscape, a house beneath a mountain. Eguchi-san pointed out a single brushstroke on the canvas. "That is the difference between beauty and nonbeauty," she declared with great authority.

We came upon another painting, which seemed oddly unfinished—a purplish burst of flowers in one corner, and the rest of the canvas empty.

Eguchi-san sighed with pleasure. "The emptiness is what makes the painting full."

I marveled now at a painting of a cherry blossom tree by a river. Nothing more—simple and elegant. It had been painted some six hundred years before, but was still vibrant with life. "It's so beautiful!"

Eguchi-san studied the plaque beside the painting thoughtfully. "Come. Let's go," she said, taking my hand.

"Where?"

The next thing I knew, we were on a train, heading north into the country. I was hungry, so Eguchi-san took a clementine from her pocket. When I reached for it, she held it back: there was an art to the eating of a clementine, as in all things, and it had to be observed.

Eguchi-san stripped the rind from the clementine, piece by piece, never hurrying. Then she slowly, carefully punctured the inner skin at the top and peeled the fruit down on the sides, so that the sections opened up like a flower. She held out the flowering clementine in the palm of her hand, and I dug into the juicy flesh. Somehow the slow, patient ritual had lent a febrile intensity to the experience. I devoured the clementine in gulps.

We got off the train at a country town, Echigo-Yuzawa. We walked down the road, Eguchi-san hobbling along on her cane unhurriedly. "Eguchi-san," I wondered, "do you know this town? Have you been here before?

"No."

I grew a little worried. "Do you know where we're going?"

She shrugged, as if to say, "No. But yes."

Before long, the road turned along a river. We walked along the river, and as we turned a bend we suddenly came upon it: the scene from the painting. There it was, the very same tableau, everything still there, just as the artist had seen it so long ago—the cherry blossom tree, the blue sky, and the river. All unchanged.

"Six hundred years," said Eguchi-san.

WITHIN three months of arriving in Tokyo, I was speaking Japanese better than I could speak English. In a way, it was my first language. Nevertheless, I felt uncomfortable and out of place at Nishi Machi, the International School that I attended. It may have been because Eguchi-san made me wear seven pairs of brown underpants every day—one on top of the next. This had something to do with her deeply held religious beliefs. It appears that the number seven and the color brown are both considered lucky in certain strains of Shintoism. Still, on hot days, I would have traded some of that luck for a little more ventilation. Using the bathroom was a strategic nightmare.

Nobody actually sells brown underwear. It's probably the one color in underwear you'd like to avoid. So Eguchi-san would have to create brown underwear, by dyeing my white underwear. She'd get a big pot of water, boil it up, and unwrap these cakes of brown dye. I can still hear that crinkly unwrapping sound now—not as glamorous an evocation as Proust's madeleines perhaps, but just as potent. Then Eguchi-san would mix the dye in the water, drop in the pairs of panties—more like granny pants, to be honest—stir the mix, and voilà! Instant nerd wardrobe.

You don't know what self-conscious is until you've walked around school with seven pairs of brown granny pants under your skirt. The slightest gust of wind and I would have had to commit hara-kiri to save face.

I was extremely shy as it was, and I did my best to fit in unobtrusively with the other kids in the class. There was one girl, however, Yuki, who upended this strategy. She was kind of a tough girl, aggressive and self-confident. I just didn't get along with her, and I avoided her as much as I could.

This wasn't easy. Dad and Yuki's mother were acquaintances, and there were many visits between our home and theirs. Somehow it came to be accepted that Yuki and I would be playmates. This arrangement did not come naturally to either of us; it was forced upon us, and we both bridled at the indignity.

In any comparison between Yuki and me, I always came off the worse. Yuki was prettier, Yuki was more confident, Yuki was more athletic. And Yuki was smart. A very good student. I was not. In fact, I was a very bad student.

You could blame the cultural divide, I suppose, but I believe my dad had something to do with it. You know how some parents are overly supportive, filling their kids with overbearing self-confidence? Dad took a different approach. He had a special nick-name for me: the Idiot.

"Here comes the Idiot!" he'd say when I walked in the door. "The Idiot's home!"

He obviously had little respect for my intellect. He would never let me read. I didn't know why; I assumed he just thought it was a waste of time. If he saw me pick up a book, he'd scoff and take it away. My mind wasn't meant for profundity. Everything needed to be kept simple and stupid. I never questioned him.

By now you may have deduced that my dad was a hard man to figure: loving one minute, distant and aloof the next two weeks. I never seemed to be on his radar.

For example, every summer, I'd visit Mom in America and she'd take me on a shopping spree, buying me all kinds of clothes for the school year. I'd look great in September.

By February, I'd grow out of everything, and nothing would fit anymore—my skirts, my shoes, nothing. I desperately needed new clothes, but Dad wouldn't buy me any. "I can't afford it," he'd say. He could afford anything for Miki—fur coats, evening gowns, expensive jewelry—but my needs would have to wait till next summer. It was almost as if he didn't see me.

Yet . . .

There were times when he made me his whole world. Dad loved to cook, and he would keep me at his side in the kitchen while he threw together an improvised gourmet meal. He loved to cele-brate the sensory aspect of cooking. He had a little herb garden by the window, and he would take a sprig of thyme or tarragon and crush it between his thick fingers, and he would say, "Smell! Smell!" I would smell, and I would smell some more, until it infringed on his sacred cooking schedule. "It's time to throw it in the pot! Now! Now!" I'd toss in the herbs, and feel as though I'd made an important contribution.

After the food had been cooking awhile, he'd hold out a ladle to me: "Sach, taste this. What does it need?" I had no idea, but I was thrilled that he seemed to value my opinion. I would make some kind of guess—"Rosemary?"—and he'd say, "Let's try it!" And it usually worked.

When dinner was ready, we'd sit on the floor, Japanese-style, and he'd savor his glass of hundred-year-old wine—Dad always insisted on having the best—and all would be very right with the world. . . .

My father and I would make a fishing trip a few times a year, just the two of us. This made it very special to me; these are some of my favorite memories with him. I seldom had Dad to myself without Miki glowering over his shoulder, like a demon in a Japanese woodcut, but here it would be just us, the fish, and the wilderness.

The train ride into the Japan Alps would take about eight hours. We would head way up north, near Hokkaido. It was an endless but exciting journey. About three-quarters of the way up, after riding through miles and miles of ordinary countryside, we would enter a tunnel—a magic tunnel, I always thought—which seemed to go on forever, and after chugging through it for maybe half an hour, we would suddenly emerge into a different world: a spectacular ice-covered fantasyland, with ten-foot-tall drifts and little fairy-tale houses half-buried in snow. And silence. A silence so pure and complete you couldn't even hear the train engine anymore. It was as if the snow were swallowing the sound. I took that journey through the magic tunnel many times, and every time, the stunning moment of emergence took my breath away.

It was usually dark by the time we got to the mountains, and sometimes we'd stay at the Kanaya Hotel, which was an ultra-first-class hotel, old and venerable (meaning creaky), with huge ballrooms and winding staircases. Here the royalty and visiting heads of state would take their leisure, and the cream of Japanese high society would gather in their Western tuxedoes and floor-length gowns to fox-trot and tango the night away.

Other times, Dad would just start up the Jeep and we'd head off into the mountains in the dark. We'd go up as far as we could, and when the roads became impassable, we'd strap on snowshoes and backpacks and continue on foot, navigating by moonlight until we reached the frozen crater lake at the top of the mountain. We'd pitch a tent on the side of the mountain, on the most level ground we could find, and camp out there for two or three nights. It was absolutely freezing, sleeping on top of the snow, but we wore thick woolen sweaters suffused with natural lanolin oil; they had a powerfully rancid stench to them, but they kept us warm. Exhausted, I would fall right to sleep, albeit slightly terrified that we might slide off the mountain in the middle of the night.

Dad would wake me up at 4:00 A.M., and we'd hustle out onto the frozen lake. The first order of business was to cut a hole in the foot-thick ice. Using a long ice pick, Dad would chip away at the ice with methodical ferocity. In the meantime, I'd go into the nearby woods to gather sticks and logs for a fire. When I got back, he'd still be chipping away, until finally a circle of ice dropped with a satisfying splash into the water.

Next, Dad would build a fire on the ice. Once the wood was blazing, he'd scoop water out of the ice hole with a small coffeepot. He'd boil the water, simmer it, toss coffee grounds into the pot, stir it up, let the grounds settle, and then drink straight from the pot. He called it cowboy coffee. It was especially good, he said, when sweetened with a dollop of whiskey from his hip flask.

Time to catch breakfast! Dad would grab his fishing pole and squat alongside the ice hole. The morning was the best time to catch trout, when the fish were hungry. And he would catch them—fish after fish after fish. His delight would grow with each catch. This, I think, was when he was happiest, when he was truly in his element. In his heart of hearts, he probably wanted to be Hemingway.

Laying his pole aside, he'd pick out one lucky fish for breakfast and slap it down by the fire. I'd watch, horrified and yet fascinated, as the trout flopped around on the ice, gasping and thrashing. I was so relieved when it finally died.

Dad would scale the trout with a Swiss army knife and then rub rock salt into the skin of the fish. He'd always use gourmet rock salt from France—nothing but the best. The salted fish would go directly on the fire, and cook through. "Hot, hot," Dad would say, gingerly peeling the meat from the trout and handing it to me, having carefully picked out the bones first. And we'd eat, and it would be delicious.

Then we would go back to the tent and sit. For the most part, we wouldn't speak to each other. Dad would read a book. I wouldn't, since Dad didn't like it when I read books. So I just sat.

Then he might put the book down and start telling a story of his adventures. He would tell me about his travels in Cambodia, and the ancient village of Angkor Wat, and his friend Prince Sihanouk. Then he would drift off, and there would follow maybe three hours of silence, and then he'd start up again, reminiscing about Turkey or maybe a trip he took to Siberia. Vivid, fantastic stories.

That was how it went for the rest of the day, until darkness fell.

Little bursts of talk, long silences the rule. I found myself mostly bored, eager for him to put down his book and start another tale. The days were alternately fascinating and excruciating.

Those mornings, though—those frozen mornings of icy mountain air and coffee smells and salty fish—they were quite wonderful.

On New Year's Eve, Dad, Miki, and I went up there and stayed at the Kanaya Hotel together. There was an old shrine, a relic from the Tokugawa era, at the top of the mountain, and it was a tradition to climb up through the snow at midnight to ring in the new year. Paths were cut through the five-foot drifts, and I would have to make my way up the steep snow wearing my special New Year's outfit, made of layers of thin silk and sashes and topped with a thick silk kimono with a beautiful flower print, an obi (a wide band around the waist woven with strands of gold), and the ceremonial shoes (called geta) with ornate thongs and three-inch bamboo clog soles.

At the top there would be an open-air market, and the vendors, batting their sides with their mittened hands for warmth in the subzero temperatures, would sell barbecued burnt corn, barbecued octopus, and oden, a special soup made with marinated fish cakes, potatoes, and seaweed.

You would buy a wish for the new year, in the form of a ribbon, from the shrine priest, and then tie the ribbon to a tree branch, and the wish would always come true. At midnight, they would ring the massive ten-foot-wide bronze bell, and it would peal out for miles. I would clap my hands over my ears to keep my brain from vibrating. The next morning, we'd have a classic New Year's Day breakfast at the hotel: raw octopus, cinnamon toast, and English tea.

It would be nice to claim that these were moments of life-shaking import for me, moments for epiphanies that elevated my relationship with my dad to a new level of intimacy—but they weren't. Mere isolated glimpses of warmth and affection, they were far outnumbered by days and weeks of neglect, when Miki held a far more important place in my father's heart.

The word they use now is *disconnect*. Nothing seemed to add up with my dad. He could be overly controlling, and yet profoundly indifferent. Sometimes he valued my opinion; more often he branded me an idiot. He had a particular brilliance for keeping me off-balance. I never knew where I stood. My tent was pitched on the side of a mountain.

So why? Still that big confounding question. Why was I in Japan? Why did my father bring me halfway across the world just to ignore me? What was the point?

Well, Dad was a very clever man—you might call him an operator—and there was *always* a point. But it was very well hidden, and it took me a long time to find it.

CHAPTER 2

Of Mockingbirds and Fox Gods

On those few occasions when they stayed at home, Dad and Miki had an amusing little game they liked to play. If the phone would ring from America, they would react in mock horror:

"The Dragon Lady is calling!"—the Dragon Lady being my mom—"It's the Dragon Lady again!"

I could tell they were doing this partially for my benefit, and I wasn't exactly sure why, but since they were feeding me and tending to my general well-being, my sense of self-preservation advised me to join in the conspiracy. "Oh, no, it's the Dragon Lady!" I'd shriek, shrinking from the phone in dismay.

Clearly I was meant to regard Mom with a mixture of terror and amused condescension. She was this comical gargoyle across the sea, fearsome and terrible but safely tucked in some subterranean cave far away.

Still, I loved her, and whenever I visited her, Mom didn't seem so bad. In fact, she was a lot of fun.

It started at the airport in Los Angeles, always a big production number, with Mom rushing up to me at the gate and giving me a big, all-encompassing hug. "Oooh, I missed you so much! Look how you've grown!" We'd walk through the airport holding hands, swinging them back and forth joyously. Once we got into the car, she'd say, "Okay, let's have some fun!"

And we did.

She loved taking me shopping for my school clothes. Or going to the movies. Or walking along the beach.

I remember wandering the Malibu beach for hours with her, staring at tide pools. She would pick out a little sea urchin and poke it with her finger, and it would curl around her finger, and she would shriek every time. It always surprised her.

After a long walk on the beach, we would stop on the way home at Wil Wright's ice-cream shop in Encino. We'd go there practically every day—Mom was a real ice-cream junkie—and she would take a tactile joy in gulping down a hot fudge sundae. You know how kids can mysteriously manage to smear chocolate all over their faces when they eat, almost in defiance of the laws of physics? That was Mom. She'd look up and smile at me with a naughty glee, her teeth a dark, gooey mess.

Sometimes we'd head down to the local Piggly Wiggly and eat free cookies from the bakery section. They weren't supposed to be free, mind you, but Mom had no qualms about stepping around the counter and grabbing a cookie from the tray. If she really liked it, she might buy a bag to take home, but otherwise, she'd eat her fill and move on. No one stopped her; she was a celebrity, after all.

There were also times we would just hang around her Encino home and play games and eat popcorn and other goodies. She used to make the best open-face peanut butter and jelly sandwiches in the world. She'd take two slices of white Wonder bread—we didn't have Wonder bread in Japan; we didn't have bread in Japan—and spread Skippy chunky peanut butter on top. Then she would make little craters in the peanut butter with a spoon and fill them with pools of jelly. Absolute heaven.

Whenever there was a thunderstorm at night, Mom would let me climb into her king-size bed. Then she'd sweep open the blue velvet curtains on her full-length windows, revealing a spectacular view of the San Fernando Valley. Having set the scene, she'd scamper back to the bed and jump under the covers, and we'd huddle together and watch the storm march across the valley.

She would tell me the tale of the Lightning Princess. I don't know where this story came from—I think she made it up—but she would tell it with such verve and wonder, calling upon all her acting talents, that it would spring to life in front of me. I think that's where I first began to understand the magic of storytelling:

Once upon a time, she'd begin, with such relish that you could see just how much she had missed the joy of telling her only daughter a bedtime story every night, of recounting the wondrous tales of Jack and the Beanstalk and Little Red Riding Hood and Hansel and Gretel:

Once upon a time, there was a beautiful princess, who lived on top of the tallest mountain in the world. And she was known as Princess Lightning. Because when she was happy she would laugh a merry laugh, and a great flash of lightning would flood the sky!

But when she was mad, a dark scowl would come over her face, and then the lightning would come screaming out of the sky in a jagged bolt of terror. Zap!

Now, whenever a storm came across the valley, the mighty Princes of Thunder, who were all in love with the princess, would call her name from the dark clouds, and they would ask her for a kiss, because she was so beautiful. "Kiss me, please, O Princess Lightning!" they would plead.

But she never would. Sometimes she would laugh, and blind them with a joyous flash of lightning, and sometimes she would screw her face up with fury and just chase them off with a crackling bolt! Zap zap zap! So when you hear the thunder rumble after the lightning, that's the princes rolling away in fear. For no one could ever capture the heart of the feisty, independent princess. (Even then, my mom was grooming me for the feminist revolution.)

Then a burst of lightning would brighten the sky, and Mom would squeal with delight. "Look, she's laughing! She's laughing!" And we would both cover our ears to protect them from the princes' doleful thunder. And I would feel so safe with her.

IN the early 1960s, my mother was sitting on top of the show business world: she was a major actress, a knockout entertainer, and an international celebrity. In short, a star. While she'd had her first successes in the late 1950s, it was *The Apartment* that put her on the map and made her a force to be reckoned with. She was nominated for an Academy Award for the second time, and she deserved to win.

"I would have, too," she insisted, "if Elizabeth Taylor hadn't had a tracheotomy."

Liz Taylor had made a splash that year by playing a call girl in *Butterfield 8*, an okay but not great film. Her performance was worthy of a nomination, but she wasn't really expected to win—until she came down with a serious case of pneumonia that required emergency surgery. The wave of industry sympathy that followed pushed her over the top, and she went home with the Oscar instead of Mom.

This may have been a blessing in disguise. Mom managed to

avoid the dreaded Oscar jinx and go on to a career of memorable films. Elizabeth Taylor, by contrast, became a full-time celebrity, and never really approached the level of creativity she enjoyed before *Butterfield 8*. (She did have a great Oscar-winning success with *Who's Afraid of Virginia Woolf?*, of course, but that movie is a lonely giant among turkeys such as *Cleopatra*, *The V.I.P.s*, *Boom!*, and so on.)

Mom, on the other hand, kept moving from peak to peak, because she stayed hungry. Without that ultimate industry recognition, she had something to shoot for, and she kept shooting. Maybe, with her ferocious inner drive, it wouldn't have made any difference; or maybe, having won the top award, she might have slowed down a little and spent more time with her family. Who knows?

The short-term benefit for me was that I got to hang out on her movie sets, and that was like heaven. For a young child, wandering through that make-believe world filled with music and lights and odd but endearing characters, it was as close to being in Fantasyland as you could get.

"Hellooo, Sachi!" everyone on the crew would cry; they made the biggest fuss over me, because I was so damned cute, and also because I was the star's daughter. The makeup artists would put all kinds of makeup on me, the costumers would dress me in little doll outfits . . . I was the Little Princess, and the movie set was my kingdom. It was like being in a cocoon; a safe, comforting, warm place where nothing bad could ever happen.

A lot of good was happening on the set of *Two for the Seesaw* for Mom. Along with nabbing a juicy part as a Greenwich Village kook and working with Oscar-winning director Robert Wise, she was carrying on a pretty steamy romance with her costar, Robert Mitchum. Nobody knew it at the time, of course, and I certainly didn't pick up on it on my brief visits to the set. I would see Mr. Mitchum shambling about during the shoot, and to me he was just a big guy with sleepy eyes and a gruff, gravelly voice. The possibility that there were any personal sparks between him and my mother never crossed my mind, but then again, why would it? I was just a kid. According to her, however, their relationship was deep and intense, lasted a good three years, and featured sexual assignations all over the world. The image of the languid Mr. Mitchum hopping on a plane to meet my mother in a hotel in East Africa for some hanky-panky seems a little odd, but she says it happened.

Mom has publicly stated that she and Dad had an open marriage; both were free to pursue outside relationships, without disturbing the essential and all-important love between them. I was never quite sure how this worked, at least in the early days, because Mom always kept her affairs pretty quiet. (In those days, there *was* such a thing as bad publicity.) She claims that she told Dad about the Mitchum affair, in the spirit of openness, but I don't know how true that is. I do know that Dad kept his very serious relationship with Miki a secret from Mom for some thirty years. I guess he was allowed to see other women as long as there wasn't One Other Woman.

The atmosphere on the set of *Irma La Douce* was markedly different. Mom was playing a lady who wore a very tight dress, and her costar, Jack Lemmon, played a policeman with a funny hat. I had no idea what the risqué situations and sophisticated repartee were supposed to represent, but the two of them seemed to be having a great time. Maybe that was because there was no romance between them; Mom always said that Jack Lemmon was a sweetheart, a really nice guy—and that wasn't her type at all. So they became very good friends, and remained that way.

There were stars galore roaming the sets and visiting our house in those early days. Mom was working on movies with Dean Martin, Audrey Hepburn, Cliff Robertson, Laurence Harvey; her friends included Danny Kaye and the Rat Pack regulars. For me, though, there was one young star who stood out from the rest.

He was young, impossibly handsome, outrageously charming, and possessed of an ineffable aura. When he walked into the room, it was like getting hit with a charge of electricity.

"Say hello to Warren!" said Mom.

Warren was my uncle. He was three years younger than Mom, and he had followed her to Hollywood. Both of them had fled from the suffocation of their Virginia home. My grandparents were devout Baptists, and devout alcoholics—not really a workable combination. I never heard much of the details of Mom's childhood—she didn't talk about it—but I know there was a lot of unhappiness and emotional pain there, and she couldn't wait to get out.

I assume Uncle Warren felt the same way. I'd met him before of course, on earlier trips home. He'd been trying to get a foothold in show business for years, appearing on TV shows such as *Dobie Gillis* and *Playhouse 90*. So far, breakout success had eluded him.

But now was his time. There was something new in his manner, a self-awareness, a recognition of his own impending stardom, that made him irresistibly attractive and yet warned all to keep their distance. *Splendor in the Grass*, his first film, was about to hit the screens, and there was a healthy buzz about his performance. Even if there hadn't been, Warren would have created his own buzz. The air vibrated around him.

In many ways, Warren was still a kid, but curiously he didn't have any special knack for relating to children. They didn't seem to interest him at all, until they got to be twenty or so. I never saw him without a beautiful woman at his side, or two or three. He accepted their presence as his due, wearing them on his arm as casually and inevitably as a folded sports jacket on a warm day.

I admit, as a little girl I had a big crush on him. Who didn't? I never thought of him as my uncle, or as someone related to me in any way. He was a separate force, a seductive charmer who could put anyone under his spell with a glance, and just as quickly and ruthlessly cut that person adrift.

I felt the pull of that magnetism even as a child, but I didn't rush to him and throw my arms around his strong legs. Even though he flashed his killer smile at me and his eyes sparkled with promise, there was something about him that said, "Don't come too close." So I didn't.

IN 1961 they were holding auditions for the movie version of *To Kill a Mockingbird*. The book by Harper Lee had been a huge bestseller, and everyone was expecting the movie version to be an Oscar contender at year's end. So every actor in Hollywood wanted in. Gregory Peck was chosen for the role of Atticus Finch early on—there really was no other choice—but other juicy roles were still available, including the two children through whose point of view the story was told.

Out of the blue, Mom decided that I should audition for the role of Scout, Atticus Finch's daughter. I don't know where she got this idea; it's not like I was campaigning to be a child actress. While I had no shyness about performing in front of people— there were plenty of staged photo shoots with me and Mom attesting to the fact—it just never occurred to me that I might become an actor.

Mom had conceived a vision, though, and once she shifted into producing gear, there was no way she wasn't going to make it happen. She set up an audition right there at her L.A. home, got hold of a copy of the script a few days before, and we went over the entire story, moment by moment. Mom coached me in doing a Southern accent—"but not *too* Southern," she cautioned—and she created the scene for me in detail, giving me hints about motivation, focus, presence, and so on. It was my first master class in acting, and I tried to absorb what I could. Then she added, "Just relax."

When the time came, she called me into the living room, which was filled with people from the production, including the director, Robert Mulligan; the producer, Alan J. Pakula; and the leading man, Gregory Peck. Now, if I'd known what a big star Mr. Peck already was, and what an iconic figure he was about to become on the strength of this movie, I probably would have quickly thrown up and rushed out of the room. But to me he was just a nice tall man with a warm smile. I didn't feel a bit nervous in his august company. I was just going to do a little pretending.

Mom handed me the script, and I found my mark in the middle of the living room and got into character. "Hey, Mr. Cunningham!" I said, reading from the script, making sure not to hold it in front of my face as Mom warned. "Don't you remember me, Mr. Cunningham? I'm Jean Louise Finch. You brought us some hickory nuts one early morning, remember?"

It went well. Even at six years old, I could tell that I'd won over the crowd. Everyone was full of compliments. I can still see Gregory Peck smiling at me paternally, his eyes all crinkled up. Mom was beaming, in her underplayed way. "She's good, isn't she? My daughter."

There was a lot of animated good feeling as the showbiz people filed out, and I was pretty excited about my prospects. "I did it, Mommy, didn't I? When are we making the film? Am I gonna get paid a lot of money? Will I have to leave school?"

Mom scoffed lightly, and then she assumed what she must have imagined was a gentle tone. "You know, Sachi, you're not gonna get the part."

My high spirits took a quick plunge. "I'm not?"

"Of course not. First of all, you're too young for the part. Second of all, who do you think you are, Shirley Temple? This was just for the experience. I wanted you to learn how to handle rejection."

Oh.

As it turns out, I didn't get to process this valuable lesson right away, because, against all odds and my mother's casual pessimism, they actually offered me the part, but Eguchi-san, who'd come along on the trip, protested the whole idea; she contended that it would be too traumatizing for me—a mere child, Japanese-raised, meek and humble as I was—to be suddenly thrust into the glare and the insanity of Hollywood. It could scar me for life. My mother put up a token argument, but in the end she reluctantly agreed with Eguchi-san.

So I stepped aside. The role moved on to Mary Badham, who was wonderful in the film, and it's now hard to imagine anyone else having played the part.

The summer of 1961 over, Eguchi-san and I went back to Japan, but this time with an added bonus: Mom was coming with us. She was doing a film called *My Geisha*, shooting on location in Tokyo. The producer of the film was none other than my own dad, Steve Parker. This was his big bid to be a player in Hollywood. The plot was a typically flimsy 1960s comedy, with my mom playing an American actress who pretends to be a geisha so that she can land a role in a movie being directed by her husband (a vague echo of my parents' own situation).

I was thrilled to have Mom with me in Japan. She stayed with us at our Tokyo home throughout the shoot (while Miki repaired discreetly to the separate house that Dad had bought for her), and it was so exciting to come home from school every day and find her waiting for me. I had been accustomed to spending every day after school horseback riding—my great passion—but I tossed it over happily for the chance of having that much more time with her.

Mom was more thrilled, I think, to be with Yves Montand, her costar, with whom she was having an affair during the shoot. Montand was married at the time, to the imposing Simone Signoret, but it must have seemed even more imposing that Dad was sitting right there in the producer's chair. (Although I'm not sure how much time Dad logged on the actual set, or if he paid even cursory attention to the production. Dad was a wheeler-dealer; and once those wheels and deals were set in motion, he was on to the next challenge.)

Yves Montand had just ended an affair with Marilyn Monroe, and apparently had been an utter cad about it—when she waited outside his airplane in a limousine with champagne, he nonchalantly ignored her. Mom, for all her tough-minded independence, always seemed to find this type of selfish bounder irresistible.

She and Montand bonded in Tokyo, she says in one of her books, because of their both being stranded in an exotic, unfamiliar world—although he had earlier toured Japan with his one-man show, and Mom had been over to Tokyo several times with Dad.

Near the end of the shoot, she discovered that Montand had actually romanced her in response to a wager with my dad. In true Gallic spirit, he'd bet Dad that he could seduce Mom before the shoot was over—and he'd won handily. In a sense, so did Dad; with Mom occupied with Montand, he was free to conduct his own romantic affairs without worry. It was all very French.

It's interesting in retrospect to view the film's opening credits: "Shirley MacLaine—Yves Montand—in Steve Parker's *My Geisha*." Dad had really earned his producer credit: he not only produced the film, but he also produced the affair. (How my father, who had never produced a film before, managed to wangle an above-the-title credit, as if he were David O. Selznick, I'll never know, but it doesn't surprise me in the least.)

Eventually the movie ended, the affair ended, and Mom went home—to L.A. It caught me by surprise, because I had forgotten that her home wasn't my home. I'd really bonded with her in those few months. She was living with us at the house, and it was a real treat to see Mom and Dad together. Watching them interacting, smiling at each other, holding hands, I got a sense of what normal family life could be like. Once, I walked in on them in the bedroom to find them spooning in bed. I quickly backed out to give them their privacy, but it gave me a warming glimpse into the sweetness of their intimacy. (I didn't know she was enjoying the same kind of intimacy with Mr. Montand, of course.)

Mom found great peace, I think, in Japan. She used to stare at the koi pond in the backyard for what seemed like hours. I loved watching her be so calm. I can remember Dad cooking, and taking great joy in preparing a meal for her, and then all of us sitting down together. It was perhaps the last time we were an actual family.

I loved those days, and having Mom with me. I thought she'd be there forever.

After she left, I returned to my old routine: school and horseback riding and Eguchi-san during the day, lemons and loneliness at night.

On some special occasions, Dad and Miki would take me out to a fancy nightclub. This afforded me a rare glimpse into the sophisticated world of "adults." Dad and Miki would dress to the nines, I would get dolled up in my Sunday best, and we'd hail a cab and sweep up to the nightclub entrance. The doorman would open the car door for us, and we'd strut up the carpet and into another world.

The nightclubs of Tokyo in the 1960s were not much different from their American models. The music was Western and jazzy, the women beautiful, the atmosphere smoky. Cocktails flowed, jewelry flashed, dancers whirled around the floor.

When Dad stepped through the front door, everything seemed to stop. He commanded the room. He was that guy in the movies who, when he suddenly made an entrance, the maître'd would imperiously snap his fingers, the waiters would rush to seat him, and a special table would be placed ringside just for him. Everybody knew Steve Parker. He'd thread through the tables, cigarette in hand, waving and glad-handing. Dad seemed to be connected everywhere; he was the Man.

We'd take our seats, drinks would be ordered, and the entertainment would begin. There were always famous performers appearing at these nightclubs, and they all knew my father. The girl singers would often flirt with him, and sit on his lap between numbers. Miki didn't seem to mind; it was all in the spirit of fun and good times, and she loved being part of it.

One night Dad took me alone to a different kind of nightclub, off the main drag. It was a small upstairs space like a living room, where everyone sat in armchairs and the atmosphere was cozy and warm. I remember the food was wonderful—little appetizers, garlic cloves pan-fried in sesame oil, super-light tempura, salted squid in squid guts. I also remember that there were no female customers, only men. And the waiters, also male, were completely naked. This afforded them the opportunity to perform a unique service;

whenever Dad ordered a scotch and soda, the waiter would hold the drink crotch-high and stir it gently with his penis before serving. I was fascinated. Did this improve the flavor? I wondered. The waiters would perform this function only with cold drinks, of course; the hot sake might have caused some discomfort. And exceptions were made: I remember when the waiter brought me a Shirley Temple, my dad put up a restraining hand—no dick for my daughter, please. I appreciated his delicacy.

This foray into the exotic world of private clubs was kind of fun, but for the most part the nightclub scene left me terminally bored. Oh, it was exciting at first, just being in the middle of all that grown-up energy, but to have to sit there for hours, watching them drink, was crushingly wearisome. Often these were school nights, and I longed to be in bed so I wouldn't drift off to sleep in class the next day. I remember that everyone in these nightclubs smoked cigarettes—everyone; the thick smoke hanging in the air was overwhelming, and it burned my eyes. I would beg for some coffee ice cream, just so I could stay awake.

Still, I knew there was supposed to be something cool about all this. It was cool that I was just seven or eight years old, cool that Dad was exposing me to this elegant lifestyle, cool that I was taking it all in with the aplomb of a seasoned jet-setter. When all these strange women showered my father with kisses and wiggled their bottoms in his lap and pressed their surging breasts against his cheek, I was supposed to be not only okay with this, but enthusiastic and delighted.

Eguchi-san was not so cool. She was outraged. It was scandalous! Irresponsible! Dragging a young schoolgirl out to these sinful fleshpots on a school night! "I would expect as much from that Miki; she is just a teahouse servant. But what can your father be thinking?"

That was, in a way, the essential question. What *was* my father thinking?

I loved my dad, and I lived in terror of him. He was mercurial and moody, and his constant drinking made him unpredictable. Two incidents stick out in my mind from those preadolescent days. One was the Cream Puff Incident.

Cream Puffs were something of a delicacy in Japan. As with Wonder bread, there was no fresh dairy of any kind in the country. No butter, no cheese. We had to drink powdered milk.

Obviously, in a world without cream, you're not going to find cream puffs. At least not cheaply. Yet Dad loved them, and he usually got what he wanted, so he would often buy fancy gourmet cream puffs at the market.

Or he would make them himself. One afternoon, just for his own pleasure, he whipped up a batch of delicious cream puffs in his kitchen. He took round pastry shells, stuffed them with custard, and topped each with a big dollop of whipped cream. It was a very extravagant whim.

The finished cream puffs were sitting on the kitchen table when I wandered in later. There were about eight of them on the plate, and they looked absolutely delicious. I knew there was no dinner party scheduled for that night; no one was coming over to enjoy these scrumptious treats. That being the case, why not eat one? Or two?

At the most, I had three. There were still about five left.

About an hour or so later, as I sat in the living room, Dad entered. He stood in the doorway a moment. I didn't look up, but I knew he was there—and I knew why he had come.

After a studied pause, he said thoughtfully, "I wonder what happened to the cream puffs."

I stiffened. I knew enough not to answer him.

"I know there were more than five," he contended. "What could have happened to the rest of them?"

While it seemed that he was being facetious, there was nothing playful in his voice. There was rather an undertone of bottled rage, as though he were a Mob boss brandishing a baseball bat and wondering where his split of the cash was.

He waited. I waited. He sat down and stared at me. I knew he was accusing me, but he wasn't going to come out and say it. He wanted to make a game out of it.

"They couldn't have just disappeared," he went on. Then he gasped, as if a thought had just struck him: "Maybe someone came into the house and took them!" He let that hang in the air a moment. "Do you think that's what happened?"

Seeing an opening, I jumped at it. "Yes, Daddy, I think someone may have done that."

He leaned forward eagerly. "Did you see him?"

"Y-yes."

"Did he come in the front door or the back door?"

I sensed that I was stepping into a trap, so I shrugged weakly and said nothing.

Dad was thoughtful. "Maybe it was a neighbor. Did it look like a neighbor?"

"Maybe."

Dad frowned. "But why would a neighbor come into the house without knocking and take three cream puffs? No, that can't be right." He pondered anew. "Did I miscount? Maybe I made only five cream puffs to begin with."

Again I leaped at the suggestion. "I think you're right, Daddy. There *were* only five."

He pursed his lips, and furrowed his brow. "But why would I

make only five cream puffs? No, I'm pretty sure I made eight. I'm pretty sure." He stared at me again.

This went on and on. He kept throwing out possibilities and suggestions, and I kept lying to validate them, and then he would pull them back from consideration. He was toying with me, manipulating me, and I knew it, and it was driving me crazy!

Finally I cracked. "It was *me*, Daddy! *I* did it! *I* ate the cream puffs!" I broke down in tears as I blubbered out my confession.

Now, you might think that, at this point, Dad's face would have broken into a warm smile and he would have patted me on the head and said, "I know, sweetheart. I know you ate the cream puffs. I just wanted you to tell the truth."

But he didn't. His stare became only more fixed. "You did it?" he said in a voice of quiet outrage. "*You* did it? That's *horrible*. Why would you do something like that?"

I had no answer. "I don't know. I'm sorry."

"You're sorry? If you were sorry, you wouldn't have eaten the cream puffs in the first place, would you? They weren't your cream puffs, were they? Were they?"

"No."

"Then why did you eat them? Why would you do something as awful as that? And then lie to me about it? Are you a *liar*, is that what you are?"

He went on and on in this merciless vein, grinding me down relentlessly. Then he closed his eyes, shook his head, ran his tongue along the rim of his upper lip, and sighed sadly, as if his disappointment in me were bottomless.

As for me, I couldn't stop crying. Yet, all the while, I kept thinking, *They're only cream puffs!*

From that point on, though, I was terrified of eating anything in that house.

This episode of bullying manipulation, trivial though it seems, served as a necessary prelude to the Retainer Incident.

When I was nine years old, I had a retainer instead of braces on my teeth. One day, I took out the retainer—I don't remember why—and I lost it. This is the kind of thing that happens naturally to nine-year-olds.

Dad didn't see it that way.

"Do you know how much those things *cost*?" he thundered. "How could you lose something so *important*? Why couldn't you just keep it in your mouth? What's *wrong* with you? *Idiot!*"

It was only with the greatest reluctance that he bought me a new retainer; and he made it crystal clear that I'd better not lose this one. Ever.

So I promised myself I wouldn't.

A few months later, Eguchi-san and I were on a pilgrimage to her family home in the country. She wanted to visit her private shrine.

It was fairly typical for middle-class families in Japan to have shrines on their grounds. They're small and simple, but in their own way they are quite ornate, all red and gold. Eguchi-san had brought me to her family's shrine many times before. Her not-so-hidden agenda was someday to see me embrace the Shinto religion.

I was not brought up in any religion (which might strike one as odd, considering my mom's very public engagement with all things spiritual). Not Christianity, Buddhism, pantheism, not even atheism. I was a blank slate. Eguchi-san saw in me a golden opportunity for conversion; she would have given anything to lure me into the fold.

So she regularly brought me to the shrine, hoping for my eventual enlightenment. She must have thought I'd be filled with a sacred awe by those huge fox god statues flanking the shrine door. Actually, they scared the hell out of me.

Her family home and its shrine were about five miles away, and since we were walking, we had to get an early start. We were fairly close by noon, but as we were getting peckish, we stopped at a sushi bar for lunch.

I didn't want to get all that chewy fish stuck in my new retainer, so I carefully took it out, wrapped it up in tissue for safekeeping, and put it right by my side. I never let it out of my sight.

Well, I guess I *did* let it out of my sight, because when I finished lunch, I turned around to find it gone.

Gone! The retainer, the tissue paper, everything!

I was stunned, and my panic level went from zero to sixty in a nanosecond. Suddenly the image of my father, red-faced with rage, loomed before me. "You lost your retainer? AGAIN?"

I was frantic. Where could it be? Was it on the floor? Had I put it in my pocket? I raced around the restaurant, checking under every plate and napkin. Could someone have walked off with it? But who would steal another person's retainer? No, it had to be here somewhere. It had to!

Coming up empty in the dining room, I rushed into the kitchen itself, and there I spotted a large barrel of garbage, filled to the brim with fish heads, fish bones, and various chunks of fish innards—it was really disgusting. Instantly I knew that my retainer was in there somewhere. Without hesitation I dove into the teeming mess, digging my hands through the slime, pulling up bones and cans and anything that felt remotely retainer-like.

No luck. I emerged empty-handed, and cast about desperately. Were there any more garbage cans I could hurl myself into?

Eguchi-san tugged at my sleeve. "Sachiko-san, we must go. It's getting late."

"But my retainer!"

"I know, but we have to get to the shrine and then make our way home before it gets dark. Remember, if you chase two hares . . ."

I knew, I knew—I would never catch one, but I needed to catch the hare with the straight teeth.

Still, I had to agree that the situation seemed hopeless. Desolate, and smelling like a herring boat, I walked out of the sushi bar with Eguchi-san and continued on the road to her house. Whatever spiritual uplift was awaiting me there was irrelevant now, because by tomorrow I would most certainly be dead.

Eguchi-san, with her shining faith, would hear none of this. She always carried a message of hope. "Don't worry, Sachiko-san. If you pray to the fox gods, maybe they will return your retainer to you."

"Really? You think so?"

Eguchi-san nodded gravely. "The gods are very powerful. Nothing is beyond them. *But*—you must pray very hard."

Eguchi-san held out her smooth sandalwood beads. I was ready to try anything, so I took them and I prayed and prayed, over and over, and I silently made one of those desperate vows that you believe with your whole heart and yet privately assume will never be called to account: "Please, kindly fox gods, find my retainer, and I will worship you forever!"

The praying continued all the way to Eguchi-san's home. By the time we arrived I was so nervous I had to run into her house and pee—which took quite a while, since I was wearing seven layers of brown underwear.

Eguchi-san was waiting outside when I returned, and she handed me an offering for the fox gods: a small bag of dry rice. I took it, feeling that it was an awfully stingy offering in exchange for the desired miracle, but Eguchi-san understood the ways of the gods much better than I did.

To get to the shrine, I walked through a great wooden archway, down a path of bursting chrysanthemums, and past those two terrifying fox god statues. I held up the bag of rice meekly as I passed, murmuring, "This is for you. I'll just put it inside."

I walked into the small red-and-gold building, and approached the shrine. With trembling hands, I opened the small doors of the shrine to present my offering. . . .

I gasped in amazement. For there, in the shrine, on a red silk pillow, was—*my retainer*!

It had returned! The miracle had happened!

I grabbed the retainer, dropped the bag of rice in its place, and rushed from the shrine, back up the chrysanthemum path, and into the arms of Eguchi-san. "Look! Look! My retainer!" I screamed.

Eguchi-san smiled knowingly. She was not surprised at all. "The fox gods have smiled upon you."

They had! I looked back down the path at the enormous statues. Though their granite visages were still grim and forbidding, they now seemed to wear just the trace of a grin. I remembered my vow, and I had every intention of fulfilling it. From now on, I would be a Shintoist!

Now, if I'd had any common sense I would have kept this whole episode from my father, because no matter how you sliced it, it still revolved around the indisputable fact that I'd lost my retainer again. Yet, I'd been so thrilled by this spiritual intervention that I had to tell him everything. Everything!

Dad listened quietly to my story, took a sip of his scotch, and stared thoughtfully. "So now wait a minute," he said finally, trying to wrap his head around this evident miracle. "You lost your retainer at a sushi bar?"

I nodded vigorously, incriminating myself with delight. "I wrapped it up in tissue, and when I turned around, it was gone. I looked on the floor, I looked in the garbage—everywhere!"

"And then you found it, a mile away, in a shrine?"

"Yes! Because I prayed, and the fox gods found it for me, just as Eguchi-san said they would!"

"Eguchi-san said that?"

"Yes!" My pride in that old woman's marvelous transformative faith knew no bounds, and I wanted the world to know it.

Dad just nodded slowly, very slowly.

I don't know what happened next, but Eguchi-san never came back to work after that.

CHAPTER 3

ON LOCATION

So now I was alone—or living with Dad and Miki, which amounted to the same thing.

Miki didn't actually live with us. As I said, she had her own house, and that's where she usually slept each night. Or sometimes she might stay in the tatami room in our house, a small guest room that lent a suggestion of propriety. I guess it was important for Dad to preserve the illusion that he was not having intimate relations with this woman who was not his wife. Accordingly, there were never any shows of affection in front of me—no kissing, hugging, nothing. They went to great pains to hide their relationship, although it was clear even to me that she wasn't following him into the bedroom every night just to sing him a lullaby.

Whatever transpired behind the door, she never stayed. Every morning, she'd be gone, having repaired to the tatami room or stolen into the night, and Dad would emerge from his bedroom alone. Invariably, perhaps in testament to the glories of the evening before, he would be naked.

Totally naked. On a cold morning, he might pull on a kimono, but it would be uncinched and flapping wide open. That's what I generally woke up to: Dad and his naked body. I would watch with fascination as he casually crossed the room, his penis dangling and bobbing from side to side.

Admittedly transfixed by this foreign protuberance, I still wanted it covered up. I couldn't say anything, though. I had to pretend that it was cool. That it was part of the routine. I had to be cool with everything.

Maybe I should have just stayed in my bedroom, but the fact is, all nakedness aside, the early mornings were the best times to be with Dad. He'd start up a fire in the fireplace, and then make his tea. He used real bone china, and the best English breakfast tea, specially ordered from Darjeeling, India. I remember him throwing the boiling water on the tea leaves (just like with cowboy coffee), and then settling down in his favorite easy chair by the fire.

He was quiet and meditative in these times, and that, I felt, was the real him. He hadn't started drinking yet; it was the only time of the day when he was completely sober. That's why I made sure I got up early to be with him. Because once he'd had his first glass of Dom Perignon champagne for breakfast, that was it. The charming, moody playboy Steve Parker would take over, and the dad I cherished would be gone.

Sometimes I would grow so lonely sitting in that empty house at night that I'd call Yuki's parents and ask if I could stay with them for the evening. Yuki's mom would always say yes, and I'd take a cab over.

Why I chose that avenue of escape, I can't say. I still didn't really like Yuki all that much; over the years, our relationship had not moved off its initial settings. She was still a competitive, assertive alpha-female, and I was still a shy doormat. Her mom was so nice and friendly, though; she would always welcome me. She'd pay for the cab, make me a snack, and send me off to school with Yuki in the morning. It was like being part of a family.

I made my usual trips to Los Angeles every summer, and made the same adjustments to a wildly different culture. We would shuttle back and forth between Mom's big house in Encino and the bungalow in Malibu.

Mom was always entertaining, and plenty of interesting houseguests passed through our portals. One was a man with a dark mustache and an interest in the supernatural; his name was William Peter Blatty. He had written the screenplay for one of Mom's lesser films, a college movie called *John Goldfarb, Please Come Home*, and he was a neighbor down the street in Encino.

Mom and Mr. Blatty were kindred spirits, and he became a familiar face around the house. Much of the time, I found them engrossed in animated discussions of ghosts, paranormal experiences, the afterlife, and so forth. They liked to get out the Ouija board and ask questions of the infinite, and once or twice they even conducted a séance in the house.

Blatty was Catholic, and a big believer in sin, evil, and the constant presence of the devil, which Mom would dismiss with her competing theories of karma and self-actualization. So he decided to write a book that would prove to her, by the very power of its narrative, the existence of evil in our everyday world. Several years later, when *The Exorcist* was published and became a national phenomenon, he conceded that he'd taken his inspiration for the actress mother, Chris MacNeil, from Mom. He even offered her the role of Chris in the movie, but she turned it down because her agent told her the script (which won an Oscar) was no good.

The unfortunate corollary, of course, was that if the mother character was based on Mom, the daughter, Regan, must have been based on me. Maybe Blatty did use me as a reference when he was sketching the basic outlines of the character. But that was as far as it went.

I don't recall ever walking like a crab or spitting vomit from my revolving head, or doing anything untoward with a crucifix.

I will admit, though, that the photo of the little girl on the first edition of the Harper and Row hardcover book looked an awful lot like me. Mom was sure it *was* me, and she told Jason Miller, the actor who played Father Karras, as much. When this was conveyed to Blatty, he denied it. "Shirley, how could I have gotten Sachiko's picture on the cover of the book?" Mom had the answer: "You could have broken into the house and stolen it." He insisted he had nothing to do with choosing the photo on the cover, which makes its unsettling resemblance to me even creepier.

I enjoyed Malibu, not only for the beaches but for the hills and scrublands behind the house. I used to love walking back there by myself. Nowadays there might be the reasonable fear of being carried off by coyotes or cultists, but in those days it was normal for kids to wander off by themselves and explore nature.

One time, as I walked the wide carriage trail, I found a side path that cut through the brush and wound up on the side of a mountain. Ever curious, I started up the meandering path, an Alice exploring a reverse rabbit hole. As I reached the top, I came upon a plateau with a stunning vista and, of all things, a small working farm.

It was an old shack in Spanish adobe style, probably built by the owners themselves. There was a huge vegetable garden, and a corral with several magnificent palomino horses. As I walked across the field toward the shack, a stout Mexican woman in her mid-thirties emerged from the garden carrying a basket laden with corn. She had a marvelous sun-lit smile, and she greeted me in Spanish.

I couldn't understand a word she spoke, but her voice was musical and friendly; she took me by the hand and led me into the house, and before I knew it, she was feeding me tortillas and beans. Just like that, I had a new family.

After I ate, she took me on a tour of her garden, and I remember there was corn, lots of corn. You could eat it right off the cob, uncooked, sweet and delicious. She would pick strawberries and grape tomatoes right from the vine and pop them in my mouth, warm from the sun.

I don't remember her name—she was just Ricardo's mom to me. Ricardo, her teenage son, was in charge of the palominos. He was always at the corral, grooming the horses, training them, riding them bareback. About sixteen years old, he was friendly like his mom, and always smiling. She didn't speak English, but he did.

That very first day, he caught me staring in wonder at those beautiful horses. "Would you like to ride?" he asked genially. I certainly would!

Ricardo carefully helped me up onto one of the horses. There was no saddle or reins. I had to ride bareback like him. "Don't be afraid," he cautioned gently. "Just hold on to the mane and I'll walk you around the corral." He didn't know that I'd been riding horses for years. I grabbed the palomino's mane and trotted confidently around the corral, as Ricardo watched in surprise.

Moments later we were both riding bareback down the path,

right across Malibu Road and through the access route to the beach. We took off across the sand and raced along the shore. I just held on to that mane and galloped down the beach, kicking up great sprays of water. It was exhilarating.

I went back often to the farm on the hill. I'm sure no one on Malibu Road—the stars, the celebrities—even knew it was there. For me, however, it was a second home, a warm, loving place far preferable to the pretentious social scene below. Over the next couple of summers, Ricardo and I would spend many happy hours riding along the beach on our palominos, splashing down the shoreline. It was idyllic and entrancing, and completely platonic. I was the little girl in love with nature, Ricardo was like my watchful big brother, and we were romping through a wholesome tableau straight out of a Disney movie. I was completely happy.

SOMETIMES my visits with Mom would dovetail with one of her location shoots, and she would bring me along. Thus, in the winter of 1966, on my Christmas break, I found myself flying to Paris, where Mom was filming *Woman Times Seven*. For some reason, Yuki came along with me. I'm not sure why; as I said, we weren't really friends, but somehow it had become accepted that we would spend our free time together. Why Mom would want to bring her to Paris, though, I couldn't say. I assume she got to know her a little in Tokyo when she was filming *My Geisha*, and Dad must have talked about her quite a lot. Still—kind of a mystery.

Anyway, it turned out that Yuki and I had a fabulous time. We stayed at Mom's lavish town house on the glamorous Avenue Foch, and we were virtually unsupervised. We had the run of the house—and we ran. I remember the two of us jumping up and down on the fancy beds, bouncing off the walls, raiding the kitchen at night, and gorging ourselves on crème brûlée and French pastries. Yuki's aggressive, take-what-you-want attitude was starting to appeal to me.

We explored Paris, too, sometimes with guides, sometimes on our own. I remember watching the extravagant floor show at the notorious cabaret Lido. It was clearly a show geared for adults; I don't know what we were doing there, two unworldly clueless ten-year-olds, but it was certainly an experience. Most memorable were the chorus lines of statuesque half-naked women parading across the stage with tassels on their breasts and huge sprays of feathers sprouting from their heads and their behinds. Yuki and I giggled through the whole show.

WOMAN *Times Seven* was an episodic farce in which Mom played seven different roles in short vignettes illustrating the tantalizing enigma that is Woman. It had one of those all-star international casts, and was directed by the great neorealist filmmaker Vittorio De Sica. He was a great, warm, avuncular presence with aging matinee-idol looks, who nurtured my mom, flattered her, and lavished her with attentive compliments and adoring glances.

He was always over at our town house, and I would watch from the living room as they cooked together in the kitchen, laughing, teasing, bestowing light grazing touches as they passed each other. De Sica would burst into an Italian street song, and then he would suddenly take my mother in his arms and hug her, and Mom would gaze up at him worshipfully like a little girl.

I thought he was wonderful—his huge beaming smile was so full of love for everyone and everything—and I hated leaving the shoot and going back to Tokyo, because I feared I would never see him again. And I didn't.

• • •

THE following year, Mom was in England working on *The Bliss of Mrs. Blossom*, and again I found myself on location. Her costar was Richard Attenborough (with whom she did *not* have an affair, I can pretty safely say). Nowadays best known as the director of *Gandhi* and the dotty entrepreneur in *Jurassic Park*, Mr. Attenborough back then was a marvelous actor who had that amazing English ability to do anything: character roles and leading men, comedy and drama, war films and musicals. He was also a lovely gentleman. He was very sweet to me when I was visiting the set. He had a special nickname for me: Poppy. I don't know where it came from, but whenever I ran into him in the years that followed, he would immediately greet me as Poppy. He still does.

The warmth and genuine sweetness of De Sica and Attenborough reminded me of that side of my dad, which I had seen less frequently over the years. The days of ice fishing and tall tales were growing more and more distant in my memory. When I got back to Japan, I felt a powerful need to reconnect with him. I wanted to forge a stronger bond.

That may have explained why I was a little overeager to see him one morning as I waited for him to emerge from his bedroom. He'd had an especially tiring night out, and was sleeping in. I waited anxiously in the living room for him to come out and start the fire and make his tea—"Come on, Dad. Where are you?" I muttered to myself—and finally I couldn't wait any longer. I ran down the hall and burst into his bedroom without knocking. There he was, in bed—with Miki.

She had forgotten to wake herself up in the middle of the night and sneak away. Now she had committed the unforgivable sin; she'd allowed me to see her in my father's bed.

There was alarm on Miki's face when she sat up. "What are you doing in here?" she hissed at me angrily, as my father stirred beside her. She waved me off, hoping I would retreat before Dad spotted me, but it was too late. A fleeting look of surprise and embarrassment crossed his face when he saw me and got his bearings, and then a dark, frightening anger settled over him. He grew furious, but not with me. He turned his glare on Miki.

Miki cringed instinctively, and then tried to deflect his rage. "She should have knocked," she said feebly, but in an instant Dad had seized her by the arm and tossed her out of the bed. She screamed as she hit the floor. Then, before she could get to her feet, he was upon her. He slapped her face hard. I was stunned by the shocking impact of his hand against her cheek. As she reeled back against the wall, he followed her, slapping her again and shouting terrible things at her. He pounded her on the back until she slipped to the floor, and then, as she lay slumped in a heap, he kicked her over and over.

It was an awful thing to watch—and the fact that it was Miki, whom I truly hated, being beaten so savagely made it seem even worse. To know that my father could summon such explosive violence was devastating to contemplate. (When would it be my turn?) Why was he doing it now? To protect his image in front of his daughter? To demonstrate that he was a good man who had been seduced by a worthless slut?

I couldn't watch anymore, and fled from the room. The beating went on. I could hear Miki's screams and the dull thuds of my father's blows. Then there was silence, and only Miki's low, muffled sobbing. Moments later, Dad was pulling Miki through the living room, her clothes hastily thrown on. He flung open the door, pushed her out, and slammed the door shut. Then he returned to his bedroom.

Not another word was said. I knew enough not to mention it. I quietly got ready for school and left.

The real value of violence, as all the great tyrants know, lies not in punishing the individual, but in delivering an object lesson of fear and subjugation to everyone else. Very soon their relationship would resume its normal equanimity, as if nothing had happened.

For me, it was devastating. Suddenly I apprehended the true depth of my father's unstable fury, and it terrified me. I would do anything not to have that rage turned on me. So I became, if anything, more docile and eager to please. Walking on eggs became my default mode.

It was around this time that Mike Parsons died. Mike was a friend of my dad's in Japan, and also a business associate. (For Dad, friendship and business always seemed to go hand in hand.) They were big drinking buddies.

Dad told me that Mike was quite the womanizer, but I knew that Mike was gay. I wasn't supposed to know this, but once, at one of Dad's parties at the Shibuya house, I wandered into one of the bedrooms, and there was Mike kissing another man. Really kissing him. No doubt about it.

This was never talked about, because in those days homosexuality was still something to be shunned and despised. So Mike led a secret life, too.

At that time, Dad had a business office in Hong Kong. I don't know what kind of business it was, and I don't know if Mike was involved in it.

One day, Mike Parsons was found dead in Dad's Hong Kong office. Shot to death.

I remember the authorities questioning Dad, and Dad being a little anxious about it. I was filled with a bewildered protectiveness: "Why are they asking Dad these questions? He doesn't know anything about it."

Did he? Nothing came of it, no charges were filed, and Mike Parsons was never mentioned again, but in the back of my head, I wondered why intrigue and violence seemed to touch upon Dad's life from every angle.

AS I approached my teenage years a natural rebelliousness was rising in me. Oh, I was a model of good-girl behavior in general, but every now and then a mood came over me, and I would decide to push the boundaries.

In a very small way, mind you. I didn't smoke cigarettes or hang out with boys or down shots of sake.

No, I started reading.

Dad didn't want me to read books. He felt it was a waste of time. I was an idiot, anyway; what was I going to learn? So I read surreptitiously, whenever he wasn't around (which was often). I'd steal into his study and pick out a book, leaf through it, see if it grabbed me. Dad himself was an omnivorous reader, so there was plenty to choose from.

I was about twelve when, one day, I came upon a copy of Ayn Rand's *We the Living*. It was the story of a young girl in postrevolutionary Russia who refused to let the repressive state tame her independent spirit. It hooked me right away. I understood this girl. She was struggling and straining against her bonds, much like me. I kept reading, and couldn't put the book down. I nestled into my dad's armchair, legs curled up under me, and got lost in another world.

Hours later, I was still reading when I heard my father come home. My first instinct was to jump out of the chair and shove the book back into the shelf before he saw me, but I didn't. I was utterly absorbed in the world of the novel, and I didn't want to leave it. I kept reading.

Behind me I heard the knob turn, and then the door open. I

knew it was Dad. He stood in the doorway, motionless. He didn't say anything, but I could feel his disapproval. I was breaking the rules.

It was too late to hide the fact, and I knew I would do well to rise meekly and acknowledge my folly, but some kind of defiance had taken hold of me. I wouldn't stop reading. I wouldn't even look up at him.

The door closed, with a reproving curtness. I heard Dad move into the room. I could peripherally see him taking off his coat, and methodically hanging it over a chair back. Then he sat down on the couch and stared at me. He would normally have settled into his armchair after a long day's work; but I had the armchair, and I wasn't moving. I kept reading.

Dad slowly took off his shoes, letting one and then the other clomp to the floor. He stared at me. I didn't look over, but I knew he was staring, waiting. It occurred to me that I should have been performing my ordinary duties: getting him a scotch and soda, fetching his newspaper, kneeling beside him and rubbing his feet. That's what a daughter was supposed to do.

But I was being a bad daughter, right in front of his eyes. I don't know why I had chosen today to push the issue, but it seemed elementally right. Kira, the girl in the novel, was fighting Communist oppression and soul-crushing poverty. I was inspired.

Of course, he had a hundred pounds on me, and thirty years of experience, and a whole culture of Japanese patriarchy behind him. My will was nothing compared to his. He knew that the longer he stared and said nothing, the more extreme the pressure on me—and that, eventually, I would crack.

But I didn't want to crack, the way I had over those damned cream puffs. It hadn't helped. So I stared doggedly at the book.

I was only pretending to read, by this point. I couldn't concentrate now. I could feel his anger collecting and rising to a boil, and sooner or later it was going to erupt on me full force. But when? In what form? Would he scream hateful things at me, or lock me in my room, or would he yank me from his chair and start beating me, mercilessly, as I'd seen him beat his lover?

I knew now that I'd made a mistake embarking on this foolish course, but there was no way to back out of it. I was stuck.

I waited. He waited. We were at an impasse, one that could end only disastrously.

Then Miki came into the room.

Miki's contempt for me had only grown since the bedroom incident. Not only had I been the catalyst for the beating, but I had witnessed her humiliation, and she despised me for that. Not for the last time, I was catching the fallout from being an innocent bystander.

Miki stood beside my father and glared at me, arms folded. Another staring contest. Finally she spoke: "Isn't it time you helped me with the flowers, young lady?"

I had to respond now, and I knew it would be suicidal to act snotty or defiant when my father was still coiled like a cobra. So I murmured, "Okay," and slowly put the book down. Defeated, I followed Miki out of the room.

I should have been grateful to her: she'd defused the situation and helped me avoid a lethal showdown. I doubt that was her intention—clearly she was trying to belittle me with her patronizing tone—but nevertheless, the end result was that I had escaped the apocalyptic wrath of my father, and lived to see another day.

I never picked up *We the Living* again. I still don't know how it ends. It would be many, many years before I finished another book.

WHY wouldn't my father let me read? I couldn't fathom it. After all, he read all the time. He knew what books could do for you—

expand your horizons, engage your intellect, accelerate your maturity. It was as though he wanted me to stay a little girl.

Yet, at the same time, he seemed to be pushing me toward adulthood.

"Are you wearing panties?" he would ask.

"Um—yes," I'd reply, embarrassed by the question.

"Take them off."

"Why?"

"It's good to air your vagina."

Dad encouraged me to go without underwear whenever possible. He thought it was far healthier to be open and exposed to fresh air than confined in restrictive suffocating cotton. Perhaps he was reacting to Eguchi-san's seven-layer panty overkill. I found both choices extreme, but Dad had established his own morning nudity as a precedent, and I couldn't argue with him.

He also liked me to open the buttons on my shirt when we were in public. I don't know why; he was always teasing me about being flat-chested—"Two fried eggs, coming up!" he'd say—so it's not as though I had something to show off. Besides, I was shy—after his taunts, who wouldn't be?—and I liked to keep my blouse buttoned to the top. He insisted I unbutton it down to my prospective cleavage, though. I'd acquiesce until he turned away, and then I'd hurriedly button up again.

I remember, when I was about twelve, going to see *Hair* on Broadway. Dad was one of the many producers, and we had great seats, third row center. That evening, he instructed me not to wear underwear. I felt extremely uncomfortable about this—it was Broadway, after all, back in its glamour days, when everyone was dressed to the nines. Going without panties in such an august venue struck me as almost criminal.

There was so much nudity on the stage that my secret subversiveness seemed almost quaint. I had seen naked strangers before, at the Japanese baths—I'd been to the Lido, for God's sake—but to have so many of them so close to me, proudly displaying their wares . . . Well, I guess I was supposed to feel liberated, but it kind of grossed me out. Especially all the pubic hair. Yuck!

Dad was clearly enjoying it, and enjoying the fact that he could watch such explicit, far-out things with his own daughter. So hip! So cool!

I thought nothing of these things at the time—that he made me go without underwear, and exposed me to adult entertainments beyond my understanding. After all, it was the Age of Aquarius. The way he would slow-dance with me on the nightclub floor, cupping my behind with his hand and squeezing—it didn't mean anything, right? He was my dad.

When I was around seven or eight, Dad would sit beside me on the couch and say, "Let's play the tickling game." "No!" I'd scream, but it was too late—he had his fingers digging into me, and I was shrieking with laughter. I was so extremely ticklish that the slightest touch would set me off. I'd plead, "No! No!" Because I couldn't stand it. I hated it.

He'd think I was joking, because I was laughing so hard, and he'd keep going. I'd fall to the floor, hoping to get away, but I was too weak with laughter to move, and he'd follow me, and the tickling would continue. I didn't want to tell him to stop, because he was having so much fun, and I didn't want to hurt his feelings, but it was awful, awful . . .

He would stop, finally—and then it was a new game. A licking game.

He would start licking me. All over my body. My arms, my neck, my feet . . .

That felt good—but I didn't like it. I didn't like that it felt good.

Then there were many nights when he'd say, "You can stay with me tonight," and I'd get into his bed.

Then he would climb into bed beside me and spoon with me, snuggling up behind me and throwing his arms around me. It was so warm and cozy, except . . . What was that hard thing behind me, poking against my butt? Did it belong to Dad? Was it the dangly thing I saw every morning when he came out to make the fire? It seemed so mushy before. How did it get so sharp?

I found it annoying, and shifted away. But Dad pulled me back, and snuggled even closer—and that sharp thing pushed its way between my legs . . .

What happened then? Did it go any further? I don't remember. My mind has blocked it out. I believe that he would just hold me close and we would snuggle throughout the night. That's what I want to believe.

When he was finally snoring, I would sneak out of his bed and hurry back to my own room. I would sleep much better there, but I always made sure I rushed back to his bed in the morning before he woke up. I didn't want him to know that I'd left him during the night. It might have hurt his feelings.

CHAPTER 4

CHARTERS TOWERS

My childhood in Japan came to an abrupt end in the fall of 1968. There was no drama involved: nobody died, no earthshaking scandal erupted. I had reached the awkward age of twelve, and in another Dickensian twist, I found myself suddenly transported to the other side of the world—Bexhill-on-Sea, England—to boarding school.

The funny thing was, it was my idea. At least I thought it was. Dad was often telling me how wonderful boarding school was. He made it seem so romantic and adventurous: "You get to have your own room, and you can do whatever you want on your time off, and you get to live in a whole new country by yourself . . . it's like being a grown-up." That really appealed to me. I wanted to show Dad that I was a big girl. That I was practically an adult. I was cool, not needy.

So when the time came, I suggested going to boarding school, but it was Dad who cleverly implanted it in my head, as if I were the Manchurian candidate. I suspect he was growing wary of my rebellious side, and a mouthy pain-in-the-ass teenager in the house (even a meek, mildly defiant one) was just going to cramp his free-wheeling style.

Or perhaps Miki was behind it. She may have planned all along to have me sent away the moment I reached a disposable age.

In any case, I was now out of their hair, and any guilt my dad may have felt about neglecting me in the past could be dismissed. I wasn't his responsibility anymore.

The curious thing—curious to me even now—is that I didn't go off to boarding school alone. Yuki went with me—and Dad was paying for it.

The story I heard from Yuki was that my dad and Yuki's dad used to drink together at the Press Club in Tokyo. Between libations, Yuki's father had confided to Dad that one of his dreams was to send Yuki and her brother, Kenji, to boarding school in Europe. He had the money for it, safely tucked away in a Swiss bank account. Then he died of a swift-moving cancer, and he neglected to give the account code to the other members of the family beforehand. The money couldn't be retrieved; it may be sitting there still.

So there was no money for Yuki's education, but Dad remembered his friend's dream, and he took it upon himself to send Yuki to boarding school, in tribute to her father's memory. It's an uplifting tale, and it may even be true.

MY new school was named Charters Towers—or, in the accepted local pronunciation, "Chah-tuz Towz." It was a stuffy, dreary, very traditional English school, the kind of place where the teachers wore long black gowns and those funny hats that looked like popovers, and you had to walk single-file from class to class, as if you were doing a community theater production of *Oliver Twist*. The discipline was similarly Victorian; if your skirt was one inch higher than school regulation, they caned you.

If you've ever seen a British period film or *Masterpiece Theatre*— one of the many versions of *Jane Eyre* would suffice—you've seen Charters Towers. There were the same long, dark hallways; the communal tables in the dining rooms; the wide winding stair- cases; the huge stained-glass windows; and the freezing cold rooms, impossible to heat. It was Hogwarts without the magic.

Still, I considered myself happy there. It was grim and gloomy, but at least I had company. It was an all-girls school, so there were no boy troubles, no hormonal distractions. The teachers were strict and humorless, but I was used to that from my days in Japa- nese schools. Plus, they had their amusing qualities.

The math teacher, for instance, was so absurdly pompous that I would burst out laughing the minute he walked into the room. Unfortunately, I couldn't stop. I became so disruptive that he made me wear a dunce cap and sit in the corner, facing the wall. That only made me laugh more. It seemed the more he punished me, the more I laughed. Soon I was dreading going to math class, be- cause I knew I was going to start laughing and never stop. He would grow furious, and I would laugh even more. It was agony, but I couldn't help it!

Then there was the infamous Mr. Gerard, the geography teacher, who would take long, self-important strides across the yard in his mortarboard hat, his leather shoes slapping loudly on the pavement. With every self-important step, he would let out a fart. I guess he couldn't help it. A more self-conscious man might have taken smaller, more judicious steps, but Mr. Gerard could not suppress his essential heartiness, so he strode on purposefully, farting as he went. The smell would collect under his flowing robes and then gently waft out as he clipped along. You didn't want to be caught in his wake.

It was a colorful setting, Bexhill-on-Sea. Near Hastings (where a pretty famous battle was fought), it sat right on the southern coast, and looked out on the English Channel. The air was fresh, the country green. Plus, there was a Woolworth's in town where you could buy candy.

The downside was the constant, monolithic cold that permeated the rooms of Charters Towers. You couldn't get away from it; it burrowed into your bones. The only way to get warm in that dank, clammy world was to bury yourself under a thick comforter made of eiderdown. That was heavenly. I would crawl into bed and pull the eiderdown around me, and suddenly the world was soft and blissful. Whenever I wrapped myself in one of those comforters, I felt happy. I felt loved.

So much so that today, I confess, I'm an eiderdown addict. I collect eiderdown comforters at every opportunity; they're my great extravagance. I must have a dozen of them around the house. I get them imported from overseas—made from genuine Hungarian goose down, they cost a fortune. Still, they're worth it. Whenever I wrap myself in eiderdown, I feel loved.

An unsettling aspect of the English school system was that when you reached the age of twelve, there was a special exam to decide the course of your future studies—it would determine which kids belonged on the fast track and which didn't (perhaps the inspiration for Harry Potter's "Sorting Hat"). The smart girls who aced the test were sent into Science and Math. The not-so-bright ones were directed into Cooking and Sewing.

So Yuki and I had to take the exam the year we arrived. I

wound up in Cooking and Sewing; Yuki went to Science and Math. She had again confirmed her position as the Smart One, the better version of me.

WHEN we checked into Charters Towers at the beginning of the school year, we had to surrender our passports, our money, and our airline tickets for the trip home. These were locked up in a special box, and we would collect them again at the end of the semester. Because we were traveling together, Yuki's and my things were stored together.

When the winter recess rolled around, however, we didn't go home. Instead, we went to visit my godfather in Ireland. He was a producer and screenwriter named Kevin McClory. In the 1950s he'd been an assistant director on *Around the World in 80 Days*, where he met my mother—she played the Indian princess Aouda— and they became good friends. Later he developed a screenplay with Ian Fleming, based on Fleming's character James Bond. Fleming novelized the screenplay as *Thunderball* without crediting Kevin, and that resulted in a lawsuit and a nice settlement. Later, in 1965, when *Thunderball* was made into a film, Kevin got the producing credit.

This is why he now had a stately mansion in Connemara, with servants and horse stables; and that's where Yuki and I spent the Christmas holiday, like little Irish princesses. For two girls fresh from the dungeons, this style of living was incongruously upscale and elegant. Every day, we were served high tea on silver trays, with crumpets and cucumber sandwiches. And every day, we would put on our cute riding outfits and go galloping across the wild green countryside. All the stable boys had crushes on us, and I watched and learned as Yuki toyed with them and put them through their paces. She was a master of her craft.

It was all very idyllic, and over all too quickly. We were soon back in the dank, dreary confines of school; a splash of cold water in the face, except it was cold all over.

It wasn't until we slogged to the end of the spring semester, and it was time to go back to Japan, that we went to the school office to retrieve our airline tickets. There was one small hitch, though: the tickets were gone.

"Excuse me," I said, after rummaging through the storage box, "where are our plane tickets?"

The matron looked at us blankly. "Did you have plane tickets?"

"Yes," I said, "they were both in this box."

"Mine was in my white purse," said Yuki helpfully. But her white purse was gone, too.

The matron shrugged. If we put the tickets in the box, then they should still be in there. "Are you sure you didn't keep them in your dorm room instead?"

This was a crazy question. Why would we have done that? All students were required to hand in their airline tickets. It was a rule, and if you broke a rule at Charters Towers, you were punished. Neither Yuki nor I was going to risk being caned just to keep our plane tickets as souvenirs.

This was as much guidance as the matron was going to provide. If the tickets were gone, they were gone. She knew nothing about it; she washed her hands of it. End of story.

For us it was just the beginning. Losing a plane ticket in those days was a serious business. There were no e-tickets or computer backups in those days; a paper ticket was like cash, and if you lost it, you were screwed.

Yuki and I had no idea what to do next. We were effectively stranded in England. While the school notified our parents, we got on the train to London without a plan of action. I guess we had this vague, youthful hope that maybe by the time we got to Victoria Station, everything would be solved for us. If worse came to worst, we could always go back to Connemara.

My real fear was that my father would come all the way from Japan to sort things out, and in his exasperation he would unleash his titanic, unreasoning anger on us. So I was naturally relieved when my mother showed up at the station instead.

I shouldn't have been.

Mom greeted us coolly—no hugs or kisses. There was nothing bubbly or effusive in her mood. She brought us both to the nearby Grosvenor Hotel, where she'd reserved a penthouse suite. Then she put Yuki in one of the bedrooms, shut the door, and locked it.

Mom turned on me and stared hard.

"So, what did you do with the tickets?"

I was so surprised by the question that I was initially speechless. "What did *I* do with the tickets? I didn't do anything with them, Mom. They just disappeared."

Mom nodded. "Uh-huh." She paced the room a moment. "They just disappeared . . ." She stopped and gave me a significant glance. "Like your retainer, I suppose?"

"My retainer?"

"Your father told me all about it. We don't have any secrets, you know. You lost your retainer, so he bought you a new one, and then you lost that, too. Didn't you?"

"Well—yes, but that was because Eguchi-san tricked me."

"I'm not talking about Eguchi-san. I'm talking about *you*. You lost the retainer, but it wasn't really lost, was it?"

"No. Because Eguchi-san took it."

"Exactly."

My head was starting to spin. I couldn't follow her logic, which may have been her intention.

"So maybe the tickets are lost," she went on, "and maybe they aren't." She let this hang cryptically in the air.

"What do you mean?"

"I mean, maybe you know what happened to the tickets, and you're not telling me for some reason."

What reason was she talking about? "I'm kinda confused, Mom."

"I'm confused, too," she replied. "We bought the two of you expensive plane tickets, and now they're gone, and nobody knows anything about them. They must have gone somewhere, right? They just didn't get up and walk away by themselves."

True point. I couldn't argue with her on that one.

She folded her arms. "So, do you have something to tell me?"

Did I? I couldn't think of anything. So: "No."

Now Mom gave me the Look. The Look was one of her most trusted weapons. It signaled suspicion, righteous anger, contempt, and a steely determination to ferret out the truth. Her mouth would tighten, and her eyes would narrow to a squint, and you could see cold fire flashing within. She was like a basilisk lizard eyeing its insect prey.

I was getting the Look now, and I knew that whatever I had said so far, it was not what she'd wanted to hear. She was waiting for something else.

"Sachi, we're not leaving this room until we find out what happened."

"But I don't know what happened, Mom."

"I think you do," she said finally. "I think you cashed those tickets in and you took the money. That's what I think."

I was stunned out of my shoes. *I* cashed in the tickets and took the money? *Me?* First of all, I didn't even know this was possible. Could you actually do that? My next question was, *how* would I have done that? What was the process for cashing in airline tickets? I had no idea, and I was astonished that my mother would think I did. It was like suggesting I knew how to score a kilo of heroin.

I told her as much. "I didn't do that, Mom. I don't know *how* to do that."

"Maybe you don't know, but I think it's very possible that Yuki does."

Oh. I suddenly realized what the stakes were here, and why Yuki and I had been separated. We were like two members of an underworld gang, rounded up in a police sting, and now we were being held for questioning. Yuki was the brains of the gang, I was apparently the stooge, and Mom was the head detective in charge of the investigation. This lavishly furnished bedroom in a legendary five-star hotel had become my interrogation cell.

I started getting dizzy. Plus, I was starving. I hadn't eaten since we left Bexhill.

"Mom, I'm really hungry. Can we order room service?"

"Not till we get to the bottom of this." She was pacing again. Mom had never played a cop before, so she was probably relishing the opportunity. She resumed the interrogation, peppering me with questions, trying to trip me up. But she couldn't break me, because there was nothing to break.

Finally, she gave up in frustration. "Okay, let's see what Yuki has to say." She left me and headed for Yuki's bedroom.

"Mom!" I called. She paused at my door and looked back expectantly. "Can I get something to eat, please?"

She looked at me a moment. "No," she said, and shut the door and locked me in.

Now I was really confused. What? *No?* I wasn't going to eat?

Because my plane ticket was missing? That was silly. Surely Mom had spoken in a moment of pique. She would bring me a sandwich when she came back. Surely. In the meantime, I drank water from the bathroom tap. That would tide me over for a little while.

About half an hour later, she returned from Yuki's room. Empty-handed. I don't know what went on with Yuki, but Mom didn't look satisfied.

The questioning began again. Why did you take the tickets? Where did you sell them? How much did you get?

Mom paused a moment, and then dropped her little bombshell: "You know, Yuki says it was all *your* idea." I knew she was lying about this—Yuki would never have folded so easily—but I was so frazzled and Mom was such a good actress that I believed her anyway.

"It was not my idea!"

"That's what I thought," Mom went on silkily. "Yuki was really behind it, wasn't she? She's the one who wanted the money. Why? To send home to her mother? I know they're very poor. That was the reason, wasn't it?"

I'd seen this movie before—she was trying to play us off each other—and I wasn't going to fall for it. I would never betray Yuki, no matter how disloyal she was to me. No, never!

Although I did start to wonder . . . *Maybe Yuki did take the tickets. Maybe she did send the money to her mother. She was certainly capable of it, wasn't she?*

So the interrogation went on, all day and into the night: Mom shuttling back and forth from one room to another, browbeating us, squeezing out odd bits of information and relaying them back to the other prisoner. When it was time for bed, she locked us both in our rooms, without feeding us, and promised to continue the discussion in the morning—which she did.

I honestly don't know how long this went on. I remember it as being three days. Yuki thinks it was only a day and a half. Maybe so, but I just recall being hungrier than I'd ever been in my life. Plus, I couldn't sleep, both from the anxiety and the hunger pangs.

Yuki said it was exactly like one of those World War II movies, where the good guys were interrogated by the Gestapo. There was no physical torture (except for starvation!), but the psychological manipulation was so intense that Yuki was on the verge of despair. It was the closest, she says, that she'd ever been to entertaining suicidal thoughts.

And all this terror was being whipped up by my mother, that sweet, kooky gamine beloved the world over. I began to see where the Dragon Lady epithet might have a basis in truth.

Finally—after holding out as long as I could, and seeing no end in sight—I cracked. Totally. "Yes, it's true, we did it, we did it!" I bogusly confessed.

"*You* did it?" Mom asked pointedly.

"No, it was Yuki's idea." Yes, to my shame, I threw Yuki under the bus.

"Why?" Mom pursued.

"Why?" I quickly recalled all the malignant little seeds she had planted, and responded accordingly. "Because . . . her mother had no money, and she needed to pay her rent. So we took the tickets, and Yuki found a place to sell them. She's the smart one, you know. Not me."

Mom nodded. "She has a devious mind."

"You're right, Mom. You can't trust her!"

Mom pondered a minute, then left the room. A moment later she returned with Yuki. "Okay, Sachi, would you repeat what you just said?"

"Repeat . . . ?" I hadn't counted on this. Yuki, who looked

worn down but still had an air of defiance about her, waited curiously. She knew she had nothing to worry about, because she hadn't done anything. What could I possibly say?

"Yuki did it!" I said, pointing at her. I was like one of those hysterical girls in *The Crucible*, picking out witches right and left to save her own skin. Then, when Mom pressed me, I repeated the entire story, just as I'd originally invented it.

Yuki was at first astonished; then she threw me the dirtiest look I'd ever seen. I could see that whatever friendship we'd managed to forge was instantly over. She denied the charges and raised a mild protest, but she seemed to recognize immediately that she couldn't win. It was my word against hers, and my own mother was the judge.

Mom gave Yuki a short, dismissive lecture—"I'm very disappointed in you"—and took her back to her bedroom. It was very quiet in there, and I wondered what could be going on. Was Mom calling the police? Was she making Yuki sign a confession?

When she returned, her bright, bubbly smile was back. "Now, what would you like to eat?"

I had a hamburger, medium rare, with thinly sliced red onions and tomatoes and Dijon mustard. The bun was toasted. Pickles and crispy French fries on the side, and a hot chocolate. It was the best food I'd ever tasted. In fact, give me that exact meal and an eiderdown comforter, and I would be in heaven.

I didn't see Yuki at the hotel after that. I discovered later that Mom had arranged her flight back to Japan. She and I were going to head back to the United States in a day or so. Everything was back to normal—but it wasn't. That night, the guilt kicked in big time. What had I done? How could I have told such a story? What would happen to Yuki now?

I couldn't sleep. I was racked with remorse. I had to tell Mom the truth. I went to her room and woke her up, at about three in the morning. In retrospect, I probably should have waited for a more civilized hour, but I had to come clean now. I had to be absolved.

"That wasn't the truth, Mom!" I recanted. "Yuki didn't take the tickets. I just made that up so I could have something to eat. I don't know what happened to the tickets. They just disappeared!"

There was silence for a moment.

"So, you were lying?" she said finally.

"Yes!"

"So, you're a liar."

This wasn't going the way I wanted. "Yes . . ." I continued, losing a degree of my confessional zeal.

"So, how do I know you're not lying now?"

"Because . . . I'm not."

Mom stared at me. She was probably giving me the Look, but it was too dark in the room to feel its coruscating effect. "We'll talk about it in the morning."

She walked me back to my room. All the way, I insisted that Yuki and I were both innocent, nobody had stolen anything, the tickets had just disappeared. That was the absolute truth!

Mom pushed me back into my bedroom, and shut the door. I heard it lock.

WE flew to New York the next day and stayed at another fancy hotel, where I was again locked in my bedroom and denied food. "You can come out when you decide to tell me the truth."

I couldn't believe what was happening to me. I'd been punished for telling the truth, and then when I finally lied, I was set free—until I told the truth again and was tossed back into my cell. Should I just lie again?

No, I couldn't. I knew I wouldn't be able to live with myself.

Out of desperation, I took to checking my suitcase, over and over again, scouring every corner of it, praying for the lost ticket somehow to materialize. It couldn't be in there, of course, because I'd never put it in there in the first place. I had plenty of time on my hands, though, and who knew? Maybe there would be a miracle! It was as if I were expecting the fox gods to do me an extra favor and exert their magical influence across the ocean.

A few days later, we moved on to Los Angeles. I was eagerly looking forward to the flight, just so I could get some peanuts to eat.

Back in Encino, I was given the run of the house, but my relationship with Mom had gone from cold to ice-bound. She wouldn't speak to me. I was a thief and a liar, and I was heading for a huge demotion in the next life.

What really scared me was that soon I would be going back to Tokyo to confront my dad. Let's face it: if Mom could react with such unreasonable fury, Dad might spontaneously combust.

It was while I was starting to pack up for the flight when I looked into the corner of my empty suitcase, and—

There it was! The plane ticket!

I picked it out of the corner of the suitcase and stared at it in amazement. How . . . ?

I didn't know how. I still don't. I'd searched that suitcase from top to bottom, maybe hundreds of times, and there was no way it could have been there. But there it was.

I was stunned. My heart was pounding. I had to show Mom right away. I rushed down the hall to her room, but then, when I confronted her closed door, I stopped dead, terrified. How would she react? Would she hug me to her and apologize for doubting me? Or would she still freeze me out?

I knocked gently. "Mom? Mom?"

There was no answer. I tried the doorknob. Locked. I knocked again. "Mom?"

After a long silence, I heard the lock on the door click open. I waited for the door to open. It didn't.

I don't know how long I stood outside her door—afraid to walk in, afraid of my mother—but I had to go in. I had to tell her.

She was sitting in her king-size bed surrounded by magazines. Self-help magazines, women's magazines, entertainment magazines. She was reading one now.

I sat on the edge of the bed and waited for her to look up at me. She didn't. She gave no recognition of my presence whatsoever.

"Mom," I said with a weak hopefulness, "I found the ticket."

She didn't respond. She kept reading.

I went on. "It was in my suitcase. I don't know how many times I looked in there, a million, and it wasn't there. But then I just looked, and there it was."

This again seemed to make no impression on her.

I held the ticket up. It was my last gambit. "See?"

Finally Mom looked up, stared at the ticket, and regarded me with a cool indifference.

"Leave," she said.

I stared at her in disbelief, hoping I'd misheard her, hoping she would say something else.

"Leave the room."

So I left. I don't remember leaving, I don't remember where I went afterward—I probably fled back to my room—but I remember feeling that something seismic and terrible and irrevocable had taken place between my mother and me. We had had our first break.

I called Yuki soon after to give her the news about the ticket turning up. Her response was a rather scornful "No kidding."

It was apparently too late to clear her name, because the story was already out in her Tokyo neighborhood. It seems my dear "stepmother" Miki had quickly spread the rumor that Yuki's mother had masterminded the theft from afar, instructing her daughter to steal the tickets and cash them in, so she could send the money back home to her. It was pretty close to the story I'd told Mom. Miki must have heard it from Dad.

Both Yuki and her mother suffered a good deal of ostracism and social persecution because of this story, so I couldn't blame Yuki for being angry at me. In fact, she had no reason ever to forgive me for what I had done, except that she had been there in that hotel suite. She knew what had happened.

Even today, Yuki and I still wonder about those tickets. Where did they go? Did one of the matrons take them? Or are they still sitting somewhere in that office in Charters Towers, collecting dust?

More mysteriously, how did that other ticket get into my suitcase? I could have just overlooked it, but that seems close to impossible. Was it even the same ticket? Did someone plant it there? Who? Why?

A few days later I returned to Japan, where I feared even harsher retribution from my father.

But no, he was not troubled at all. In fact he took it very much in stride. "So you lost the ticket." He shrugged. "Things get lost."

I was shocked. "Really? But all that money . . ."

He waved it off. "Pah—money! As long as you got home safe, that's the main thing."

I was bewildered by his sangfroid—also relieved—but still, I wanted to make sure he understood my side of the story. "It wasn't my fault, Daddy. I gave them my ticket at the beginning of the year, and then when they opened up the box, it was gone!"

He nodded. "Look, Sachi, it's not important. Even if the ticket weren't gone . . . even if you did cash it in . . ."

"But I didn't!"

"It doesn't matter. I know you must have had a good reason for doing what you did. Look, you finally found the ticket, right? So it's over."

I could see he didn't believe my story. "But—"

"Don't worry about it, Sachi. When you get to be eighteen, I know you'll tell me the truth."

I don't know what being eighteen had to do with it, but six years later, when I turned eighteen, I sought my father out and told him again, in pretty definitive terms, that I'd been totally innocent in this affair, and so had Yuki, and that the tickets had just disappeared. That was the pure, unvarnished truth.

Dad nodded knowingly. I thought I saw a trace of pride in his smile, as though he were thinking, *She's sticking to her story, even after all these years. Cool.*

CHAPTER 5

FROM HERE TO ZAGREB

returned to Charters Towers the next year, as did Yuki. The Strange Affair of the Lost Tickets slowly faded from memory, and our friendship resumed its usual comradely competitiveness.

I was thirteen now, in full-rigged adolescence, and naturally inclining toward romantic dreams and schoolgirl crushes—and since I was surrounded mostly by fellow schoolgirls, my first big crushes involved females. (I wasn't going to get all dreamy-eyed over the flatulent Mr. Gerard.) I wasn't unique in this regard: all the younger girls at the school had big crushes on the older girls. This had nothing to do with sex. It was all very innocent and pure of spirit. Yet the power of the emotions, the from-the-heart intensity, was so overwhelming and all-consuming that some girls would hyperventilate, get hysterical, go into catatonic trances of longing.

My great crush was Sarah, a prefect with bright red hair and freckles, who was maybe two years older than I. She was so sweet and so friendly. I was crazy about her. I don't know if she realized the depth of my infatuation, or if she even suspected my interest. She probably had her own crush on somebody older. That's how it worked: the love kept spiraling forward in a great, continuous daisy chain of unrequited desire. The hallways were thick and humid with yearning.

I was unaware of anyone else's passions, being totally absorbed in my own little drama. Sarah would pass me in the hall, and my heart would leap. Sometimes she'd smile at me, and I'd lose my breath. If she happened to touch me, if even just her clothing brushed against me . . . electricity! A week's worth of daydreams!

Eventually the obsession faded, and I moved on to the next infatuation. I had lots of crushes at Charter Towers. About the only girl I didn't have a crush on was Yuki. We knew each other too well.

The following year, I switched schools—and found myself in Switzerland. Aiglon College was located high in the Swiss Alps, not far from Montreux and Lake Geneva. It was a spectacular location, a magnificent series of chalets set in a picture-postcard Alpine valley cradled by tall, snowy peaks.

Also spectacular, for me, was that Aiglon was a coed school. This was one of the reasons I petitioned Dad to leave Charters Towers. The all-girl ambience was starting to feel unhealthy to me. I remember telling him quite seriously, "I want boys."

And I got them: an international smorgasbord of boys in blazers. I soon discovered that while I liked girls, I *loved* guys. They were so cute, and funny, and full of energy.

And they loved me. Perhaps because I had such an open innocence, they were always flocking around me, flirting in a sweet way. I adored the attention, but I was still shy and deferential in my Japanese way, so not much happened. Except in my head.

I really had a great time at Aiglon. It was sunnier than Bexhill, nowhere near as cold and dank and dispiriting. The food was wonderful, and there was all that Swiss chocolate. And the mountains, and the forests. And the boys.

My grades were still terrible, true; I was an abysmal student. Then again, my father had already convinced me I was an idiot, and I had demonstrated no capacity for learning at any level, so I didn't care. I was *supposed* to be stupid.

So instead of going to class, I would sneak off to the Alps. I'd go skiing, or rock climbing, or skipping through fields of wildflowers, doing my best Heidi impersonation. In the spring, I'd slip out of the dorm at night and climb up the forest path to a glacier lake, and I'd skinny-dip in the moonlight. It was crazy and irresponsible, I know, but it was quite wonderful.

The great love of my Aiglon College days was Gabriel Connolly. I'll never forget him: a short, dark-haired British kid, sort of a Dudley Moore type, who had a mad crush on me. He thought I was gorgeous, and I thought he was funny, so it was a great match. Gabriel was from Liverpool, and he was probably on scholarship, because he had a slightly unrefined, street-smart air about him, so different from the other privileged kids at the school. A tough, manly Dudley Moore.

One night, I was in my dorm room on the fifth floor, lying awake in bed fantasizing about marrying Gabriel Connolly and having the perfect life. My roommate, Katie Sokoloff, was sleeping peacefully. Katie was from Greenwich, Connecticut, from wealthy, entitled stock; ironically, she was very good friends back home with the man who would become my husband some twenty years later. Right now, though, she was just the girl snoring in the other bed.

Suddenly I heard a light tapping on my window. I knew who it was right away—my Romeo, my dashing cavalier! He had climbed up the side of the building in the dark, using a rope. I couldn't let him in, not with Katie right there, so I climbed out. We went down the rope together—five stories, mind you—with Gabriel carrying me in his strong arms. It was the quintessence of romance.

Together we went into the woods and climbed up to my favorite glacier lake. All shyness gone, we took off our clothes and went swimming in the nude. The water was ice-cold and thrilling. When we came rushing out of the frigid lake, Gabriel wrapped me in a blanket. Then we kissed: my first real kiss, with tongues and everything. The cold had made the blood rush to the surface of my skin, and I was suddenly boiling hot. The rush of sensations was overwhelming: the cold, the heat, the full moon, Gabriel's lips, Gabriel's hands, the sweetness, the tenderness . . . I thought I would pass out.

That's as far as we went: a little petting, a little swooning. This was plenty far for me. We came back down the mountain, hand in hand, and climbed back up the rope, and he delivered me safely to my bed. Another kiss or two, and he was gone. While Katie slept on.

No, I'll never forget Gabriel Connolly.

THE first moments of 1971 found me at the New Year's Eve party at the Kanaya Hotel, high on a mountaintop in the Japan Alps. I was fourteen years old, and Dad was dancing with me. I now loved dancing with him, because he made me feel so grown-up and special. There was a disco ball overhead, scattering dreamy patches of light everywhere.

As we circled the dance floor, Dad pointed out an elegant European woman sitting at a table.

"That woman is quite beautiful. Don't you think?"

He turned me around on the dance floor so that I could see. Yes, she was beautiful.

"She reminds me of Eleanor Parker," he said. "The actress?"

I shrugged blankly.

"She was in *The Sound of Music*. She played the Baroness."

"Oh." Of course I remembered her. Everybody hated the Baroness.

"I was good friends with her," Dad said.

I looked at him in surprise. Who? The woman at the table?

"Eleanor Parker," he elaborated. "She was very special."

At the same time he was telling me about Eleanor Parker, his hand slid down from my waist and patted my fanny—and stayed there.

That struck me as very odd.

"She was a real woman—lovely, sophisticated, a classic beauty," he said, still holding on to my bottom. "You should watch some of her movies. You'll see what I mean."

I was getting some very confusing signals. Why was Dad grabbing my butt this way, as if I were his girlfriend? And why was he going on and on about Eleanor Parker? I sensed that he was conveying a message to me: that this actress was his idea of a truly desirable woman, and he was telling me—he wanted me to know—that I didn't come close to measuring up to her. I needed to be sexier and more beautiful if I wanted his approval.

Yet, why would I need that kind of approval? I wasn't his lover. I was his daughter, wasn't I?

IT was the end of my second year at Aiglon. I was fifteen years old and waiting to go home. I wasn't sure who was coming to pick me up, Mom or Dad. There hadn't been any communication or instructions—I wasn't even sure where they were—but I knew someone was coming. So I packed up my suitcase and waited.

The rest of the students were already leaving. Some had their parents pick them up; others took the bus to Lausanne and grabbed the train, heading off to various parts of Europe. The school was emptying out.

Still no sign of my parents. People were starting to get a sense of my plight. "When are you leaving?" they'd ask.

"I don't know," I'd say bravely. "But pretty soon. It won't be long now."

"Are you okay?"

"I'm fine!"

Of course, as soon as someone asks you if you're okay, you start to realize that maybe you're not okay. *What happens if nobody shows up? And the college and the dorm rooms are all shut down? Where will I sleep?*

At the same time, I was sort of enjoying the drama of the situation. I was like young Ebenezer Scrooge, left behind at the Christmas break. Nobody wanted me home. Nobody cared! At the same time, it was the perfect opportunity to be swept away in a wild European adventure. I was exhilarated by the prospects.

It was the next day now, however, and the last students were trickling out. Even the staff was leaving. I began to sense that I was in real danger of being abandoned there. Who was going to take care of me? I was starting to panic. As the last few students waved goodbye, I waved back cheerfully. I didn't want to share my agitation. I didn't want to make trouble.

Finally, my schoolmate Jane Wise, the last soul on the premises, was going off to catch the train at Lausanne. She saw me sitting by the front steps. "Are you okay?"

I thought about giving her a reassuring nod and sending her

untroubled on her way, but I couldn't keep my upper lip stiff any longer. "I don't know," I answered plaintively. "I don't think anyone's coming to pick me up!"

"Well, you can't stay here," she said.

I looked around at the empty grounds. She had a good point.

"Why don't you come with me?" Jane suggested. She was joining her family in Trieste, Italy. Her father was the American ambassador to Czechoslovakia, and during his mission they were living in Prague. So they were meeting up halfway for a few weeks of summer vacation on the Adriatic coast.

"Trieste?" I pondered.

"Sure. You can try to call your parents from there."

It seemed to make sense. I didn't want to be a burden on Jane and her family—she was a year older than I, and we weren't exactly close friends—but there didn't seem to be any other choice.

So we went down to Lausanne and caught the train to Trieste. Jane paid for my ticket. It was an all-day trip, as we had to make the trek straight across the top of the boot to eastern Italy.

At the train station we met Jane's mom and dad, and her sister Ann. We went to a luxury hotel in the heart of Trieste, and I stayed in Jane's room.

I knew I was incredibly lucky to be there. Jane's parents paid for everything. We spent the days at the beach, which was right at the northern tip of the Adriatic Sea. There were lots of beautiful Europeans, male and female, cruising the sands in the tiniest of bathing suits. I remember everyone kept asking me if I wanted ice cream.

I didn't want ice cream. I didn't want anything. I had a very numb feeling inside, which at night was replaced by a pain around my heart. I didn't know what was causing it, but my heart was hurting.

So much so that I could barely sleep—and when I did, I would wake in the middle of the night with a deep, profound feeling of sadness. Yet, I didn't know why.

I didn't voice any of this to Jane or her parents. I felt guilty enough freeloading on them; the least I could do was maintain a cheery disposition. That was the Japanese way.

One night, I woke at around 2:00 A.M. There was the pain again, the pain in my heart. I got up quietly. Something was telling me I needed to leave. I needed to go out.

I quietly got dressed. I put on my tight blouse and my miniskirt—and no underwear. Not one brown shred.

I went into the next room, where Jane's parents were sleeping. I saw her mom's high heels under the dresser. I took them and sneaked out of the room. Outside, I slipped on the high heels and left the hotel suite.

Downstairs, I crossed the hotel lobby. I felt the doorman watching me quizzically as I stepped out into the warm night. I knew that if I looked at him, he would stop me. So I didn't look. I headed down the sidewalk and turned the corner, and now I was on my own.

The Trieste streets were empty and quiet. My high heels click-clacked on the cobblestones as I made my rudderless way through the city, strutting along in my sexy, tarted-up outfit.

Unwittingly, and yet as if by design, I found myself in the seediest section of town. There was nightlife here; people were moving in the shadows: large, indistinct shapes; muted snatches of their conversation echoed against the buildings. Who were they? Thieves, perhaps; drunks, prostitutes. A dark, threatening sexuality was in the air. Men and women were humping openly against the building walls. Other men circled around, eyeing me prospectively as I walked along. Some would move closer; some would even stand in my path and make me swerve around them.

Now the prostitutes emerged from the dark, gathering in pockets and glaring at me with territorial hatred: "Who is this little bitch, in her miniskirt and high heels, and what is she doing on our turf?"

What *was* I doing there? What was I thinking? I don't know. It was all very dreamlike and Felliniesque, without the saving grace of comic absurdity. I knew I was in danger—I could feel it all around me—but I didn't really care.

I was being adventurous, the way Dad had suggested. I was having an experience.

Basically, I think I wanted to die.

So I stopped on that dark, dangerous street, vulnerable and surrounded, and waited for something to happen.

Finally, one aged prostitute detached herself from the group and approached me. She was in her sixties, maybe older, wearing garish clothes that clung unattractively to her body, her face caked with makeup. Her eyes gleamed savagely in the glint of the street-light. I felt a sudden, paralyzing terror—this is it. She's coming to kill me. She's going to rake me with her clawlike nails, slash me open with the stiletto hidden in her garter . . . I couldn't move. I was trapped in my death wish.

When the old woman got very close, she put an arm around me and asked, in a gentle voice, *"Dove abiti, cara?"*

Somehow she had grasped exactly why I was there, and what I really needed. My eyes filled with tears, and I started to cry. She hushed me, cradled my head against her bosom, and gently turned me around and walked me back to the hotel. We didn't speak much—I had had some French in Aiglon, so we could manage a few words here and there—but most of our conversation was spoken with our eyes.

Back at the hotel, the doorman was waiting in the lobby. I can imagine what a sight we were, the two of us dressed up like ladies of the evening, and one the genuine article. By all rights, he should have barred the old prostitute at the door and called upstairs for Jane's parents to collect me.

But he didn't. Somehow he knew exactly what was going on. He and the woman traded glances, and there was one of those miraculous moments of unspoken human communication. He nodded and stepped aside, letting us pass. He was probably relieved to have me back, and grateful to the woman for her kindness.

Back in my room, the woman undressed me and put me to bed. When she saw that I'd been wearing no underwear, she tsked disapprovingly, but kept her silence, so as not to waken Jane. Like Katie Sokoloff, Jane was a sound sleeper and never stirred.

The woman tucked me in and sat by my bedside a moment, stroking my hair, whispering soft, comforting words. Then she bent down, kissed my forehead, and left.

I never saw her again.

AFTER a week in Trieste, we took a ferry south to the coast of Yugoslavia, where we stopped at another beach resort on the Adriatic, and stayed about two weeks.

I don't remember much about this time, except that there seemed to be an awful lot of Germans on the beach. Most of my days were spent on the phone, trying to contact my parents. After hours of blind-dialing, waiting on operators, listening through bad reception, getting tantalizingly close and suddenly losing the connection altogether, all I could safely determine was that my dad wasn't in Tokyo, and my mom wasn't in Los Angeles. This narrowed the field of inquiry somewhat.

It seemed I was on the phone all day every day, and getting

nowhere. I was miserable, and still haunted by a feeling of vague sadness—and feeling guiltier all the time for taking advantage of the Wises' kindness. They had been incredibly warm and gracious, but sooner or later I knew I was going to wear out my welcome.

We left the coast and drove up to Zagreb, the capital of Yugoslavia. From here the Wises were taking the train home to Prague. I just couldn't tag along anymore. The moment of truth had arrived.

Or rather, the moment of untruth. I rushed up to them on the platform with a big patented smile on my face. "Finally," I told them brightly. "I got hold of my dad! He's sending me money right away, so everything's fine. You guys can go ahead without me. I have to wait here for the money."

None of this was true, but the Wises bought it. Or at least they said they did. They could leave me now with a clear conscience. There was nothing unusual in this, by the way. In those days, it was quite normal to see teens traveling by themselves all over Europe. The Wises weren't abandoning me. They were letting me enjoy my independence.

They boarded the train, and I waved cheerfully as it chugged away. "Goodbye! Thanks for everything! Goodbye, goodbye!"

So, now, instead of being stranded in Switzerland, I was stranded in Yugoslavia. What an idiot.

There was a hotel across from the train station. I walked over and went into the hotel bar. I sat on a stool, put my head on the bar, and started crying. What was I going to do now?

There was an elderly couple in their seventies at the bar. They were sitting close and chatting intimately, with a relaxed, casual familiarity that indicated they were married. There was something a bit rustic and out of place about them, so perhaps they had ventured into the city for a romantic date night. If so, my sobbing at the bar may have put something of a damper on their ardor.

In any case, they got up from their stools and came over to see what was wrong. They spoke only Yugoslavian, so even my little bit of French wasn't going to help me now. Still, they saw my distress, and much like that prostitute in Trieste, they understood without words.

They sat beside me and comforted me, and somehow managed to construe that I was stranded and had nowhere to stay. So they brought me up to their hotel room and had a cot set up for me, and I stayed the night with them. This was, all in all, a remarkable thing.

I had already imposed on one family for the last three weeks, and I really didn't want to start all over again. I had no idea what to do next or how to proceed, though, so the next day, when they insisted, through some universal gestures and inflections, that I go back home with them, I meekly accepted.

We drove into the Yugoslavian countryside to their farm, a good five-hour ride. I could see when we arrived that they were of very modest means. It was a run-down working farm, with lots of vegetables and chickens. Everything was old and rusty, but it all worked.

I stayed with these wonderful people for about two weeks. I helped out with the chores: milked the cows, fed the chickens, shared the cooking with the old woman. There was plenty of work to do, and I slept really well—no pain in my heart at all. It got cold at night, but they had the Hungarian eiderdowns!

I loved that couple. They treated me like their daughter, and the setting put me in mind of that palomino farm up in the hills of Malibu, with Ricardo and his mother: simple, hardworking people who were full of a love of nature and life. There were no pretensions, no demands, just a regulated sense of peace and harmony.

The old man had a great deal of work to do on the farm, but he would always take time out from his busy day to drive me down to the local post office so I could make my calls in my ongoing attempt to locate my parents. After an hour or so without success, we'd head over to the local bakery for a treat. I remember the pastries were denser and less refined than the fluffy ones you'd find in the French or Swiss bakeries. These were earthier, more typical of the people, whom I found to be unfailingly cheerful and friendly in spite of their inescapable poverty.

Still, much as I enjoyed this new world and these new friends, I was growing desperate to find my real family. I called and called. Finally, one day, instead of dial tones and static, I heard a familiar, English-speaking voice at the other end of the phone: "Hello?"

I was stunned. "Dad?"

"Hey, Sachi! Sach the Pach! What's up?" His voice was sunny and gregarious. He sounded as if he hadn't a care in the world.

I felt an immediate need to match his good spirits. "Nothing. I was just calling to say hello," I answered, without a trace of irony.

"Where are you?"

"Um—I'm in Yugoslavia."

He laughed. "Yugoslavia? What are you doing there?"

"Oh, just hanging around." I was being very cool. "Uh— where are *you*?"

"I'm on the boat," he replied casually. The "boat" was his private yacht, *Happy Pappy*. It turned out he'd been sailing the Mediterranean, just off the coast of Greece, all this time.

We made a little small talk, and then I mentioned that I needed some money to get home. Or wherever I was going.

Dad was quiet a moment. "You know, your mother is shooting a television show in London," he said. "You should go see her."

"London?"

"I'll wire you the money."

"Oh, okay."

I told him exactly where I was, and he said he would take care of everything: problem solved. "Enjoy your summer!"

I hung up. I should have been vastly relieved, I suppose, but instead I came away feeling unsettled by this surreal collision of three wildly incongruent worlds: Dad sailing the Mediterranean, Mom shooting a TV show in England, and me stuck on a chicken farm in Yugoslavia.

My surrogate parents drove me to a bank in Zagreb, where the money was wired. Then they brought me to the airport, and we said goodbye. I couldn't have expressed my gratitude sufficiently even if we'd spoken the same language, but I think they understood how I felt. They were stoic, unemotional people, but I owed them so much—God knows what would have happened to me if they hadn't come along and helped me. I kept in touch with them over the years, and sent them a Christmas card every December, until they both passed on about thirty years ago.

I arrived in England and found my mother on the set of her new TV show. *Shirley's World* was her attempt to break into sitcoms. In it, she played a globe-trotting photojournalist with a crusty but charming editor played by English actor John Gregson, and it was shot on location all over the world. The main base was at Pinewood Studios, just west of London.

The show was not destined to be a success—in fact, it was an outright flop—and Mom seemed to sense this even as they were shooting it, because she was in a foul mood on the set, and didn't seem to be getting along with anyone.

She was delighted to see me, of course: "Hi, sweetie! What are you doing here?" I didn't bother to tell her that she had forgotten to pick me up in Switzerland. I was afraid it would upset her. At the same time, I think I was afraid that it *wouldn't* upset her. She might have even wound up blaming me for the oversight.

Anyway, we had a nice visit, for about a day or two, and then she shifted back into work mode, and I suddenly became a great inconvenience. She had enough problems dealing with this god-forsaken show; she didn't want to have to deal with me, too.

She called the headmaster of Battisborough, the boarding school I was transferring to in the fall—I don't know why they had decided to move me out of Aiglon; maybe because they couldn't remember where it was. "My daughter is here in London," she told him. "Is there something you can do with her?"

The next thing I knew, I was on a train to Devon.

Battisborough House was run by Anthony Fiddian-Green, who used to be in charge of the girl's dorm at Aiglon. So I already knew him and his lovely wife, Susan. They had taken over this run-down centuries-old stone mansion and were in the process of fixing it up for the fall term.

For the rest of the summer, I became their errand girl and all-around handyman. I helped clean up the dusty rooms, paint the walls, wax the floors—whatever needed doing, I did. I stayed in the house and ate my meals with them and became a temporary member of their family (my third of the summer!).

Battisborough, in the county of Devon, is an absolutely beautiful spot, right on the southwest coast, near Plymouth. Looking south to the English Channel, the house sat on a green sward not far from a series of dramatic rock cliffs and coves abutting a deserted coastline. As I recall, there were never any people around, only sheep. I would often navigate the narrow sheep paths through the brambles and gooseberry bushes and down the steep cliffs, and take long walks on the lonely windswept coast, exploring Bugle Cove and Mothercombe Beach. I had long grown accustomed to being alone, and I felt totally in my element wandering barefoot in the sand with the wind whipping my hair and the spray of the ocean misting over me.

I didn't go back to Japan that summer. (There was no one there, anyway.) I stayed at Battisborough, and as the fall term began and the other students—including boys; hooray!—arrived, I resumed my studies.

Not that I studied much. Battisborough was based on the Summerhill model. Summerhill School was founded in Suffolk, England, in 1921 by A. S. Neill, a Scottish writer who believed that children flourish most without adult authority. His progressive school stressed freedom and autonomy. So, at Battisborough, you were defined by your own idea of success. There were no bells; you went to class any time you wanted to, and if you didn't want to, you could just play. It was, for most kids, an ideal situation.

It wasn't for me. Much as I bridled at authority, I was lost without it. Given the choice, I never went to class. My grades sank to a level not even imagined before.

Yet, in spite of my low academic performance, I was considered the most responsible, level-headed kid at the school. Some of the other kids were messing around with drugs and alcohol. They came from money, so there was plenty of acid and LSD and cocaine floating around the dorms.

I didn't touch any of it. My biggest vice was going for walks on the beach. So my bond rating was pretty high. Everyone in the faculty trusted me—and I took advantage of this.

There was a separate cottage on the grounds; I used to walk by it on the way to the beach. Nobody was staying there, and it seemed to be going to waste. I would have loved to have that cottage as a dorm room all to myself. At the moment, I was rooming with an American girl named Anne Hearst (younger sister of Patty Hearst, who was famously kidnapped by the Symbionese Liberation Army just a few months later). Anne was nice enough, but I liked the idea of being on my own and independent.

I brought up the idea of the cottage with Mrs. Green (we never bothered with the "Fiddian" part; they were always "Mr. and Mrs. Green" to the students). Mrs. Green, who was very fond of me, discussed it with her husband, and they agreed that I was trustworthy enough, so I moved into the cottage. I loved that place. It was small, but there was a kitchenette with a hot plate and an electric kettle. There, I was completely, serenely alone—except for one fateful night.

It was my second year at Battisborough, the spring of 1974. I was seventeen years old, and the new great love of my life was Bradley Foster. There were only about eighteen kids at the school, half of them of the male persuasion, and most of those were pretty dicey. Brad was head and shoulders above the rest, the pick of the lot, and it was my good fortune to have nabbed him. He was tall, handsome, and very sweet.

This particular evening, Brad sneaked up to the cottage to be with me. The door was on the ground floor, so there was no need for ropes or climbing out of windows. I just let Brad in, and we immediately went at it like teenagers in heat—which is exactly what we were. We were so mad with passion that I forgot to close the curtains.

We were doing some heavy making out, and pretty soon I realized that this was going to be a historic encounter: we were going all the way. We moved from kissing to groping to grinding with amazing speed. As if by magic, my clothes were off, and so were his, and we were wrestling on the couch, and it was happening, we were going for it, we were right at the brink . . . !

Then the door flew open—forgot to lock it!—and there was Mrs. Green, staring at us, mouth open in shock. We were caught, caught dead. There was no hope of coming up with an adequate excuse, not with the two of us stark naked, our limbs intricately intertwined.

I hastily covered myself with a couch pillow, while Brad grabbed his clothes and hid behind them. Mrs. Green took in the lurid scene for a moment, her eyes fixing me with wounded outrage, and then she turned and stalked off into the night.

I threw Brad out of the cottage and then, guilt-stricken, rushed up to the main house. I burst in on the Greens and apologized profusely to them. I felt terrible, I had betrayed their trust. How could I have been so selfish and ungrateful? I tearfully admitted my guilt—"I'm sorry, I'm sorry, I'm sorry!"—and begged for their forgiveness.

I didn't get it. Mr. Green just said he was "very disappointed," and left the room. Mrs. Green wouldn't even look at me; she stared at the wall and said nothing.

Brad and I broke up after that. Much as I desired him, close as he had come to adding a seminal chapter to my sexual history, he had been an accomplice in the most humiliating episode of my life, and I just couldn't be with him anymore.

AT exam time, we had to take both the British and the American tests to determine our college worthiness. The SATs were not culturally neutral; they were definitely slanted toward American mores and idioms. If you hadn't been raised in the United States, you just wouldn't do as well—and I didn't.

I did, however, score very high on my French and English A-levels, which were extremely hard and served as the best barometer of whether you belonged in college.

This encouraged me to look forward to college with a new-found purpose. I was going to really apply myself from now on. I was going to be a model student. I hadn't picked out a college yet, but wherever I went, I was going to shine.

So it was with pride and relief that I received my diploma from Battisborough. Mr. Green gave me a stiff, cursory handshake, and Mrs. Green averted her eyes as I passed. I didn't care: I was out, I was moving on. The graduation ceremony was small, but it was beautiful and inspiring.

Neither of my parents came.

CHAPTER 6

"You're on Your Own Now"

In June of 1974, Mom was performing her act in Las Vegas. That was her reason for missing my graduation.

I completely understood. In those days, before the second coming of Atlantic City and the glut of casinos all over the country, Las Vegas was a world of glitz unto itself. When you played Vegas, you were at the peak, the center of the entertainment universe. And you couldn't just walk away from that, even to attend your daughter's graduation.

So, since Mom couldn't come to me, I went to her. I was a high school graduate now, practically a grown-up. It was time for us to establish a real, mature mother-daughter relationship before I went off to college.

I'd been to Las Vegas as a young girl, when Mom was hanging out with Frank Sinatra and the Rat Pack. Back in 1960, Dad was producing a show called *Holiday in Japan*, a musical revue extravaganza starring the biggest Japanese singers and dancers of the time; it more or less introduced postwar Japanese culture to the West. *Holiday in Japan* played a month at the New Frontier Hotel and Casino, which, with the Flamingo and the Desert Inn, was one of the few Vegas-type hotels on the Strip at that time. The Strip itself was in fact just a strip, a wide dirt roadway. Las Vegas was a different proposition back then. There was a lot less neon and a lot more sand.

I don't remember the Japan show at all, but I remember the wind, and the cold. It would be dry heat during the day but freezing cold at night. For some reason, while I was visiting Dad during *Holiday in Japan*, we didn't stay in a hotel. We lived in makeshift tents in the desert, and slept on cots. We had to walk across the sand dunes to get to the hotel where the revue was being performed. Our feet would sink in the shifting sands, while the wind buffeted us from all directions, and we had to use outhouses to relieve ourselves. When I would wake up in the middle of the night having to pee, I dreaded going out into that cold, and the blowing wind. Whenever I did screw up my fortitude and make a run for the outhouse, I was constantly dodging the huge tumbleweeds that rolled past. They scared me, and for good reason—they were as big as I was.

Vegas had a lonely, mysterious feeling then. There was an overpowering sense of nothingness. Yet for some reason, I found it enchanting. I particularly loved the mornings, when the red sun would paint the sheer cliffs of Sunrise Mountain.

So I was completely unprepared for the jolt of energy that hit me now, in the Las Vegas of 1974, virtually the minute I stepped out onto the tarmac. The lights, the people, the cars, the sense of money and power and pleasure—the very air thrummed with electricity. It made me sad. It wasn't quiet, like before. I couldn't hear the wind anymore.

As I sat at a front table in the theater where Mom was performing, I found myself surrounded by celebrities, politicians, high-rollers, and the like, all in tuxedoes and gowns and gaudy leisure suits. They were all there; they had all dragged themselves away from the casino tables and the roulette wheels just to see my mom in action.

And she was worth it. A complete entertainer, she did all her songs from *Sweet Charity*—"I'm a Brass Band," "If They Could See Me Now"—and some funny specialty numbers, and those brilliant Bob Fosse dances with the top hat and black tights, and "It's Not Where You Start, It's Where You Finish," a new signature song for her from the musical *Seesaw*, which was based on *Two for the Seesaw*. (Show business is a curiously circular kind of world.)

It was a great act. Mom owned that stage, and she knew it. And every now and then she would look down from her kingdom and give me a wink, with a big, glorious smile on her face. She was enjoying herself immensely, and she wanted me to share in the fun.

And I did. I was so proud to see her up there that it literally made me shake. The waiters would ask me if I wanted another Shirley Temple, but I couldn't even speak. If I could have, I would have said, "Forget about the drinks. Look at my mom!" She was so special, and she made me feel special, knowing that I was a part of her, that her spirit and her talent lived within me, somewhere. Just the thought that we were connected took my breath away.

After the show, I waited in the dressing room while Mom greeted her fans. There was always a line of people outside the door, armed with papers, posters, anything for her to autograph. They would wait patiently, sometimes over an hour, just to pay homage to her. Every now and then the professionals, the important people, would be ushered through the crowd to see her. Sinatra, Dean Martin, Jack Lemmon, Danny Kaye—they would blithely cut the line and step into the dressing room for a casual chat that might last fifteen minutes, an hour, or more.

While everyone else waited. This upset me, because I felt for all those ordinary people out there who just wanted to show their appreciation. I knew what it was like to be kept waiting. I wanted to say, "Mom, shut up. There are people out there who want to see you!"

At the same time I was empathizing with the outsiders, I was also enjoying the thrill of being on the inside, with the special people. If they were special, that meant that I was special, too. More than that—I was cool.

When Mom did finally make time for the public, she would be a most charming host. She'd chat, she'd laugh, she would happily pose for photos. Then the moment would come—you could see it in her eyes—when she was done. Her face would go blank, she'd turn off the thousand-watt smile, she'd give you the cold stare, and you knew you'd been dismissed—and woe betide those who didn't pick up on the signals, because then she'd happily spell it out for them:

"Excuse me, but I have a life, do you? Have a nice day. Go win some money."

That night, having vanquished her fans, Mom closed the door, sighed wearily, and then turned to me with exaggerated deliberation. I could tell from her manner that there was a dramatic moment coming. She stepped forward and took my hands in hers.

"Sachi, sweetheart, I'm so proud of you. I really am." She waited a moment to let this sink in. I understood in a limited sense that the important point here was not that I had graduated from school, but that she was proud. Her emotional response was center stage right now.

Mom turned to her dressing table and picked up a thin jewelry box with a red ribbon stretched around the corners. She waited a beat, and then handed the box to me. "Here."

I took the box and opened it.

Inside was a diamond necklace.

I was stunned. It was spectacular. It must have cost a fortune.

"Oh my God! Mom—it's amazing!" I held it up, and saw the dressing room mirror lights glittering in the prisms of the stones.

"Those diamonds are from Belgium," Mom said. "Belgian diamonds are the best in the world. I had them shipped here specially on a private jet."

"Really? Just for me?"

"Just for you." She wrapped her arms around me and gave me a big hug. "Congratulations, baby!" We rocked back and forth, and I luxuriated in the moment.

Then she stepped back and added a casual fillip: "You're on your own now."

It took me a moment to process this, and I realized that there was a hidden weight to these unexceptional words.

"On my own? What do you mean?"

Mom sat at her dressing table and began removing her makeup. "Well, I mean, you've graduated, there's your gift—good luck. Do you have any plans?"

"Plans? Well, I was hoping to go to college . . ."

Mom looked over her shoulder with a get-real expression. "College? What for?" She laughed pleasantly. "How can you afford college anyway?"

"Well, I thought maybe . . ." I made a hopeful gesture toward her.

She rejected my fanciful notion in short order. "Ha! Don't look at me. You have to make your own way in the world, sweetheart. That's what I did, and look where I got." She made a sweeping gesture to include the trappings of her room, the photos with fellow celebrities, the good-luck telegrams, and, beyond that, the golden world of Las Vegas itself. "That's the key to happiness. When you do it all on your own it means so much more. You'll see."

I was trying to see, but I have to admit, it wasn't easy taking the long view. I just couldn't make sense of it. I wasn't going to college? Why had I just spent six years in expensive prep schools if I wasn't prepping for anything? What was that all about?

For the record, I asked Dad to pay for college, and he said no, too—which was odd, because all through my teenage years, Dad had contended that I would be the perfect candidate to work at the United Nations in Geneva. "You have so many languages under your belt, you have a broad way of thinking, you're not judgmental, you don't have any religion to screw you up, you understand and embrace differences in people, you empathize with others. You would be ideal." I thought so, too. Still, how was I going to get to the UN without a college education? I was no genius, but I knew that I couldn't make it from A to D without a few stepping stones in between. Take them away, and where was I?

I watched impotently as Mom wiped the cold cream from her face and started applying another round of makeup for the real world. My first instinct was to flee in tears, but then I thought better of it and decided to appeal to her maternal advice-giving side. "But, Mom, what am I gonna do instead?"

"Oh, don't worry," she said cheerfully. "Something always comes up." Mom stared critically at her visage in the mirror, adjusting her mascara. "And you know, sweetheart, if you ever get short of money, if you're ever really desperate, you can always sell the necklace."

I never sold it, no matter how desperate my situation was (and it got pretty grim at times). I always kept the necklace in a compartment in my purse and carried it around with me wherever I went. I was terrified of losing it. It was only when I was married and settled in a house of my own that I felt confident enough to leave it in a jewelry box—and there it is, still.

MOM did give me one other unexpected gift that summer. It was after her show closed and we went back to Malibu. The Malibu house was actually a huge apartment building that Mom had built for herself. It was a two-story structure right on the sand, and she rented out some of the apartments downstairs. She lived upstairs, in an ever-expanding suite of rooms.

There were always guests in the other rooms, and some of them stayed so long they were getting their mail there. One such omnipresent couple were Phyllis and Eberhard Kronhausen, renowned sex therapists and art curators. They had written all kinds of books—*The Sexually Responsive Woman*, *Pornography and the Law*—and they'd organized a museum show, the First International Exhibition of Erotic Art. They were generally considered standard-bearers for the sexual revolution of the 1960s.

They had latched on to my mom in a big way. Mom embraced them as liberating figures, not just sexually but philosophically. Looking back, I think they gave her permission to be free with her life, permission she never got from her own very restrictive Baptist parents. Phyllis and Eberhard were anything but restrictive. Extremely full of themselves and their "anything goes" credo, they were eager to spread the gospel of the *Kama Sutra*. That's all they talked about: sex, sex, sex, in every conceivable facet and permutation.

They gave me the creeps. I think I was also jealous of the attention they got from my mom. It made me angry that they were sponging off her and using her as a meal ticket (I was even angrier some years later when I discovered that she bought them a farm in Costa Rica). I just wished there was some way I could protect her from these kinds of people.

I avoided them as much as I could. Luckily it happened that my old boyfriend Brad from Battisborough (who was now back as my new boyfriend) lived in San Francisco, just a few hours away, and he was visiting for the weekend. So I could spend all my time with him.

It was inevitable that at some point my path would intersect with that of our live-in guests. One afternoon, we found ourselves all colliding in the living room: Mom, the Kronhausens, Brad, and me. The grown-ups were looking very sophisticated and knowing. I sensed at once we had stumbled into a potentially volatile situation, so I tried to hustle Brad out of there as quickly as possible, but it was too late.

"Sachi, is this your boyfriend?" Phyllis asked.

"Yes, this is Brad." I made all the necessary introductions.

"You've been going together a long time?" asked Eberhard, fixing me with an owlish eye.

"About a year, maybe. Off and on. Here and there."

"Have you had sex yet?"

I felt my face flush. I didn't look at Brad—I didn't want to embarrass him any further. "Sex?" I responded, laughing lightly. "No! Of course not." I chuckled some more, just to underscore the point. This seemed like the only rational response: to treat the question like a joke. Obviously they were parodying their reputation as sexual gurus, right?

As I looked at Phyllis and Eberhard Kronhausen, and Mom, they all stared back at me with earnest curiosity.

"No? You've never had sex?" Phyllis asked. "*Ever?*"

"No," I admitted sheepishly.

"Don't you think it's time you did?" her husband asked.

Now I did look at Brad, because I instinctively felt the need for an ally. He had an incredulous what-the-hell-did-I-get-myself-into expression on his face. I don't think he'd had a lot of experience with bizarre eccentrics.

"You're how old—seventeen?" Phyllis asked.

"She'll be eighteen in September," Mom offered.

"Well," Phyllis said, with a perplexed shrug, "you're practically an adult. What are you waiting for?"

"You're at the bright dawn of your sexuality," Eberhard pointed out. "This is the moment to explore and experience."

I nodded politely. "Okay, well, we'll think about it." I took Brad's hand in mine, to show that we were pledged to making a serious effort.

"I think you should do it right now," Eberhard stated.

Brad and I instantly let go of each other's hands. "Now?"

"You know," Phyllis said, directing her comments to my mom now, "it would be a fabulous opportunity for Sachi, to have her first introduction to sex with all of us here as a support group. We could talk about it afterward—discuss what happened and why—and validate her feelings."

Eberhard agreed. "Guide her through the trauma, and celebrate the joy."

Phyllis was getting excited. "She could really benefit from our expertise."

Mom was leaning forward, lips pursed thoughtfully. I tried to read her face. Which way was she going to break? Surely she wouldn't agree with this nutty idea. Surely.

Now Mom nodded warmly. "I think it's a wonderful idea." *So much for surely.* "I wish someone had been there for me," she added.

I started inching toward the exit.

"And on a professional level," Phyllis said, "it will be instructive for us to observe this crucial rite of passage as it happens. It's a win-win."

All eyes then turned on me expectantly, waiting for my endorsement.

"Uh, I don't think I want to do this."

"But you *should*," Eberhard said with solemn gravity.

Phyllis chimed in: "Better this way than in the backseat of a car or in some dirty alleyway—no offense, Brad, I don't know you, but statistics show that for most people the first time can be very unpleasant. Lots of psychological scars result."

"It's not my first time," Brad said.

"Even better. You can help her through this, too."

"We're all here to help you, sweetheart," Mom said, beaming.

I felt like Mia Farrow surrounded by the Satanists in *Rosemary's Baby*. There were three powerful personalities bearing down on me, forcing me to their collective will, and I couldn't fight them off. How to negotiate this situation? I couldn't say I didn't want to have sex with Brad, because of course I did. Besides, how often do you find your own mother coaching you to lose your virginity?

"Well, I guess . . . if you think it's all right . . ."

"Of course it's all right!" Phyllis said.

"In sex, everything is all right," Eberhard assured.

As if to prove their point, they fetched some books from their room. These were books they had written themselves, about erotic art and sexual fantasies, and they were liberally illustrated. We sat on the couch and Phyllis flipped through the pages with me. "This is a good position," she suggested. "Oh, and this one allows for maximum penetration. You could try this one, too. You're young and flexible." Many of the positions seemed to entail a lot of squatting and bending and standing on your head.

"Take the book with you," Eberhard suggested.

So, having been given our assignment, Brad and I went down the hall to my bedroom. It was as dry and unerotic a prelude to sex as I could imagine, but I went along with it because I didn't want the Kronhausens to think I wasn't cool.

"And if you have any questions," Phyllis called, "we're right out here."

"We'll be waiting," Eberhard said.

My room was pretty cramped. We had to use the lower tier of a twin bunk bed. It would have been a lot more comfortable in Mom's expansive bedroom, but that would have been a little too weird, even for her.

We took off our clothes and climbed into the bunk. We weren't going to use any of the Kronhausens' fancy positions; it was hard enough to pull off the missionary position in that tight space. I remember being pushed up against the wall, my neck bent sideways, as we started going at it. There was no foreplay to speak of. People were waiting.

There was also no birth control to speak of. Brad didn't use a condom—I don't think I ever saw a condom until I was in my late twenties—and I certainly wasn't on the pill. At the time, I didn't realize how odd it was that my mother was encouraging me to have sex and didn't express any concern that I might get pregnant or contract a social disease. I guess everyone just got caught up in the giddiness of the moment.

Except Brad. I felt sorry for him. I don't know what was going through his mind. He couldn't have been enjoying this; it was more like an onerous duty. (Although I don't know that a seventeen-year-old boy could ever not enjoy sex.)

I was very thin by this time. I'd been losing weight steadily, and now, at five foot six I was about eighty pounds. Although I didn't realize it, I was suffering from anorexia. I don't know when it started—I'm tempted to think when I was put on that starvation diet after we lost the airline tickets, but I can't say for sure. Somewhere along the line, I had just stopped eating, and by this time I was pretty bony. I couldn't have cut a very seductive figure for poor Brad—there was very little there to arouse him—but he gave it the old college try nonetheless.

Suddenly I felt pain inside. "Wait, stop!"

"What's the matter?"

"Something hurts."

Brad apologized and said he'd try to be gentler. He started again, and— "Ow!"

I was terrified. Why was this painful? Sex was supposed to be a pleasant experience, wasn't it? Was there something wrong with me?

Brad, drawing on his measure of experience, explained the situation to me. I was a virgin. My hymen hadn't broken yet.

"My hymen? What are you talking about?" I really had no clue. They hadn't taught us about this at boarding school—and the celebrated sex therapists in the next room had forgotten to mention it.

Brad tried to explain. "The hymen is like a membrane that stretches across the—you know. And the first time you make love . . ." I eventually got the picture. He promised to go very easy. Over and over, though, he would bang up against it, and I would yelp, and he would pull back. It was getting annoying.

"Look," said Brad, "we don't have to do this . . ."

"But I want to," I said. I really did. I couldn't go back out into that living room and face my mom and her friends and admit failure. I wanted their approval. I wanted to be cool.

"Okay, well . . . On the count of three, then, I'll push really hard and break it, and it'll probably hurt a lot, but then it'll be over."

The scenario didn't sound too appetizing, but it had to be done. "Okay, let's do it." I lay back and braced myself against the wall.

Brad got into position. "One, two, *three!*" He lunged into me, and oh my god! It hurt like hell. I thought I was going to die. It was all I could do to keep from screaming.

But it was done. Brad held me tight. He felt so sorry that he'd hurt me. He kept saying, "I love you, I love you," over and over.

Then, to my horror, I looked down and saw blood on the sheets. Now what? Had he perforated something important? Was I having an early period, or hemorrhaging to death?

Brad calmed me down and reassured me that it was all very natural. I really was so lucky to have had such a patient, understanding guy for my first time.

And he was right: it didn't hurt anymore after that initial thrust. In fact, it felt pretty damn good.

Once our mission was accomplished, we had to face the next hurdle: reporting back to the Kronhausens. We dreaded the thought; there was something so weird and cultish about them. We hid out in the bedroom until we heard a light knock on the door, and Mom's voice: "Is everything okay in there?"

We emerged from the bedroom and went out to the living room, where Phyllis and Eberhard sat placidly on the couch.

"So, how did it go?" Phyllis asked.

"It was great."

"Did you achieve climax?" Eberhard asked.

We both nodded vigorously. They smiled smugly.

I hated them.

THE one positive result of this strange interlude was that I fell madly in love with Brad. He had been a model of chivalry throughout the ordeal, and now I was crazy about him. Brad was my first real lover, and I wanted him to be the only one—and he wanted me.

So after he went back home to San Francisco, I made plans to join him. We were going to live together.

I told Mom the good news, fully expecting her to share in the excitement. She didn't.

"You're only seventeen. You can't move in with a man. You're not ready."

"I was ready enough to sleep with him. It was your idea!"

"That's different," she contended. "I was helping you become a woman. Sexual maturity and emotional maturity are two different things. You don't want to get tied down in a serious relationship now. You have your whole life ahead of you."

"But it's not like I have any other plans. I'm not going to college," I helpfully reminded her.

She ignored this point. "Besides, you don't love him."

"Yes, I do!"

She smiled understandingly. "I'm sure you have feelings for him. But let's give it some time. If he really loves you, he'll wait for you."

I didn't want to wait. I was in love with Brad, and we were

going to live together. Mom had pushed us into bed, and now she would have to live with the consequences.

A few days later, as I was preparing for my great life move, Dad called out of the blue from Japan with some exciting news: he'd lined up a job for me in Tokyo, as a television newscaster.

A newscaster! On television! I couldn't believe it. I'd never really thought about doing anything in show business—not since my role in *To Kill a Mockingbird* got shot down—but once the offer came in, I suddenly realized that it was the one thing in life I wanted to do. *Had* to do. I knew I'd probably gotten the job by trading on my mom's name, but I didn't care. It was a gig! I was going to be a star!

Yes, I would now have to give up the idea of living with Brad in San Francisco, and that gave me serious misgivings.

"Hey, opportunities like this don't come around that often," Mom said. "You have to jump on them." She reminded me, "If he loves you, he'll wait."

Armed with these time-tested clichés, I called Brad and told him I was heading back to Japan, and we'd have to postpone moving in together, but it would only be for a short while, and if he loved me . . . It all sounded like total bullshit. I knew if I left, things with him would be over, and so did he.

I think it broke Brad's heart when I went back to Japan. I know it broke mine. He was the love of my life—and it would be a long, long time before I found another one.

WHEN I arrived back in Tokyo in the fall of 1974, there was no one waiting for me at the airport. That struck me as a little odd, but—whatever. I took a cab to the house—and there was no one waiting there, either. In fact, there was no one waiting for me in the entire city. Dad and Miki were gone.

What about my newscaster job? I called the television station. No one seemed to know what I was talking about.

I was getting that stranded feeling again. In my heart, I sort of knew that my parents had used this job as a pretext to get me away from Brad. Still, I'd assumed that at least there would *be* a job.

At this point, I guess I could have flown back to Brad and continued the life I'd dreamed of, but I didn't. For one thing, I didn't have the airfare. More significantly, I was still being guided by my Japanese upbringing, which, in the face of all obstacles and disappointments, counseled stoic acceptance. My father had summoned me back home, and it wasn't in my nature to question that. If I were to leave now and go against his unspoken wishes, he would lose face. Being Japanese is a complicated business.

So as I'd come to Tokyo for work, I would simply find work. As it happened, the local noodle shop was looking for waitresses. I'd never waitressed before, but I'd never been out of school and broke before, either, so I took the job.

Noodle shops are a staple of Japanese casual dining, much like coffee shops in the States, and they're not to be confused with teahouses. While the customers in both emporiums are overwhelmingly male, they don't go to noodle shops for relaxation or ritual observances or stimulating conversation. They go for noodles and sake—and that's it. There are no geishas flitting about, being charming and flirtatious, and floating the vague possibility that there might be a little something extra available for the right price. The men wouldn't be interested anyway; they kept their noses buried in their noodle bowls, and for the most part they left the waitresses alone—but not me.

Maybe because my body was more substantial than that of the average noodle waitress—even with anorexia, I was bigger and curvier in certain critical areas—but I was constantly getting pinched and pawed and squeezed by the clientele. I tried to maintain a polite smile and ignore them, but it was getting increasingly hard to serve the soup when I was being fondled at one end and goosed at the other.

The other waitresses were sympathetic to my plight, but also a little envious. Their behinds were generally flat, while my all-American ass stuck out like an increasingly sore thumb. "How does it do that?" they'd marvel in the dressing room as they helped me put on my kimono. All the waitresses had to wear kimonos, and there were several layers, which had to be draped just so. It took me a while to get the hang of it, but even after I did, they still helped me dress. It became a bonding ritual between us. I loved hanging out with them. The dressing room was like a women's haven, where they could relax, have a smoke, and talk about their lives, and their husbands, and sex. When I complained about being pinched, they tried to figure out ways to flatten my breasts and behind, wrapping them tight with linens and so forth. Nothing helped. I still got groped. More than once the chef came charging out of the kitchen, cleaver in hand, to protect me.

I didn't stick with the noodle shop long. I heard that there was a need for ski instructors up north. I'd been skiing ever since I was a child, and my tenure in Switzerland had really sharpened my skills, so I got a children's ski instructor license and spent the winter of 1975 in the Japan Alps teaching kids how to ski.

When the season ended, I went back to work at the noodle shop. The gropers were still in season, so with summer approaching, I started looking for a new job somewhere. Anywhere.

Anywhere turned out to be New Zealand. It was winter down below, the skiing was sensational, and they needed ski instructors. I took the next plane.

If you've seen the *Lord of the Ring*s movies, you know how spectacular the New Zealand scenery can be. When I landed at Christchurch and took the bus southwest to Queenstown, I was astounded by the natural beauty surrounding me on all sides. Towering snowcapped mountains, primeval forests, glacier-cut fjords—you name it, they had it. Queenstown itself was a beautiful resort town on the shore of Lake Wakatipu, right at the edge of the Southern Alps. The lake was so crystal clear you couldn't tell the mountains from their reflection in the water. Gold had been discovered there in the 1860s, and the ensuing rush created a boom for the area. They still had some working mines when I was there.

The head of the ski school in Queenstown was a young American named Larry Lasch, who also taught in Vail. I got my adult ski license from him, and taught throughout the summer. The skiing in New Zealand was beyond amazing. The mountains were so high that, instead of taking the endless tram lifts, people would fly up to the summits in helicopters and ski all the long way down.

The setting was incredible; the pay wasn't. I didn't make enough to stay at the ski resort, so I found lodgings on a nearby sheep ranch. The owner, Hildy, was a single woman in her sixties, tough and independent, with sinewy arms and a weather-beaten face. She had hundreds of sheep on her ranch, and she was busy looking after them from dawn till dark. So she was more than happy to let me stay there for free, if I cooked for her.

I cooked a lot of lamb. She had chickens on the farm, so every morning we had fresh, warm eggs with bright orange yolks. The butter was delicious; Hildy churned it herself.

Hildy also made classic New Zealand sweaters, from her own homegrown wool. She taught me how to shear the sheep. I would hold the sheep under the crook of my arm and take a pair of shearing clippers and run them right along the skin of the sheep. I still remember the feel of the soft wool as it gently fell over my hand and piled up at my feet. We would gather the sheared wool into huge baskets and carry it into the spinning room.

Hildy and I would sit by the spinning machines and pull heaps of raw wool from the basket and shape it into a ropy string. We'd feed the string into the spinner, and it would come out as spun wool. It was still in a natural state, sticky with lanolin oil. Hildy would knit the wool into chunky sweaters, which were super-warm and so comforting. The sweater wool was grayish and dirty, but you couldn't wash it, or you'd lose the lanolin, which repelled water and insulated you from the cold.

Hildy gave me one of these sweaters as a gift, and I wore it constantly. The smell and the sticky feel of the lanolin reminded me of those trips I made with my dad up into the mountains of Japan, when we'd go ice-fishing and sit huddled in the tent while he spun magical tales of his past.

I missed him. I wanted to see him again.

AFTER three months in New Zealand, I returned to Tokyo. Dad wasn't there, but he had left a forwarding phone number.

"Hey, Sach the Pach! What's up?"

"Hi, Dad. Where are you?"

"I'm in Hawaii. I'm doing some business."

"When are you coming back?"

"Oh, I don't know. Soon."

Soon could be next week, next Christmas, or whenever he got bored with the palm trees. I didn't want to wait. I was on a personal crusade to reconnect with my family, and I wasn't going to be denied. I scraped the plane fare together and went down to

Honolulu. I knew Dad kept a suite at the Halekulani Hotel on Waikiki Beach. Wouldn't he be surprised when he saw me?

Once again, Dad surprised me. He was already gone. Where, I had no idea.

So now I was stranded in Honolulu. Not the worst place to be stuck, granted, but when you're broke and alone, a picture-postcard sunset can offer only so much in the way of gratification.

I was really starting to feel sorry for myself. Nobody cared about me, nobody loved me! I was swimming in self-pity, and I desperately wanted attention.

So I came up with an ingenious idea: maybe if I pretended I was sick, my parents would rush to my side to help me. It worked in the movies all the time, right? I couldn't make it anything really serious, because I wanted to recover fairly quickly, so I fell back on my Queenstown experience and manufactured a skiing injury: I'd messed up my knee badly, it was dislocated or torn up or something, and I was in real pain.

It was a good story. I called Mom.

"You hurt your knee skiing?"

"Yes," I said, adding a little tremble to my voice.

"You hurt it in New Zealand, and it's just bothering you now?"

"Well, it was always bothering me, but now it's getting much worse."

"Have you seen a doctor?" she asked.

"Uh—no . . ." This was not going exactly the way I planned.

"Well, go see a doctor, for Christ's sake."

"I can't afford a doctor," I quickly replied.

There was a silence on the other end. I was half-afraid she was going to tell me to sell my necklace.

"I'll pay for it," she finally said. "Just make sure you send me a copy of the bill."

That was as far as we got. At least she was offering to pay for something I didn't really need.

Now I was in a bit of a fix: I had to get a doctor's bill to verify that I'd been injured in the first place, or Mom and Dad would know that I was lying (which would only confirm their earlier suspicions about my suspect character).

So I went to one doctor, and another, and another. They couldn't find anything wrong with my knee (perhaps they should have been checking my head). I knew they wouldn't, but I felt that now that I had talked my way into this situation, I had to see it all the way through. The more doctors I saw, the more impressive my injury would appear. Eventually I would be miraculously cured, that would put an end to the episode, and we could all move on.

It was the fourth doctor who threw a wrench in the works. He examined my knee carefully, bending and extending it over and over. He took a barrage of X-rays. He made some very ominous-sounding grunts and mutterings.

"Miss Parker," he finally intoned grimly, "it appears that you have a torn cartilage in your knee."

"I do?" I tried to mask my surprise. "In my knee?"

He held up the X-ray, pointing to the seam of my knee. "See right here?"

I couldn't see anything. There wasn't supposed to *be* anything. "So, is that bad?" I asked.

"Well, it's going to require surgery sooner or later. Sooner is better."

"Surgery?" I looked at him, trying to see if he was hiding a tiny smile, but he was very grave and doctorly. "Are you sure?"

"Oh, I'm sure."

So I had the operation.

I knew it was completely unnecessary, but I couldn't say that because I didn't want the doctor to think I thought he was pulling a scam, which of course I did because he was. But I was pulling a scam, too, so we were even. Besides, maybe there *was* something wrong with my knee. How did I know?

There's an underlying irony here that eluded me at the time. One of the most famous of showbiz stories is how my mom got her big break because of a bad leg. Carol Haney, the dancing lead of *The Pajama Game* on Broadway, broke her ankle, and Mom came out of the chorus to replace her. The popular story goes that Hollywood producer Hal Wallis was sitting in the audience that very night, immediately spotted her star potential, and signed her, a complete unknown, to a movie contract.

Actually, that happened a couple of months later—she had already been playing the role to acclaim and was pretty well known by the time Wallis saw her—but the basic story is the same. One minute a nobody, the next minute a star, and soon she was doing her first film with Alfred Hitchcock. Sometimes it happens that fast.

Maybe, subconsciously, I was hoping for history to repeat itself. My bad leg would remind Mom of how she had profited over someone else's misfortune, and she would overcompensate for the lingering guilt by showering me with maternal affection, and I would finally become important in her eyes . . .

Or maybe I was just being an idiot again. Either way, it didn't work. Even after my operation, all I got was a "Get Well" telegram.

When I went for a post-op checkup, the doctor was considerably pleased with his work. "That's coming along just fine. But you know, you'll probably have trouble with that knee down the line."

"I will? But you just fixed it."

"Yes, but once you go into that area and start cutting around . . . things get compromised. Eventually you might need a knee replacement."

He got that right. Thirty years later, I had surgery for the partial replacement of a knee that was never damaged to begin with.

Chapter 7

Into the Wild

O nce I stopped limping, I went to work at the Halekulani. My father maintained a suite there year-round, and he and Miki stayed there whenever they were in Honolulu. Dad was treated at the hotel with all the cachet of a visiting dignitary: he would saunter through the lobby, shaking hands and doling out tips, with the same stylish swagger that my mom commanded on a Vegas stage. This was his kind of show business, and he loved it.

In spite of Dad's rock star status at the Halekulani, however, I couldn't even land a waitressing job there. It was very upscale, they hired only the best, and my noodle-shop résumé failed to impress. I was offered a job as a bus girl, and I humbly took it, even though it paid almost nothing. Until I could gather enough cash in tips, I had to live in a seedy part of Honolulu, at the apartment of one of the hotel waitresses. Her name was Shigeko, she was a Nisei (second-generation Japanese American), and she let me stay for free, until I could get back on my feet.

Of course, I could have just stayed in my dad's suite, but he didn't make the offer. I guess he considered it his private sanctum. Besides, while I often made room-service deliveries to the other guests, the management made it clear to me that Dad's suite was off-limits to me. Whatever his business was, he didn't want me sticking my nose in it.

I didn't care. I was close to him; that's what mattered. At least we would be together on my nineteenth birthday.

That very morning, I got a call from Dad. "Sach! Happy birthday! Listen, I wanted to do something special with you tonight."

I recalled all those endless, tedious nights in Tokyo bouncing from nightclub to nightclub. Now I was old enough to enjoy them. "Okay!" I said eagerly.

"But I can't. I'm in Italy."

"Italy?"

"Business trip." I could hear now the long-distance sound in his voice, a little tinny and displaced. "Sorry I can't be with you on your birthday. I feel terrible."

"That's okay . . ."

We were interrupted now by the operator, a woman who spoke in Italian, and she and Dad traded a few Italian phrases. Long-distance calls in those days were not the smooth exchanges we have today. There was always an operator, the sound was scratchy and crackly, and every now and then there would be a *beep-beep-beep*—all of which I listened to now as I waited for him to get back to me.

"So when are you coming back, Dad?"

"Oh, next week, maybe," (scratchy crackling) "or the week after" (*beep-beep-beep*). "But listen, honey, you just have a great day today, and I'll make it up to you. Okay?"

"Okay . . ." Click. Dead air. He was gone.

So I was spending yet another birthday alone.

Still, I wasn't about to feel sorry for myself. Last time I tried that I wound up in surgery. Instead, I decided to give myself a little birthday treat.

Since Dad was off in Italy, it seemed the perfect opportunity to breach the sanctum. What harm could it do, after all, just to sneak into his room and poke around a bit?

I charmed the key from the hotel clerk and took the elevator up. I felt a momentary qualm as I slipped the key into the lock, but I knew this would be my only chance.

I pushed the door open, and peered in. I expected to be overwhelmed by lavish furnishings, spectacular views, solid-gold bathroom fixtures, that sort of thing.

Instead I was overwhelmed by a thick cloud of marijuana smoke as it billowed toward me. There was pulsing jazz-rock music playing on the stereo, the kind you might hear in a porno flick. As I moved into the drifting haze, I became aware that there were a bunch of people in the room, and very few of them were wearing clothes. Naked bodies were bouncing up and down furiously on the bed, in a merry synchronized humpfest. In the tangle of limbs I couldn't tell if they were men or women or what—but I knew one of them was Dad. Back from Italy in record time.

I ran from the room in horror. Luckily Dad never noticed me, or if he did, he never let on—and of course I never busted him on it. Somehow, my sneaking into his room and spotting him in a pot-smoking orgy seemed a far greater offense than his lying to me about being in Italy on my birthday.

What amazed me most in retrospect was the way he'd faked that phone call, with all its long-distance authenticity. The scratchiness, the tinny voice, the beeping . . . and I'd *heard* him talking to an operator. Who played that Italian woman? Was he doing all the voices himself? Who was the real actor in this family?

DAD owned land on the Big Island of Hawaii, in Napo'opo'o, where it is said that Captain Cook first landed when he discovered the Hawaiian Islands. How Dad was in the position to own such an important piece of real estate, I don't know. That was just his way.

One time I visited Napo'opo'o with him and we took a drive in his white Jeep Cherokee to Kailua, about a half hour away, and cruised around looking at the scenery. I thought it was just a spur-of-the-moment outing, but then he pulled into a parking lot outside an accountant's office. He said he had some kind of business he had to discuss, and he told me to wait for him in the car. I didn't want to wait in the car: it was too damn hot, and there was nothing to look at, and I was bored.

Dad was annoyed, and he got very short with me: "Stay there!" he snapped.

So I sat in the car while he went inside. While waiting, I noticed a manila envelope on the front seat. The flap was open. *I shouldn't look in there*, I thought. But it was hot, and I was in a bad mood, and I wanted to be entertained by something. So I peeked in the envelope.

Inside were a bunch of loose, glittering gemstones. Diamonds, to be precise. There must have been a hundred of them. I'm no diamond expert, so I didn't know if they were cut, or finished, or raw. Yet they were diamonds. I knew that.

Why would Dad have an envelope of diamonds in his front seat? Whom did they belong to? Where were they going? Was this part of Dad's business? What business?

I didn't know, and I wasn't going to ask. What I did know was that just one of those diamonds would have come in handy for me right around then.

AS soon as I could afford it, I moved out of Shigeko's apartment and got a place of my own. She was a lovely woman, and I was tired of mooching off her. On the other hand, I couldn't quite swing the deposit on my new place, so Shigeko helped me out by paying the first and last month's rent, no small sacrifice on a waitress's salary. God bless Shigeko—she was one of those uncanonized saints, like the prostitute in Trieste and the Yugoslavian couple, people who came into my life at just the right time and gave me an enormous lift and a sense of hope when I really needed it.

And I needed it now. I was living in perhaps the most dangerous part of Honolulu. I had no money and no friends. I remember this time as being perhaps the lowest point of my life.

I could barely afford to eat. At the Halekulani we would get one meal a day, lunch, and I made sure never to miss it. Aside from that, I would often stroll through the mall, where the food merchants gave away free samples. I'd go from stand to stand gathering up samples; that would be my dinner.

At the coffee shops, there would be no charge for refills, so I would drink five or six cups of coffee in a row. In my anorexic mind-set, I thought this was good for me. The laxative powers of coffee helped me to purge myself of the toxins, the pain, the loneliness. Every trip to the bathroom was an opportunity to feel clean and emptied out, the darkness gone. In my situation you had to take the positives wherever you could find them.

Still, there was no escaping the depressing reality of Apartment 315. Little more than a tenement apartment, it was a tiny space infested with roaches. I cleaned and cleaned, but there was no getting rid of them. I couldn't afford bug spray; and anyway, being Buddhist in philosophy, I didn't want to kill a living thing. So I gave them all names instead, and we did our best to coexist.

My apartment overlooked a tiny shack right below, where a family of native Hawaiians lived. Every single night, they would have a barbecue in their backyard, and every night, I would watch them from my window and live through them vicariously, peeking through the leaves of the palm tree that framed my view. They had a big family—big in every sense; there wasn't a thin one in the bunch. The aunts, uncles, and cousins would come over every night, swelling the ranks and bringing food for the pot luck dinner. It was always a huge feast: poi, lomi lomi salmon ceviche, banana leaves stuffed with pork . . . They'd party into the night, drinking and getting rowdy, and dancing around the bonfire. They were as poor as all get-out, but they seemed immensely happy.

I wanted so badly to join them. I was hoping someone would notice me and call me down from my balcony, just like in the movies. I would eat and dance and become part of the family, and marry the handsome chubby son, and we would hula off into the sunset.

It didn't happen. I stayed apart and alone.

I remember one night sitting on the floor of my apartment watching the roaches scurry along the wallboard, feeling utterly empty. I stared at my phone, waiting for it to ring—which was a futile exercise, because the service had been cut off for nonpayment. Didn't matter. Nobody ever called anyway. Next door, the party was raging into the late night, everyone in the family laughing and getting rowdy, and reminding me that I had no family of my own.

I knew suddenly, with fierce clarity, that I should kill myself. My life was a failure, nobody cared about me, I was completely alone and forgotten. So why go on? Who would miss me? Who was I kidding?

I wasn't sure how to go about it. I didn't have any sleeping pills, so I couldn't try Mom's method from *The Apartment*. There were knives in the kitchen, of course. I could probably hang myself with the belt from my robe. Oh, if I only had some bug spray . . .

There were lots of possibilities. As it happens, I was too depressed to do anything about it. So I just sat there, all through the night, thinking about being dead.

THEN everything changed, in the blink of an eye. Two eyes, actually, both gorgeous—and they didn't belong to a Hawaiian or a Nisei; they belonged to an Australian.

His name was Luke Garrett, and the minute he sat down in the hotel restaurant, I knew I wanted him. He was Hollywood handsome, with blond hair, broad shoulders, and a great tan. All I could think was, *Oh my god, who is that?*

As it turns out, I already knew who he was. We had met years before, in Australia, when I was about twelve or thirteen. My dad was business partners with Luke's dad, who had a cotton plantation in Weewaa, which proudly calls itself the Cotton Capital of Australia. The plantation house reminded me of Tara in *Gone With the Wind*, with its Corinthian columns and winding staircase, crocodile-filled bayous, and black Aboriginal laborers doing all the menial work. The surrounding countryside was barren and dusty, with unpaved dirt roads and far-off mountains. Whenever I see old Westerns on TV, I think of Weewaa.

Young Luke was a teenager then, sixteen or seventeen. I probably had a little crush on him, but it was nothing earthshaking.

This time was different. Now I was seeing him from a fresh, sexually informed perspective, and the earth was shaking plenty.

At first I was a little embarrassed; I didn't want Luke to know I had turned out to be a bus-girl. At the same time, it gave me a perfect excuse to engage him.

I wanted to look my best when I did, so I put on some extra makeup, hiked up my skirt, and flashed my most charming smile as I approached him and bent over him: "Coffee, sir?"

He nodded, and I promptly spilled hot coffee on his pants. Oh, totally on purpose. It was very artfully done—all around the crotch, without burning anything important. I sputtered apologies as I dried him off, conscientiously patting down the area in question . . . Then I looked up at his face. "Why, aren't you Luke Garrett?"

He flashed his own charming smile back—and just like that, we were off to the races. I don't know if you could call it a whirlwind romance, but it moved mighty fast. A few dates, and then Luke had to return to Australia. Then he came back to get me— and asked me to marry him.

I never said yes faster in my life. I couldn't believe my fairytale luck. I was Cinderella, rescued from the drudgery of busing tables by a genuine Prince Charming, who would sweep me away to his enchanted kingdom across the sea.

Dad was delighted with the match. He remembered Luke from years before, and he was very pleased that our families would be united. Even Miki seemed to approve, which surprised the hell out of me. She never ever wished me well, but now she was beaming like a proud mom. I guess that was Luke's roguish Aussie charm at work. He could win anybody over. They even started inviting us to hang out with them. I got to see Dad's suite again, without the naked bodies.

As much as we enjoyed the perks of a comfortable lifestyle, we couldn't tarry in Hawaii. We had a new life waiting for us, Down Under.

I'D been to Australia before, not only as a child, but more recently: piggybacking off my New Zealand ski instructor experience, I'd traveled on to the Snowy Mountains region in New South Wales. It was only for about a month or so, but it was memorable.

At the Thredbo ski resort, I was looking to teach, but there were no jobs open, so I wound up working as a maid at a local hotel. There was a whole team of maids, and we rotated jobs. My job was to do the beds, which was a step up from cleaning the toilets. On one particular day, while I was making up a bed, I noticed a curious substance on the sheets. It was creamy, like a gel, and as I bent to smell it, it had an odor sort of like fresh-mown grass.

I had no idea what it was, so I called in the other maids. "Have you ever seen anything like this before?"

They all exchanged knowing glances, and smiled. "Uh . . . yeah."

"What is it?" I asked innocently.

They laughed, and explained to me an essential component of the reproductive experience. I was amazed. I knew about sex, of course—I'd engaged in the act myself—but I didn't know that this creamy, grass-smelling stuff came out of men. Brad had never mentioned it in his hasty tutorial, and I wouldn't have noticed it anyway, what with all the blood.

That just goes to show how out of the loop, how utterly clueless, I was about sex. I knew it was fun, I knew I enjoyed it, but I didn't understand the mechanics of it, the implications of it, or the powerful omnipresence of it. Sex was all around me, and I just never saw it.

For instance, there was a handyman who worked at the motel, an older guy who was seedy looking and a bit creepy. He was always hitting on me, but I didn't really pick up on the signals. I wasn't interested in him, so I assumed he wasn't interested in me. It was only when he cornered me in a guest room and, in what I assume was a gesture of seduction, opened his pants and showed me the crabs around his penis, that I realized his true intentions.

I quit the motel that very day and moved to the nearby ski resort of Perisher Valley. Here I was a ski instructor by day and a waitress by night. The ski-lift operator was an American named Jay, who was a little older, in his mid-thirties, and sort of a hippy-dippy type, with long hair and a beard. Jay lived across the hall from me, in the rooms above the restaurant. I was rooming with a fellow waitress, Katie.

One night after work I came back to my room and found Katie in bed with a guy, having boisterous sex. Without missing a beat, she turned her head to me and said, "Get out!"

I hurriedly shut the door and found myself in the hall. I was exhausted from my shift, and now I had no place to sleep. So I knocked on Jay's door.

"Sure, you can sleep here tonight," he said. Unfortunately he had only a twin bed. He seemed like a gentleman, so I assumed it was safe.

And it was. We both climbed into the small bed, and Jay spooned me from behind. I remember I had two long braids at the time, and he held them as he wrapped his arms around me. We stayed that way all night, and nothing happened.

This seemed unremarkable to me at the time, but in retrospect I realized that Jay had acted with exceptional decency (and restraint). When I went back to Australia years later, I made a point of visiting Perisher Valley and thanking Jay for that night. He told me it had taken every bit of his willpower to hold back, but I was so innocent, he just couldn't take advantage of me. So Jay goes into the small pantheon of Nice Guys.

I wish I could put Luke in that class, too, but I can't. He wasn't such a nice guy, as I found out a little too late.

LUKE had once been a sheep rancher, but now he was a vintner—he owned a thirty-seven-acre vineyard in Pokolbin, in the Hunter Valley, the wine area of New South Wales. We moved there in the spring of 1976. Like much of Australia, it was starkly beautiful: rolling hills with mountains in the distance. The house was a two-story with a veranda, and while it was reasonably modernized, there was no indoor bathroom; we used an outhouse. There was also no dryer, so the laundry had to be hung out on a line to dry. I grew to love the smell of the clean air-dried sheets and clothes. Plus, there were chickens on the property, so we always had fresh, warm eggs.

Yet, it was a lonely place, in the middle of nowhere. The wind was always blowing. Still, it was the kind of life I enjoyed, simple and elemental. I was happy there.

Except when I was working at the nearby wine factory. Now, Luke was a proud man. I'm sure he would have balked at seeing his wife work—but I wasn't his wife. We weren't married yet; we hadn't even set a date. That being the case, he saw no reason why I shouldn't earn my keep. So he got me a job working on the factory line, putting labels on wine bottles. It was droning, stultifying work, and I hated it. I was ready to blow my brains out, but I did it for love.

. . .

MY anorexia had continued unabated all this time, and by now I was down to eighty-two pounds. Yet it wasn't enough. I still felt that I was too fat. I needed to lose more weight.

I picked up a book called *Dr. Atkins' Diet Revolution*, which had been published just a few years earlier. I was delighted to see that I could eat all my favorite foods with this diet—steak, eggs, bacon—and was guaranteed to lose weight. How cool was that?

So I went on the Atkins Diet, and gorged myself on protein—and immediately, I started gaining weight. I couldn't figure out what was going wrong—what kind of a stupid diet was this?—but I was enjoying the food too much to stop. Before long, I was back to a normal weight, and I was never anorexic again. You could say Dr. Atkins saved my life.

I don't mean to minimize in any way the seriousness of anorexia. It is a terrible, ravaging illness, and in its own insidious way a form of suicide; I was extremely lucky to escape it when I did, without any treatment, and I feel an immense empathy for those who struggle with it.

I was also lucky to find Robert. Robert—who was French, and whose name, therefore, enjoyed the elegant pronunciation "Ro-BEAR"—was the chef-owner of Robert's, a first-class restaurant down the street from the vineyard. The minute I arrived in Pokolbin, I went down to Robert's and got myself a job as a waitress. I'd paste labels at the wine factory in the morning, and then hop on my bicycle and ride down to Robert's for the lunch and dinner shift. Between Dr. Atkins and Robert's rich gourmet cooking, I got healthy very quickly.

Robert's attracted all kinds of customers: Australian ranchers, wealthy visitors from Sydney, tourists from around the world. Robert and his wife, Sally, were superbly accomplished restaurateurs. Their food was star quality and a little expensive. It was always amusing when some of the locals came in to order pub food. Once they got a good look at the prices, there was many a hasty exodus.

One fine day four cowboys sauntered in and took a table. They were fresh from the fields, dusty and sweaty, and already a few pints in. They looked over the menu and, without blinking an eye, settled on Chateaubriand for four. "And make it well done," said one of the cowboys.

Now, there are a couple of ways to cook Chateaubriand: rare and medium rare. Anything beyond that is inviting disaster: the meat shrinks to nothing, and the quality is ruined. I tried to explain this to the cowboys. "You know, Chateaubriand is supposed to be pink. If you cook it too much, it spoils the whole experience."

They didn't care. "We want it well done."

"Well, maybe you should order something else well done. Like a sirloin or a rump steak."

They grew a little testy. "We want *Chateaubriand*."

"And we want it *well done*."

I smiled brightly. "Okay, I'll talk to the chef."

I really didn't want to talk to the chef. Robbie was a sweet, delightful man, but he was also a classic temperamental Frenchman, and *très* passionate about his food and his reputation. He would cook his dishes the right way or not at all.

He fumed as I explained the request to him, his cowboy boot tapping petulantly on the floor; Robbie always wore cowboy boots in the kitchen. "I tried to steer them to something else," I told him, as he glared at me. "But they want Chateaubriand, and they want it well done."

Robbie swallowed his outrage and gave a Gallic shrug. He

then proceeded to make the Chateaubriand exactly the way he wanted: medium rare. Then he poured an extra layer of Béarnaise sauce over the sliced meat, so they wouldn't notice.

When I brought the dish to the table, sumptuously prepared and beautifully presented, the boys were generally unimpressed. One cowboy spooned the sauce aside contemptuously and looked at the slice of meat in dismay. "What the hell . . . ? This meat is rare. We want it well done!"

"I'm sorry," I said, "but the chef says it will ruin the dish . . ."

"We don't care! Who's paying for this? We want it well done!" They sent it back to the kitchen.

Robert was not pleased, but he grudgingly accepted that he wasn't dealing with informed gourmands here. He put the Chateaubriand back in the oven and cooked it to an arguable medium. Any more than that, and he wouldn't have been able to live with himself.

I crossed my fingers and brought the compromised Chateaubriand back out to the cowboys. Still too pink. They rejected it in unison: "We want it well done!"

I timorously returned to the kitchen with the meat. By now Robbie had reached his limit of understanding. "They want it well done?" he exploded, his neck veins popping. "I'll give them well done!" He took the individual slices of meat, threw them on the floor, and stomped on them, one by one, with his cowboy boots. "There! There!" he screamed. "Well done! Well done!"—and he launched into a string of French obscenities as he stomped, stomped, stomped. I didn't understand what he was saying, but I knew exactly what he was saying.

Then he scooped up the meat and threw it back into the oven, and he cooked the slices until they were black and charred and looked like hockey pucks. "There. *Now* it's well done." He drizzled on some token béarnaise sauce and handed me the platter. "Give it to them."

I was horrified. I couldn't serve this mess to them now.

"*Give it to them*," Robbie insisted.

I nervously placed the charred Chateaubriand on the Aussies' table. "Here we go," I said cheerfully. "Well done!" Then I quickly retreated to the safety of the kitchen.

The cowboys leaned forward, studied the blackened meat curiously, and inspected it from all angles. Then they started eating. We all watched from the kitchen door in disbelief.

They loved it.

I was so happy at Robert's. Sally, Robert, the whole staff—they were a real family to me. That's why I worked two shifts, to be honest. I would rather have hung out there than gone home to my fiancé.

I want to be fair to Luke. He was a very sweet and thoughtful guy when he wasn't drinking—but he was often drinking. It was part of the culture out there, and Luke was nothing if not cultured. He had a very short temper, and was prone to explosive outbursts.

I first appreciated the extent of his volatility one evening when I was sitting at the kitchen table and he walked out of the bathroom. "What's this?" he asked.

He was holding something by the tail—it looked like a white mouse with a blotch of red on it. I looked closer and realized, to my mortification, that it was a used tampon.

"What's this?" he repeated, dangling it right in front of my eyes. "What's this?"

"That's mine . . ." I said meekly.

"I know it's yours!" he screamed in my face. "Do you know

where I found it? Do you? On the edge of the *bathtub*." He spat the word out, to underscore the egregiousness of the offense.

"Oh. I guess I left it there." I reached for the tampon, but he pulled it away.

"Is that what you guess? You guess you left it there? I guess you did, too. I know *I* didn't leave it there." He was looming over me, swaying slightly, as if he couldn't contain the anger roiling within him.

"Okay, well . . ." I reached for it again, and he flung it across the room.

"Don't touch it. It's disgusting! You think I want to look at that after I come home from a hard day at work?" He was reminding me of my father, asking questions that I wasn't supposed to answer, and then waiting for me to answer, and then hoping it would be the wrong answer so he could attack me again.

I knew there was only one thing I could say that would satisfy him. "I'm sorry. I'll never do it again."

"You're goddamn right you'll never do it again! Leaving your female shit lying around, as if you owned the place. You show me no respect. No respect!" He overturned the kitchen table, the dishes and silverware clattering to the floor around me. Then he stood waiting, hands on hips, as if daring me to say anything at all in my defense.

I didn't. Because, in a way, I understood. He was a man, he was a proud product of his chauvinist rancher society, and he shouldn't have had to be exposed to inferior womanly things. It was insulting and emasculating.

And I was a product of *my* society, which had taught me to be submissive and accepting, and protective of the male ego at all costs. So I just wept quietly, and kept my head low. After a moment, I heard him sigh with disgust, and mutter, "Clean up this mess." He stalked out of the house and headed for the vineyards.

I know I should have bolted then and there but this was my first serious relationship, and I didn't know any better.

So I stayed with Luke. I don't know why. It wasn't for the sex, because we didn't have much. When we did, it was fast and furious. Mostly fast. Not a lot of foreplay: ten seconds, maybe. "Brace yourself, baby!" Wham, bam. "Now feed me."

Then I'd hop out of bed and make him steak and eggs. Anything to make him happy.

ONE day, in my continuing aspiration to be the perfect housekeeper, I was cleaning up Luke's bedroom, putting away his laundry, when, in the bottom drawer of his dresser, I found a sheaf of letters, hidden away. Curious, I took them out and started reading.

They were love letters. Sexy, impassioned love letters. To Luke.

From Miki.

I was staggered. What? *My* Miki? The evil stepmother? She was sending love letters to my fiancé? How could that be? Was he in love with her? Could such a thing even be possible?

I read the letters in disbelief. They were stuffed with high-flown romantic sentiments along the following lines: "My dearest love . . ." "My one and only . . ." "Every time the sun sets, I think of you . . ." There was some explicit sexual stuff in there, too. Just the thought of Miki and Luke engaged in such intimate couplings, even on a fantasy level, made me positively nauseated.

I felt sick in every sense. It was like being hit by a train. My heart was pounding so hard I thought it would burst from my chest.

How had this happened? Maybe Miki had caught sight of young Luke years before, on the business trips to Weewaa. Or maybe they'd first met in Hawaii. Is that why she was so happy that we were getting married? Because it would give her more opportunities to see him? For that matter, had she set up the whole thing herself? Did Dad know? Was he somehow involved?

My mind was racing, all kinds of crazy questions were popping into my head. I never found out the answers, though, because I never confronted Luke. I didn't dare. I carefully replaced the letters in the bottom drawer and closed it—and never said a word about them.

I wasn't angry. That wouldn't have been cool. I almost felt that it wasn't my business. They were sophisticated adults, after all, and this is what sophisticated adults did: they had affairs, they kept secrets, they did shockingly naughty things. Who was I to pipe up and say they were wrong? No, I was too embarrassed and scared to do anything.

Now I understood. I understood why Miki would make unexpected visits to our home, traveling thousands of miles on a whim. At the time, I'd thought it sweet of her, if a little odd. I also now understood why we were always getting invitations from Dad and Miki to join them in Hawaii, or Greece—to the yacht, the island, the chalet in Italy: all places from which I'd formerly been excluded. I had thought it was because we were such a fun, attractive couple. Now I'd watch Miki and Luke together, though, and I'd see the little flirting glances and accidental touches. What had once gone undetected was now so obvious. I wondered, whenever Luke went out for a smoke or a breath of fresh air, if a rendezvous was in the offing, if one of those feverish acts of passion described in the letters was about to be enacted offscreen—and I would watch Dad's reaction, to see if he knew, or cared.

Dad never let on one way or the other. He was the master of secrets.

I lived with the violence and the betrayal as long as I could. The tipping point, I guess, was Melbourne Cup Day. The Melbourne Cup is Australia's biggest thoroughbred horse race; it's practically a national holiday. They call it "the race that stops a nation." It's held on the first Tuesday of November (coincidentally Election Day in the United States), which is mid-spring in Australia.

On Melbourne Cup Day 1976, everyone gathered in Cessnock, a neighboring town, to watch the race at the local pub. I've forgotten the name of it: the Dirty Dingo, or something like that. All the wives and girlfriends were dressed in their holiday best (cream-colored dresses and stylish wide hats) to celebrate the great day. The only hitch was, we weren't allowed to enter the pub. In fact, there was a sign outside the pub door: "No Dogs or Women Allowed."

We had to enter through a separate "Ladies'" entrance, and wait upstairs. While the boys were downstairs watching the preliminary races, drinking pints, and getting rowdier and rowdier, the ladies were sipping tea and having a Tupperware party. It was absurd, and excruciatingly dull. I'd rather have been pasting wine labels. I hung in there as long as I could, but finally I couldn't bear another minute; I had to go home.

I came downstairs and stepped out on the porch, and stopped dead. There was a spring rain falling. Actually, it was more like a monsoon. Heavy sheets of rain were pelting down, making the dirt road a muddy, coursing river.

Unfortunately, the parking lot was behind the building, and I was in my Melbourne Cup dress and high heels. There was no way to get around to my car without getting drenched and ruining my shoes, unless . . .

Hey, I could just cut through the pub. Why not?

Well, because there was a sign: no women allowed. The sound coming from inside the pub was deafening: loud music, drunken laughter, shouting, and screaming. It sounded as if they were wrestling kangaroos in there. How would they react if I barged in on their party? Would there be a riot? Maybe they wouldn't react at all. Maybe they were all too smashed to notice. I was only cutting through, anyway. As I looked at the rain beating down relentlessly, I couldn't see any other choice. So I opened the pub door . . .

And suddenly—silence. Everything stopped: the music, the TVs, everything. Just like in the movies. Every eye was staring at me with outrage and anger.

I realized right away that I'd made a mistake. I'd violated the sanctuary. I was an affront to their maleness. I should have backed out immediately, but I couldn't. *This will last only a moment*, I thought, *and then they'll go back to their regular carousing.* Surely I wasn't worth missing the big race for.

So I took another step in, waiting for everything to go back to normal—but it just got quieter.

I nervously searched the pub for a friendly face. None to be found. Wait, there was Luke over in the corner with his pals. Surely he'd come over and defuse the situation. "Hey everyone, meet my sheila!"

Luke just stared at me, as outraged as the rest—even more so. His face was impassive, but his eyes glittered with fury. He was not happy.

So I had to face the vortex of hostility alone. I kept walking forward, one meekly defiant step after another. It took forever. Like one of those nightmares in which the door keeps receding farther and farther in the distance. I thought I would never reach it. The tension in the room was growing moment by moment. I was terrified that the men would suddenly rush forward to exact frontier justice upon me, and Luke would be cheering them on. When I finally reached the door and got outside, I realized I hadn't been breathing all that time. I rushed to the car in the rain and drove away.

That night, I waited nervously for Luke to return home. I knew there might be a scene, especially if he'd kept drinking at his usual pace. I would try to explain the situation to him, and maybe he would understand.

A long time passed between the moment I heard his Jeep pull up and the moment he finally walked in the door. He stood in the hall doorway now and stared at me, his eyes red and belligerent. "What's wrong with you?" he said with contempt.

"It was raining, I had to get to the car . . ."

"I'm in there with my mates, and you come stomping in like a fucking elephant, embarrassing me, making me look like a fool . . ."

"I'm sorry . . ."

"You're *always* sorry. You're a sorry excuse, that's what you are." I smiled at his little joke, which was a mistake. "You think it's funny?" he said. "It's *not* funny."

"I am stupid," I hurriedly agreed, trying to calm him. "I should have known better, but . . . I was tired, I just wanted to go home . . ."

"You just wanted to go home, huh?" He sneered, and threw a chair at me. "Well, now you're home. Are you happy? Are you happy?" he yelled.

As he grabbed a glass from the table to hurl at me, I fled from the room.

• • •

I decided to call off our engagement. I didn't tell Luke; that might have been dangerous. I started planning my escape. I saved up my tip money from the restaurant, and every night, I'd sneak a few more pieces of clothing into a suitcase and hide it in a closet.

My biggest problem was transportation. I needed a getaway car. I had my eye on a used pink Vauxhall in the local lot. It was a worn-out piece of junk, but it moved, and it could get me to Sydney. However, I was short five hundred dollars, and I'd never scrape that together from my waitress tips.

So I called Mom. She was in New York shooting her ballet film, *The Turning Point*.

"What?" she asked in disbelief. "You want to borrow five hundred dollars from me so you can buy some old clunker? You think I'm made of money?"

"I need it, Mom. It's my getaway car."

"What are you doing in Australia, anyway? I wouldn't follow a man across the street. You've gotta stop letting people walk all over you."

"I'm trying, Mom. I just need five hundred dollars. I'll pay you back, I promise."

She thought it over a moment. Parting with money was always a cause for serious contemplation for Mom. "What kind of interest are you offering me?"

I was confused by this question. "You know I'm always interested in you, Mom . . ."

"Interest, interest!" She sighed, and worked the numbers over in her head. "Ten percent. Compounded annually. For the life of the loan."

I didn't understand business talk at all, but it sounded reasonable to me. "Okay. Whatever. You can have twenty!"

So she sent me the money, and I bought the Vauxhall, and one sultry night, while Luke was at the pub, I got out my suitcase and drove away, barreling down the dusty roads at thirty miles an hour. It would take me eight hours to chug into Sydney, but that didn't matter. I was free.

CHAPTER 8

FLIGHT

Queensland and Northern Territory Aerial Services, or QANTAS, is the largest airline in Australia, and the second oldest in the world. With a fleet of jumbo Boeing 747 jets, Qantas in 1976 was the shining face of Australia to the rest of the world, famous for its record of never sustaining an airliner crash in its history. Nicknamed the Flying Kangaroo, it became familiar to Americans through its popular commercial of a crabby tourist-loathing koala bear munching on a eucalyptus leaf and grumbling, "I hate Qantas!"

I felt different—and by the time I arrived in Sydney, I'd formulated a clear, cogent plan for my future life: I was going to be a stewardess for Qantas Airways!

I don't know how I hatched this idea, but for some reason (and in willful dismissal of all my past history) I was completely confident that I would get the job. After all, I was eminently qualified: I had three languages under my belt—English, Japanese, and French—I was pretty, I had great legs, and I knew how to be cheerfully subservient. It was a no-brainer.

As soon as I got to Sydney, I put in my application. I then underwent a series of interviews and tests to see if I was flight-worthy.

The comprehensive Character-Personality Exam contained one section dealing with empathy. It gauged how much compassion and understanding you were likely to have for the passengers. The questions were all yes/no, and they were worded with such sophistication that you could never suss out exactly what the correct answer was supposed to be. You just had to give your honest answer every time, and hope that it rang positively with the judges.

Well, when the results came back from my empathy test, the inspectors were shocked. They said that it was the highest score in their years of keeping records. My empathy level was totally off the charts.

In fact, it was so unbelievable that they didn't believe it, and they made me take the test all over again. All different questions, but the same result. It was official: I was the most empathetic person on the face of the earth.

Now, in the grand scheme of life, I don't know if you could count this as an asset or a grave liability, but for Qantas it got me the job.

At the age of twenty, I began my stewardess training.

I know many people will scoff at that term, as if training to be a stewardess in the old days—before it evolved into the more respectably titled "flight attendant"—consisted mostly of learning how to dress, walk, and smile in a pretty, vacant, nonthreatening way (the latter need I had already mastered). The three-week training session was intense, though: lots of studying, memorizing, and more studying. There were courses on aerodynamics, mechanical engineering, aircraft maneuvers, first aid, CPR, and the intricacies of childbirth. We had to pass a Red Cross–authorized medical exam, learn to deploy air slides, and be proficient in every aspect of accident training. Serving coffee with a smile was way, way down on the list of priorities.

Most unnerving was the simulated disaster scenario, when you were placed in a mock cabin that was fitted with all kinds of special effects—smoke, flashing lights, pneumatic lifts that would shake you back and forth—and then asked to perform your stewardess duties in this chaotic emergency situation. You had to stay calm under pressure, which wasn't easy, because even though you knew it wasn't happening, it was so realistically staged that you'd become convinced you were about to slam into the ocean and break into a million pieces.

Yet I found, to my surprise, that I performed extremely well under these conditions. I actually tended to become more calm as the stakes grew higher. While I knew I had a tendency to get overdramatic in a mini-crisis, it turned out that I could really hold it together when the shit hit the fan.

Stewardess training was rigorous and exacting, but I don't deny that there was a certain emphasis placed on personal appearance. These were the last days of the glamour era of air travel—people dressed up to fly, the pilots strutted through the airports like conquering heroes, and stewardesses were still expected to be the stuff of businessmen's fantasies and *Playboy* centerfolds. We were taught how to stand, how to pour coffee with an ingratiating smile, how to bend properly in our pert little outfits. We didn't wear those little hats anymore, but our hair always had to be in an up-do, a bun or a chignon. There was a whole lot of hairspray going around.

Plus, whenever we reported for work, we had to get on the dreaded scale. If you edged one pound over your assigned weight (relative to your height), you were bumped off that flight, and you didn't get paid. This was supposedly an effort to keep the plane as light as possible, but nobody was fooled. It was, as usual, all about sex. After all, none of the male stewards had to weigh in.

While I was going through my preliminary training, I lived with my friend Margo Tolmer. Margo's father was Alex Tolmer, the founder of the Australian toy company Toltoys; he had manufactured the first plastic hula hoop, and was consequently a very rich man.

Margo was kind enough to let me stay with her for free while I was training. Soon enough I would be a working stewardess and able to take care of myself, so she didn't mind putting me up for a few weeks. Margo was a professional chef—we ate very well—but unlike Robert, she didn't have an artistic temperament. She was a down-to-earth, no-nonsense lady, and you could see she wouldn't put up with any crap.

This came in handy one day when there was a fateful knock at the door. Margo went to answer it, and then returned to me.

"It's Luke."

I instantly felt the old fear and anxiety welling within me. I couldn't believe he'd found me. What did he want? What kind of mood was he in? Did he have a weapon? I whispered to Margo, "Stay close."

I went to the door. Luke was standing outside. He wasn't angry at all. He was apologetic and contrite. He wanted me back. He wasn't sure what he'd done wrong, but we could discuss it, and he'd never do it again. He'd brought clams on the half shell (my favorite dish) and a bottle of champagne. Could we just talk?

Yes, I wanted to talk. He seemed changed: sincere, respectful, and still gorgeous. Still, from somewhere deep inside, my sense of self-preservation was roused and said no. No, I couldn't risk being charmed by him and then carried back to a life of misery. I'd seen that movie before.

So I asked him to leave. With Margo looming in the background, protective and warrior-like, he had no choice but to accede. I watched him go with mixed feelings. I hated giving up those clams.

I still don't know how he found me. It occurs to me now that maybe Miki told him where I was. I'd called them just after the breakup, my heart still freshly wounded, and Dad had consoled me in a light, joking way: "Keep a stiff upper lip, Sach"—something like that. Then Miki got on the phone and gave me her advice: "You should get a glass of wine and listen to all the sad songs you can think of, and cry and cry it all out, and you'll be fine." I said thanks, and hung up.

I was a stewardess for Qantas for over four years. It was a huge chunk of my life, which I basically spent flying back and forth across the world: London, Paris, Amsterdam, Bombay, Singapore.

Because of my languages, I always worked in first class—and in those days, first class was first class. Gourmet meals and free-flowing alcohol were the rule of the day. Service was premium. We would draw a diagram of the first-class seating and write down the names of each passenger, so that, when we served them, we could address them personally. This always gave some of the first-timers a startled shock—"How did she know my name?"

I took my job very seriously, and worked hard to be considered an excellent stewardess—and it paid off: Qantas was constantly getting letters from passengers raving about my service, and suggesting that I should get some kind of award or promotion, or at least a raise. Not that the company paid any attention, but it was gratifying to read those glowing letters in my file. It was a kind of applause.

MY Qantas years were busy and yet, in a curious way, uneventful. Because I was seldom in the same spot for very long, there was never a chance for an emotional drama or a complicated situation to play out. I'd had enough of that for the time being, anyway. I was in my early twenties. I wanted to have fun, I wanted to have adventures, I wanted to learn new things.

And I did.

I learned, for example, that if you want to quiet a crying baby on a long flight, put a little powdered valium in his bottle. The stewardesses, who always carried a personal stash for their own purposes, would approach a harried mother and ask solicitously, "Would you like me to warm up his formula?" Once back in the galley, they'd crush up a valium pill and mix a baby-size amount into the formula. It worked like a charm.

I also learned that one of the largest concentrations of Greeks in the world is in Australia. Melbourne is sometimes called "Greece's third largest city," and Sydney isn't far behind. Every spring, there would be a mass pilgrimage of Greeks back to the homeland to celebrate Easter. Qantas would ferry whole planeloads, all in a festive but reverent mood.

Now, for some reason—and I'm not promoting a cultural stereotype here, but only making an objective observation—Greeks have a tendency to get airsick. It never failed that, about a half hour into our flight, someone would start vomiting into his barf bag. Invariably this would signal a general uprising: once one passenger started, the entire cabin would follow suit. Soon everyone on the plane would be retching, in a chain reaction of mass nausea. A powerful smell of vomit would fill the air, and stay with us all the way to the Mediterranean.

There's no comic tagline to this story. I'm just offering it as a public service. If you're traveling during Eastertime, beware of planes bearing Greeks.

Another thing I learned: you know that popular cliché about how airline stewardesses were fast-living good-time girls who loved to party and sleep around? "Coffee, tea, or me?"

Absolutely true.

Why not? It was the late 1970s, post–sexual revolution, pre-AIDS, everyone had Saturday Night Fever, even the president lusted in his heart. You were flying into the most glamorous cities in the world—how many museums could you visit?

The stewardesses would get together in the galley and trade tips on their international boyfriends. "There's a guy in London who'll buy you a fur coat," "There's a guy in Amsterdam who gives away diamond rings," and so on and so forth—the unspoken corollary being "all you have to do is sleep with him."

I wasn't into that. The idea of having sex with some exotic stranger who just might pay off in silver dollars left me cold. Not that I was a total prude: I just preferred having fun with people I knew. Like the stewards.

There was a presumption in those days that any male flight attendant was likely to be gay. Well, not in Australia. The crews were staffed with rampant heterosexuals, and they were constantly on the prowl. They flirted openly with the prettiest passengers, knew all the hot spots around the world, and hit on every steward-ess in their proximity.

This wasn't difficult. In the close quarters of a plane, you're always brushing against each other, and it's inevitable that sometimes a helping hand will land on an unexpected spot, or an aisle-jutting bottom will intersect with a passing crotch. Then, when you all wind up staying in the same hotel in a strange city, it's a recipe for musical beds. I readily confess, I was right in the thick of it. As an antidote to boredom and loneliness, getting laid couldn't be beat.

Not that I cared much about the sex; I didn't even like it. Luke had cured me of that. Yet, the guys were always asking, and I couldn't say no—my Japanese training again: I didn't want to hurt anybody's feelings. They had their hearts set on screwing me, the little sweeties, and I couldn't disappoint them.

Let me hasten to add, this was only during the aptly named layovers. When we were actually up in the air, we were total professionals. None of that mile-high-club stuff for us. We left that to the pilots.

Those big jumbo 747s were like flying mansions, and they had all kinds of amenities, including a huge galley below deck, where the chefs cooked fresh gourmet meals for the first-class passengers. The galley would be empty after dinner, and on long overnight flights, it was very private—the perfect bachelor pad. So the pilots would put the plane on automatic and take a couple of girls downstairs for a personal tour of the facilities. Our job was to scope out the passengers and find the cutest, most-likely-to-be-seduced candidates.

"Hi," we'd say brightly, doing our patented stewardess bend. "Would you like to meet the captain?" We were like perky pimps—and we seldom came up empty. Airline pilots had an almost mythic stature in those days, and to get one in the sack was part of a female traveler's rite of passage.

I steered clear of the pilots—it seemed a conflict of interest; besides, I think I had a worshipful naïveté about them that precluded any erotic involvement—and only once did I avail myself of the international boyfriend list. We were flying into Bahrain, and I was told I simply had to call this marvelous sheikh who lived in the capital of Manama. He was obscenely wealthy, and if you were nice to him, he was sure to give you gold. Not a gold ring or a gold trinket, but gold. Pure gold. Lots of gold.

This sounded both fun and profitable, so when we landed, I called him up. The sheikh seemed delighted to hear from me, and sent a car to bring me to his home—his home being an ornate mansion on the outskirts of the capital. It was of the expected opulence: lavish furnishings, servants scurrying in all directions . . . and look, there was the gold, everywhere!

There also was the sheikh: a fat, middle-aged little man in a white robe and headpiece. I looked him over a moment, making a quick calculation: *I'm supposed to sleep with this guy?* Then I looked around at all that glitter and I decided, *It can be done.*

The sheikh treated me with gracious charm, wined and dined me, and then asked me if I'd like to see his camels. I'd never heard this line before, but I'd come this far. How could I refuse? So he took me outside and, sure enough, he had a stable full of camels. "Would you like to go riding?"

We went camel riding out to his country house, in the middle of the desert. It was a smaller mansion, nestled beside a picturesque oasis of palm trees. There were great heaping baskets of dates everywhere, left out to dry in the sun. We held hands as we strolled around the pond, listening to the desert breeze stir the palm leaves. Then he led me into the house. It was time, I knew, to go for the gold.

Somehow this didn't happen. I don't know why. He was definitely in the market for sex; all the stewardesses had explained the deal to me, and they spoke from experience. Yet he never tried anything. I think what happened was, he discovered that he liked me personally, and I liked him. There was a lot of mutual liking going on—we related to each other as actual human beings—and that sort of pushed the sex right off the table. After a pleasantly civilized evening, we hopped on our camels, rode back to Manama, and I took the limo back to the Gulf Hotel—empty-handed.

Well, not entirely. A few weeks later, when I returned to Sydney, I found waiting on my doorstep several spindles filled with bolts of the very finest cashmere. I had told my Bahrain admirer about my love of sewing, and he had shipped this incredibly expensive fabric, yards and yards of it, right to my home, ready to be converted into a luxury wardrobe. I promptly sewed myself a strapless light salmon floor-length gown that was to die for.

IN 1979 we were laying over in Bombay, India—now called Mumbai—when the Bombay Airport burned down. We were in no danger, but the Santa Cruz Terminal was gutted, and we couldn't fly out for about two weeks.

Now, nobody wanted to stay in Bombay itself. I'd been there several times before and was well acquainted with the almost unimaginable poverty and desperation. In the mornings, I would take a walk from my hotel to watch the sun rise over Bombay Bay. It was spectacular and inspiring; yet at the same time there would be carts going through the predawn streets piled high with dead bodies that had been collected from the sides of the road. Every morning, there would be a fresh cartload heading off to the incinerator.

Then as the day dawned, the living would emerge to take the place of the dead, and it would be difficult to say which was the preferable state of existence. The depth of misery was shocking: people half-clothed, half-starved, moving numbly through the streets as if half-alive. Most disturbing were the blind children begging on the corners: they'd had their eyes gouged out by their parents, in a bid for greater sympathy.

I knew I was supposed to move past them unseeing, but one time I got sucked in, and gave a little bit of money to a sightless child. It was a big mistake. Suddenly I was beset by beggars, who materialized from the shadows. They surrounded me, hands thrust into my face, and as I backed away, they become more angrily insistent: You gave *him* money, where's mine? Terrified, I started running away, and they actually chased me, all the way back to the hotel. I was lucky to escape with my life. Of course, I did escape. They, the poor and hungry, were still stuck there in the desperation of their poverty, waiting for the next tiny ray of hope.

So, no, I didn't want to stay in Bombay, and neither did my colleagues. We'd heard that there was an old British hotel at the top of a mountain in nearby Pune, where we could settle in until the airport reopened.

To get to the top of the mountain, we took an old train that chugged up the steep hill in a series of switchbacks, crawling along at six miles an hour. Indian workers furiously shoveled coal into the engine to keep the train moving, their bodies pouring sweat from the ferocious heat of the furnace and the pitiless noonday sun.

When we reached the top of the mountain, we found ourselves in a different world: foggy, green, full of flowers, more like Switzerland than India. It was still hot, but a soft mountain breeze made it endurable. The hotel had long been abandoned and was in a state of creeping dilapidation, but what remained was an elegant reminder of the imperial days, with high ceilings and huge overhead fans, gorgeous cherrywood banisters and mahogany wainscoting. A veranda stretched around the building, with stunning views looking out over the valley.

The hotel wasn't totally empty when we arrived: a tribe of macaque monkeys had taken up residence on the roof. We were charmed and amused by their antics, as they chased one another back and forth and swung from the gutters. We were less amused when we went out for a walk through the woods and returned to find our luggage ripped apart. The macaques had stolen all of our snacks, eaten the bananas and other fruit, and now sat on the roof picking the last remaining crumbs from the bags of potato chips and pretzels. They seemed quite pleased with themselves.

Fortunately we had a cadre of local chefs to cook for us, so we didn't go hungry. Every evening, we'd sit around a communal table, one big family, and feast on classic Indian cuisine—vegetarian, and loaded with spices. I was never a big fan of spicy food, but I grew to appreciate its merits here, where it was swelter-ing even in the shade. I discovered that the more spices you ate, the more you would sweat, and when the breeze periodically came through, the air would naturally cool off the sweat and pleasantly refrigerate your body.

The downside to this natural cooling system was that the copi-ous perspiration did a number on your body odor. Add to this the fact that I never used deodorant—my father taught me that deodor-ant was bad for your underarms; it was foreign and unnatural—and by the end of the week I was smelling pretty funky.

That didn't keep the men away, though. When you're stuck in an old hotel on a mountain in India with monkeys on the roof and no TV, the pungency of your aroma becomes a very minor ob-stacle to romance.

Now, speaking of sex and body odor, let me tell you about Pierre.

Pierre was my French lover. I had heard that everyone should have at least one French lover, so I went out and bagged one. We met in Champagne, when I had a few days on a Paris layover and decided to take a road trip. I was always going out on such expeditions; I'd seen plenty of big cities in my time, and while I enjoyed the cosmopolitan energy, I truly preferred exploring the surrounding countryside, finding out-of-the-way places by accident and stumbling upon moments of unexpected magic.

I went to Champagne because I'd heard of a wonderful restaurant down there, tucked away in the middle of nowhere, housed in an ancient stone cottage that might have been a thousand years old.

I don't remember the restaurant's name, but the dining experience was unforgettable. There was only one sitting for dinner, at one long table. The surroundings were rustic, but the table was set with stunning elegance: fine linen napkins and tablecloths, crystal glassware, candelabras, flower centerpieces—but no menus: you ate the food they served, and drank the wine they poured.

It was all exquisite. The courses went on and on into the night, and you never knew what was coming next. Each course had its own wine, which the sommelier would celebrate with a joyful exegesis. After the dinner came the cheeses and port wine, the fabulous desserts, everything homemade. I can still taste that perfect crème brûlée. I was so glad I wasn't anorexic anymore.

There were fifteen people at the table, all French; not a tourist in sight. As the courses leisurely followed one upon the other, we got to know our dining companions. There were couples present—husbands and wives (or mistresses)—but, by design, they didn't sit together. Lovers were kept significantly apart, so as not to inhibit the free flow of conversation.

This is how I came to be sitting next to Pierre. He had come with his girlfriend, but she was across the table and just outside of earshot. So he and I spent the evening chatting, and philosophizing, and flirting, and by the end of the evening, the attraction was undeniable. He left with his girl; I left with his phone number.

The next night, we had our first rendezvous, and it was the beginning of a passionate, earthy love affair—in the French style, of course. Pierre never left his girlfriend—they eventually married, and might even still be together—but every time I flew into Paris, I went down to Champagne, where he would be waiting. I didn't know a lot about him—I don't even know how he made a living. I didn't care. I had a lover in France. That's all that mattered.

As I intimated, Pierre was very much obsessed with the scent of a woman. Body smells turned him on, and he detested perfumes and lotions, anything that camouflaged what he called the "aroma of desire." To that end, he refused to let me shower for five days before I saw him. He wanted me to be natural in every way. So whenever I had a flight scheduled for Paris, I stopped showering back in Sydney. I could wash my hands and face; that was it. By the time I got on the plane, I was as ripe as a compost heap. I don't know how the passengers stood it. I know I revolted me.

Then I would arrive at Pierre's house in Champagne, and he would savor me like a fine Bordeaux, his nose twitching like a hyperactive rabbit's. After he'd assessed my general fragrance, he would push me back on the bed and his head would dive hungrily between my legs. Ah, the French! It was all very organic, and consistent with his philosophy. Pierre never bathed, either, so I got to savor his natural essence in return. We were one smelly couple.

When the festivities were over, I would finally take a shower, and after that he had no use for me. *Au revoir, mon amour*—see you next time.

. . .

FOR all my newfound sophistication regarding affairs of the flesh, I was still pretty traditional and conservative at heart. I know that's hard to square with the facts, but I offer, as an example, an incident when I was staying at the Mandarin Hotel in Singapore.

Singapore was an interesting city. They had a thriving black market there—street after street of outdoor stands where you could obtain basically any kind of drug you wanted: opium, cocaine, Valium, Mogadon (a sleep aid; lots of stewardesses took it), whatever. Many of the stewards and stewardesses were addicted, either to sleeping pills or uppers. I wish I could claim to have been above that sort of thing, but I was young; I tried them all. The only thing that saved me from a harrowing downward spiral was that none of them really worked for me. Drugs—whatever.

One night, while the rest of the flight crew was out sampling the local pleasures, I was in the hotel bar, hanging out with a tall, dark, handsome steward named Ken. I had a big crush on Ken at the time, and we were flirting like crazy, but I knew he was married, so it was all totally innocent. Even when, at one point, he asked me if I wanted to go back to his room, I didn't read anything into it. His wife was about to have a baby back home, so there was no way I could interpret the offer as anything more than a friendly gesture between colleagues.

I went up to his hotel room and we had a drink and did some casual chit-chatting. Then Ken excused himself and went into the bathroom. He emerged a moment later, totally naked.

I was perplexed. "Why are you naked?" I asked.

He grinned. "You're from Japan. How about a massage?"

"Oh," I said, relieved. "Okay."

Ken lay facedown on the bed, and I commenced massaging him from head to toe—his shoulders, his feet, his ass, everything. Then he rolled over on his back. His penis sprang up, proudly erect—which was normal during a massage. I took it as a compliment: he was enjoying my work.

So I continued the massage, rubbing his chest, his thighs, and so on. I wanted him to be impressed with my thoroughness.

"Okay," I said, with a satisfied sigh. "All done."

"Wait a minute," Ken said, grabbing my hand. "You forgot one muscle."

I was puzzled. "No, I didn't."

"Oh yes, you did."

I thought about it, retracing my actions in my head. Let's see, I massaged his calves, his deltoids, neck muscles, toe muscles . . . "No, I got them all."

He took my hand and placed it on his penis. "What about this muscle?"

I looked at him wide-eyed. "Oh, no," I explained, now understanding his confusion, "that's not a muscle. That's just a concentration of blood. It won't do any good to massage *that*."

I had such an anachronistic faith in the binding fealty of marriage, despite my parents' unconventional arrangement, that I couldn't grasp the obvious even when it was standing right there in my hand. I still didn't get it.

At this point, I think Ken was starting to realize that he wasn't going to get it, either.

I had one other unsettling moment at the Mandarin Hotel: I was heading through the lobby one day with a couple of stewardesses when I spotted a familiar face by the magazine stand. I stopped short, my heart skipped, and my stomach lurched.

It was Luke.

Jesus. What was he doing in Singapore? How had he found me? Was he stalking me?

I reached out to my fellow stewardesses for support. "Save me," I whispered.

Then, as the scene came into focus, I realized that Luke was wearing a Qantas uniform—a steward's uniform.

What? Was I seeing right? By what weird process had Luke, my macho ex-boyfriend, the sheep rancher, the vineyard owner, the son of a plantation owner, transformed himself into an airline steward?

The utter incongruity of this metamorphosis did not alter my first instinct: to turn and run. It was too late, though—he looked up and spotted me. Although he knew I'd become a stewardess, he seemed mildly surprised to see me.

"Hey, Sachi," he said, in a bland but friendly manner.

I couldn't retreat now, so I walked up to him. "Hello, Luke." I gestured to the uniform. "Working for Qantas now?"

He shrugged. "Yeah. Something different."

"Welcome to the club," I said.

We exchanged a few more pleasantries, and then we ran out of conversation. I never asked him why he'd become a steward; I didn't really care. Besides, it was clear to me now that Luke didn't care much about me, either. We had both moved on.

"See you around," he said, as I left him in the lobby. I never did see him again.

THE most memorable episode of my Qantas tour took place on a Sydney-to-London nonstop, which was about fifteen hours long. I was working the night shift. Everyone was asleep—the passengers, the stewardesses. The pilots were downstairs getting refueled. My job was to keep an eye on things, stroll the aisles, and try to stay awake.

In the middle of the night, when all was quiet, a passenger in first class started to stir. A big strapping Aussie—is there any other kind?—he'd been something of a headache earlier in the flight, drinking continuously since we left the ground and making an obnoxious nuisance of himself, until he finally slumped into a pickled coma. I'd have thought he'd be out for the duration, but here he was, rumbling about and getting his second wind. Being the only one awake, I pointedly looked away from him, not wishing to invite conversation.

Then he stood up. I assumed he was going to the bathroom—and he was. Yet he had no intention of leaving his seat to do it. Instead, he dropped his pants, turned to the side, and deposited a monstrous turd right in the lap of the woman sleeping next to him! I watched this happen in horror, but there was nothing I could do to prevent it. The bowel movement shot out so fast, like a torpedo, that I didn't have a chance to catch it in a food tray or anything. It landed in her lap with a moist plop. Then the Aussie just sat down, pants-less, as if nothing had ever happened.

The woman slept on, blissfully unaware—which was rather fortunate. He being a complete stranger, I doubt she would have appreciated such familiarity. Luckily she was wearing a thick Qantas blanket over her lap, so her dress was spared. Thank goodness for those amenities.

Still, this was something I had never encountered before—there was nothing mentioned about it in our training—and I didn't know how to react. Panicky, I woke up the other stewardesses, but they didn't know what to do, either. We all just stared at the drunken lout with his pants down and the fresh mound of excrement sitting proudly beside him. It needed to be cleared away ASAP, before it started to seep, but he was blocking all access to the woman, and no one wanted to tangle with him. Maybe this went against the Qantas code of crisis management, but when one passenger defecates on another passenger, all bets are off. We had to get the pilots.

When the pilots emerged from the cockpit, the drunken Aussie was still in his seat, pants down, and starting to sing "Waltzing Matilda"—always a bad sign. Without hesitating a moment, the pilots yanked up his pants, strapped him into a straitjacket, put duct tape over his mouth, and shoved him back in his chair. He didn't even struggle. His fate now determined, he closed his eyes and slept for the rest of the night.

My role in this drama was considerably less heroic, but utterly necessary. The offending turd was still steaming on the woman's lap. I had to remove it without waking her up, or else the resulting screams would surely ignite a plane-wide panic. So I went to work, operating with rubber gloves and the steely nerves of a bomb defuser.

The specifics don't need to be discussed here, but suffice it to say, the blight was removed, a fresh blanket installed, and overall calm maintained. Just another day in the life of a Qantas stewardess.

IN all the time I was with Qantas, I saw my mother exactly once. She'd really meant business with that diamond necklace "you're on your own" routine.

In that time, her career had gotten a good bounce with *The Turning Point*, a glitzy ballet world soap opera with Anne Bancroft and Mikhail Baryshnikov, her biggest hit in years. Then she did *Being There* with Peter Sellers, a marvelous film and one of my favorites. Her star was on the rise again. Every now and then one of her movies would play in-flight. It was odd to look up at my mother's face on the big screen—they had big screens in airplanes in those days—glamorous and larger than life, while I was pouring orange juices and carrying barf bags.

Once, we were on a rare two-day layover in San Francisco—rare because I almost never flew into the United States; with my languages they liked to reserve me for foreign countries—but we were continuing on to Europe, so, for the time being, I found myself just a few hours up the coast from my mother's home.

On a whim, I decided to visit her. I jumped on a Greyhound and headed down to Malibu. It had been so long since I last saw her there that I wasn't exactly sure what her address was, and I didn't have her phone number. For that matter, I wasn't sure how she would react when she saw me. So it was going to be a complete surprise for both of us.

When Mom saw me standing on her doorstep, she registered immediate delight. "Sweetheart! How are you?" She threw her arms around me and gave me the biggest hug. "Come on in!"

It was as happy a welcome as I could have expected. There was none of the tension I associated with our previous encounters, dating back to . . . well, the hotel room in London when I was twelve years old and the air tickets had gone missing. All the distrust, the disapproval, the withholding—it all seemed to have disappeared. Absence had made her heart grow fonder.

She showed me around the apartment—so much had changed, so much had stayed the same. We sat on the sofa and discussed our respective histories. She told me about her men; I told her about mine. I showed her my stewardess outfit, and she was impressed.

Then we went out for a walk on the beach, just like when I was a kid. Mom found a sea urchin in a tide pool and stuck her finger into it. "Ooh!' she squealed in surprise.

When we got back to the house, Mom pointed to the balcony. "See up there? That's where I met them."

"Met who?"

"The extraterrestrials. They landed over here on the sand, and then they came up on the porch, and we talked. They told me I was an Enlightened One."

I nodded thoughtfully. We were having a nice visit, so I wasn't going to spoil it by voicing any doubts about her sanity.

Besides, I wasn't surprised by the revelation. Mom had always had an abiding interest in the otherworldly, ever since Dad had given her *A Dweller on Two Planets*. So, extraterrestrials in Malibu? Why not? What's for dinner?

Mom prepared a perfect sirloin steak, with steamed vegetables over steamed brown rice. Actually I suspect the housekeeper prepared it, because Mom was no cook. She could just about boil water.

She could pour a good drink, though. She introduced me to a red wine from Chile that was absolutely delicious. "And only five bucks a bottle," she bragged. She loved a good deal.

After dinner we laughed and told stories, and drank more wine, and enjoyed each other's company. It was a truly pleasant day. I slept in my old room, listening to the ocean crashing against the shore—my old ocean, my old shore.

The only discordant note in the trip was that I was having my period at the time. I didn't share this information with my mom. It was not something we talked about.

My very first period had occurred in the dorms of Charters Towers, when I was twelve years old. It came upon me in the middle of the night, and even though Mom had been preparing me for this moment since I was nine, when it finally arrived I had no idea what to do. The blood was streaming down my legs as I wandered down the halls in my white nightdress, searching for the matron. When I finally found her, I stood before her embarrassed and mortified. She looked at me stone-faced and handed me a bulky sanitary napkin and two safety pins. "Here you are, dear," she said. "Off you go."

Off I go? Where? To do what? I knew about the napkin, but what were the safety pins for? And what do I do with all this blood? I stumbled off to the bathroom in a state of panicky confusion. As I tried to wash the blood from my underwear with hot water (nobody had told me that cold water works better), the sanitary napkin fell off the sink and landed on the bathroom floor, collecting dust and God knows what on its surface. I took a quick shower and wiped myself off with the towel. As I was still bleeding, there was now blood on the towel. I washed the towel out in hot water, and then tried to dry myself again. More blood on the towel! Screw the towel. I tackled the dirty sanitary napkin. I managed to attach the front pin, but I couldn't reach around to fasten the back pin. So I tried twisting the back of my granny pants toward the front for easier access, but then the napkin start twisting sideways, and I was still bleeding! I was almost weeping with frustration. Finally I stood out on the landing and called for the matron. She waddled slowly down the hall, and in her pleasant but brisk English way she attached the back pin for me. "Off to bed," she said, dispatching me down the hall with a firm push. I wanted to crawl into a hole.

From this initial encounter, I came to understand that menstruation was a messy, private business, not to be addressed in the public square. I was always extremely careful to conceal my monthly condition from everyone. Luke's outraged reaction to my used tampon had certainly reinforced this sense of female shame.

So when I was having my period now at Mom's house, I did my best to hide it from her. Why burden her with such unpleasantness, and spoil a perfectly good visit? But as I was removing my clothes in her huge dressing room, Mom walked in. She spotted the stained panties in my hand—the flow had been heavy and clotted, it was not a pretty sight—and was remarkably unfazed: without a word she took the panties in her hand and went to the bathroom sink, and washed them out thoroughly—in cold water— working her fingers through the thick blood without any theatrics. I watched her from the dressing room, amazed. She was just taking care of business. She wrung the panties out and put them on a chair in the sun to dry, and then she said to me, "Go take a shower." I don't think I said anything—any sound would have been a violation of the moment. I took a shower, and when I came out she handed me a pair of underwear from her drawer, and a tampon, and I got dressed.

The entire transaction was so matter-of-fact and without pretense that it stunned me. Usually Mom created a big drama over the tiniest thing, but here she was sublimely restrained, and every moment was quiet, ritualistic, almost Japanese in its simplicity. It was a beautiful experience for me: the maternal validation of my own femalehood that I'd been unconsciously desiring for the last ten years.

Later that afternoon I took the Greyhound back to San Francisco. It had been a perfect visit with Mom, and as I rode up the coast, I thought to myself, *I have to do this again—soon.*

Chapter 9

La Vie Bohème

After four years at Qantas, it was time for a change. I can cite no particular deciding factor in this—not the apparition of Luke, nor the pile of poop nor the general rootlessness of the stewardess life. In fact, I was having a great time. There was no reason at all to leave.

So I did—and moved to France.

I'm not sure why. My affair with the malodorous Pierre had long since ended, so there was no romance drawing me there. Yet I didn't want to stay in Sydney, I didn't want to go back to Tokyo or Honolulu, and I loved Paris. I loved the French people, the French culture, and I especially loved French food.

I'd saved just enough money from Qantas to afford a small studio on the Left Bank—and when I say "small," I mean tiny: there was a twin bed, a closet-size bathroom, and that was it.

Crammed inside the bathroom was a toilet, a corner sink, and a cheap plastic stall shower. There was no kitchen to speak of, just a hot plate and an electric coffeepot. I couldn't really cook there, which was ironic, because I think the main reason I'd moved to Paris was so that I could learn to cook.

I didn't take any cooking lessons per se—too expensive—but I did take a job as a waitress in any restaurant that would have me. I figured, if I can be close enough to where they make this marvelous food, I'll be able to absorb their culinary knowledge without paying a dime.

These were not gourmet restaurants, but little mom-and-pop storefront bistros and cafés. Simple and unpretentious, they turned out classic French fare—onion soups, ratatouille, roast chicken (ah, my favorite!)—for everyday diners who had no idea how lucky they were. I watched the chefs at work in the kitchen and picked up many a savory tip just by keeping my eyes open. I also picked up a rich vocabulary of French colloquialisms and swear words.

During the year I spent in Paris, I was never at any one bistro for more than a couple of months. Perhaps owing to the restlessness bred into me as a stewardess, I liked to bounce from one place to another, looking for new friends and adventures. There were a lot of Japanese tourists in Paris in those days, so my felicity with the language put me always in demand, and I never had a problem finding a job.

Wherever I went, though, I found myself immersed in the world of food. I would get to work early in the morning to help the chef prepare, and go shopping with him at the open markets to pick out the best fruits, the best fish, the best overall ingredients. Then I'd spend the entire day at the café, watching the cooks put together their simple masterpieces as I flitted in and out of the kitchen. I'd be there fifteen hours a day, and the staff would become my new family.

Then, after a few months, I'd be done, and I'd look for another bistro. I just wasn't the settled type. When I saw the movie *Forrest Gump* in 1994, I was startled to recognize something of myself in the title character's constant searching for a place to land. Of course I wasn't as out-to-lunch as he was—I don't think—but I was, like him, always looking for the next box of chocolates.

Oddly enough, in that full year I spent in Paris, I had no boyfriends to speak of—and consequently, no sex. In Paris! It was a criminal waste of natural resources, agreed, but I just wasn't interested. I did a lot of walking instead.

There was so much snow in Paris that winter. I remember the vendors hauling their pushcarts through the snow, peddling fresh warm crepes with butter, sugar, and lemon. My favorite was the *crème de marrons*, a delicious crepe filled with pureed chestnuts. Strolling along the cobblestones of the Left Bank in my beret, eating my hot crepe, I felt quite the quintessential Parisienne.

IT was in the midst of this cold winter that Dad and Miki descended on Paris—not to see me, of course. It may have been for business reasons, or maybe they just wanted to dine at Maxim's. That's what they would do on a regular basis: hop on a jet and eat their way around the world. It was surely just a coincidence that we were sharing the City of Light at the same time.

Nevertheless, when he found out I was in town, Dad invited me to join them at Maxim's—which was fun, but very much on the superficial side; we all strained to be festive, and I found it difficult to look at Miki without picturing her in bed with Luke. I figured it would be a quick hello-goodbye-see-you-around, but as we left the restaurant, Dad invited me to stop by their hotel room the next evening.

I happily took this as a sign that Dad was reaching out to me. As with my mom, I hadn't really seen much of him during my stewardess years. I was endlessly busy, of course, but I would have made time to see him if he'd ever proffered the invitation. He didn't. I think my breaking up with Luke, his old business partner's son, had annoyed and embarrassed him. Somehow, by saving my life, I had done something shameful again.

We would put that in the past now, though. I'd already reconnected with Mom, and now I'd do the same with Dad.

Dad and Miki were staying at the George V Hotel, right off the Champs-Élysées, one of the great five-star luxury hotels. I got there early in the evening. It was the classic dark and stormy night, the cold rain coming down in buckets.

I walked into the lobby—I'd been in some beautiful old hotels in the past, but this was the absolute, sumptuous peak—and announced myself to the imperious concierge at the desk. "I'm here to see Steve Parker."

Once again the mention of my father's name worked like a magic incantation. The concierge's studied indifference vanished. "Ah, oui, Monsieur Parker! And you are . . . ?"

"I'm his daughter."

He was even more impressed. Suddenly *I* was somebody special, too. "Right this way, mademoiselle."

He ushered me personally to the elevator. It was one of those old clanky elevators with the metal gate that pulled across. It had its antique charm, but tonight I preferred to take the stairs. The grand staircase was wide and spiraling, with plush carpeting. It was like walking up to heaven.

Dad and Miki were staying in the penthouse. This was yet

I Love you!
Mom

Mom holding me
when I was a newborn

Me and Mom on
Malibu Beach

On the set of
Some Came Running

Photo shoot at age two
for *Look* magazine

Dad greeting me at
the Tokyo airport

My friend the cherry tree

My father and me in
front of Tokugawa Shrine
in the Japanese Alps

Eguchi-san, my Japanese governess, and me

My father, mother, and me on set

My elegant silk kimono

Yuki watching me knit
at Charters Towers

Miki, Dad, and
me at dinner

Me in my Quantas
stewardess uniform and
the diamond necklace my
mother gave me, with Dad

On the set of
Manhattan Express

Me and Mom on
the red carpet

Me and Mom

Me and Mom at a
movie premiere

On the set of *The Witch of the West Is Dead*

another irony that escaped me at the time. Because I was living in a penthouse, too; the only difference being that mine was a hovel the size of a shoebox. Yet I never thought anything of that. I never questioned the fact that while I was living in bohemian squalor, a mile or so away my father was ensconced in outrageous luxury. This was just the way of things: I accepted it as normal. It was as if I felt that, with my record of false starts and abject failure, I deserved no better.

Maybe I even felt I didn't deserve to take the elevator, and that's why I took the stairs. Whatever the reasoning, it was a long climb, and by the time I got to the top floor, I was a little winded. Instead of knocking right away, I paused outside my dad's hotel room door to catch my breath—which is why I was in the position to hear a conversation going on just inside the room.

It was Dad and Miki. I could hear them clearly, every word.

I sometimes wonder what would have been different in my life if I had taken the elevator that night and bounded right up to the door and knocked right away. If I had not overheard my dad and Miki talking inside, unaware of my presence in the hallway, I would have missed one of the pivotal moments in my life.

Dad was crying.

I had never heard him cry before. It shocked me—I can still remember the icy chill that shot through my body. The sound was alien, and devastating. If my father was crying, then something was terribly wrong, wrong with the life he had created, wrong with the world that I understood. He was a strong, confident man—he was Hemingway—and to show weakness was not merely out of character for him, but inconceivable. His cries that evening were awful to hear: raw and animalistic, the wail of some broken, faltering creature that was trapped and confused and twisted with despair.

"I don't know who I am anymore," he was sobbing. "I don't know anything. I feel like I'm going crazy!" His voice was high and stressed, so unlike his usual smoothly modulated baritone. It was hard to believe it was my dad in there, but I knew it was.

Miki was trying to soothe him. She did not have a soothing demeanor, so her calming words sounded forced and slightly desperate. "It's okay, Steve. I have you, I'll take care of you, don't worry, it's all right . . ."

"No, I can't keep this up anymore! I can't do it!"

"Yes, you can, you can," she insisted. I could hear that Miki was not just being supportive; it was terribly important for her own sake that Dad hold it together.

"Who *am* I?" he cried. "Who *am* I? I can't remember anymore!"

"It's okay . . ."

"No, it isn't! No, it isn't! Who am I?"

I listened with transfixed horror. I couldn't knock now. They would know that I'd overheard.

I couldn't leave, either. They might hear me walking away, and anyway, they were expecting me; I was supposed to be there.

I stayed and waited for Dad to calm down. He couldn't sustain this howl of emotion much longer, and I have to admit, I was fascinated by what I was hearing. I had no idea what he was talking about—Who was he? He was my father, he was Steve Parker, he was the husband of Shirley MacLaine, he was a rich, successful businessman, that's who he was—but I sensed in his anguish the first intimations of a secret life emerging, an alternate reality that I had probably always suspected but never dared recognize. Now all my doubts came swimming to the surface, and the pieces of an unsuspected puzzle were slowly clicking into place. It wasn't totally clear yet; the answer was still out there, but those obsessively repeated phrases—"Who am I? I can't do this anymore! Who am I?"—were pointing the way.

Who was my dad? What did he do? How did he get to be where he was? I assumed I knew the answers, but when I thought about it now, there were many small gaps and great blank stretches unaccounted for.

I knew he wasn't a totally honest man. He had lied to me more than once in my life—the last time on my birthday, when he told me he was in Italy and had faked the phone call, complete with Italian operator. Then there were all the other episodes, the lingering doubts and inconsistencies—the death of Mike Parsons, the loose diamonds in the front seat of the Jeep—all those shadows lingering in the back of my head.

As I listened to my father agonizing over his identity, I felt an uneasy pang of recognition. How often had I wondered the same thing: Who am I? Who am I supposed to be? Who did I become, instead of myself? Underneath the layers of Japanese humility and self-effacement, the docility beaten into me in Australia, the eagerness to please in my Qantas days, the malleable personality adapting to meet each new situation—underneath all that, who was the real Sachi?

It had gotten quieter in the room now, and it seemed safe for me to enter. I knocked on the door.

Things got even quieter, and then, after a pause, my father called out, "Be right there!" in his strong hearty voice. He needed a moment to compose himself, I suppose, and Miki had to get the room just right.

Finally the doors opened—into a huge, gorgeous space, with a king-size bed on one side and sofa and chairs on the other—to reveal Dad, himself again, whoever that was, looking suave and cosmopolitan in his smoking jacket. "Hey, Sach the Pach!" Miki looked frazzled, and gave me a stiff smile; in other times, I might have taken this for hostility, but now I knew she had just pulled my dad back off an emotional ledge, and her nerves were raw.

I sat on the sofa, and we had a drink and exchanged pleasantries. They were both distracted, though, and so was I.

My mind was racing. I had found myself in a unique situation: I knew something about my dad, and he didn't know that I knew it. I actually had the advantage over him. Plus, unlike before, when I would tactfully withdraw from any confrontation, I was eager this time to get some answers. He had tantalizingly cracked open the door to his reality, and I wanted to push through before it closed again.

So I waited for the right moment, waited until everyone was relaxed, before I said, "Dad, can I ask you something?"

"Sure, honey," he said, sitting back in his chair with his scotch, legs crossed.

So I asked: "What do you do for a living?"

It was the essential question, the key to every mystery surrounding my dad, and I had calculated that this was the perfect time to ask it, when his defenses were down, when he was hurting and vulnerable, and ready to face the truth.

I was wrong.

All the civility drained from his face in an instant, and the lights seemed to get dimmer, as if the energy were being sucked out of the room. He gave me the dirtiest look I'd ever seen. I heard Miki gasp in surprise, but I didn't look at her: my eyes were fixed on Dad, as were his on me.

"What?" he finally asked, in angry disbelief, his voice as cold as ice.

I could see I had made a colossal mistake—it hadn't been the right time to broach the subject at all, and it would probably be in my best interests to backpedal as fast as possible.

Yet I couldn't. I wasn't a kid anymore; I was twenty-five years old, and I wanted answers. I looked around at this luxury suite and I asked myself, *How can he afford all this? And the yacht, and the island, and the trips around the world? How?*

So I repeated the question, with a little less confidence: "I was just wondering, Dad, what do you do for a living? Because I really don't know."

The room grew darker. Dad held himself quite still, but I heard the ice cubes clinking in his glass as his hand trembled with contained fury. The tension in his body radiated outward and gripped the whole room.

I'd crossed the line now, big-time, and I knew it. I'd been raised to respect, to accept, and not to question—but now I'd questioned, I'd cast doubt, and (most unpardonably) I'd com-pounded the shame: I'd done it in front of Miki.

Really, I just wanted to know what his job was. What was wrong with that? I knew he had produced a couple of movies and Broadway shows, but that wouldn't have supported the lifestyle he and Miki had been living for all these years.

Dad said nothing. He let his dark silence speak for itself. That was his favored strategy. He would let his unsaid displeasure settle over me, and work its insidious magic.

This time, however, I wasn't cowed by his glare. I wasn't go-ing to backtrack and start apologizing and asking forgiveness. The old routine wasn't working, and he could see it.

So he glanced significantly over at Miki—his enforcer—and she knew what that meant. Take care of this, he was telling her. Go for the kill.

She rose from her chair and advanced on me. "How dare you?" she said, sputtering with outrage. "How dare you ask such a rude question of your father? Who do you think you *are*?" (Ah, that was the question.) "You have no right to ask such a thing! A daughter does not speak like this to her father. It is disgraceful! You are a disgraceful child! You should be ashamed! Ashamed!"

All of this was spoken in Japanese. She wanted to denounce me in the language of my childhood, for maximum effect. Since my father, despite his many years in Japan, didn't speak the language, he had no idea what she was saying, but he could probably guess the basic thrust from the fury in her voice and the violence of her gestures, and he seemed quite content with the performance.

"You want to know what he *does*?" she went on, almost choking on her bile. "Look around you! He is a success, that's what he does! What do *you* do? Where do *you* live? Your father treats you like a princess, which you don't deserve, and this is how you thank him? You are lucky he lets you in the door! I wouldn't! You think you are special? You are not special! You are nothing! You disgust me, you ungrateful little . . . bitch!" She spat out the last word with special relish. Miki was getting meaner and nastier, because she knew Dad couldn't understand her. She was going for the kill, all right, hoping to finish me off.

I should have leapt up at this point and thrown it back in her face: *Look, I know what's going on! I heard my father crying, I heard him wondering who he was, wondering how he could keep up all this pretending. Pretending what? What's real around here and what's bullshit? And who are* you *to lecture me? You're not my mother! You're my father's mistress, a teahouse servant—and, by the way, I know you were sleeping with my fiancé! So who's the bitch now?*

That's what I *should* have said. It would have been a great scene in a movie.

Of course, I said nothing. For all my defiance, I was still bound to the culture I was raised in. Miki had pushed all the time-tested buttons of guilt and shame, and I responded accordingly.

When she finished her tirade, I got up quietly from the sofa, gave Dad a hug, walked past Miki, and left the hotel room. I didn't say a word. Neither did they. They never made a move to stop me.

I walked slowly down the stairs, measuring each plush, cushioned step, as the staircase spiraled down and down. When I came out of the hotel, it was still raining, and I walked home in the rain.

For all that, he never did answer my question.

CHAPTER 10

THE Good DOCTOR

I wanted to get my breasts done.

Not that there was anything wrong with them. They looked fine—a bit smallish perhaps, but firm and proportionate. And none of my boyfriends complained. As Luke would charmingly have put it, "Anything more than a mouthful is a waste, anyway."

I was self-conscious just the same. Dad had always teased me about my "fried eggs," and I guess I always felt inferior in that regard. Any boost in my self-esteem would be welcome about now.

I got a recommendation for a plastic surgeon from Anastasia Gratsos, a close friend of Miki's, and the wife of Constantine Gratsos, known as "Costas." Costas was involved in the shipping business, and he was also the right-hand man of Aristotle Onassis. We're talking connected.

So when Anastasia called with the name of a plastic surgeon, I knew I was getting top-of-the-line. Dr. Jeffrey Dietrich had an office in Illinois, just outside Chicago. He handled models, actresses, the rich and the super-rich.

I was none of these, but Anastasia told me to come over to the States to meet the doctor, and I could figure out how to pay for it later. I saved up my money and took a cheap flight from Belgium to New York. I stayed with Anastasia for a few days, and then took the train to Chicago.

Dr. Dietrich's clinic was actually outside Chicago, a fancy modern building in the woods. Dr. Dietrich was a handsome, assured man in his late forties, commandingly in charge but with great personal warmth—just the kind of doctor you might see on television. Since the vast majority of his patients were women, he knew how to charm them and put them at their ease—and being the susceptible romantic that I was, I happily allowed myself to be charmed.

"What seems to be the problem, Miss Parker?" he asked as we sat in his consultation room. His eyes were sky blue and penetrating.

"Well, I'd like my breasts to be a little bigger. Not a lot. I mean, there's nothing wrong with them the way they are, but I think they could be a little more, you know, full. Round. Whatever." His steady gaze made me nervous, and I couldn't stop babbling. "But I'm no expert. What do you think, Dr. Dietrich?"

He smiled. "Call me Jeffrey."

I was ready to swoon right there. "Okay, call me Sachi!"

We went into his office, and I took off my shirt and showed him what I had. He could not have been more solicitous and gentlemanly, handling me with great care and observing all professional boundaries. Still, I was topless in front of a very attractive, wealthy single man, and it was giving me ideas.

After our meeting, I had to get back to the city and catch a morning train back to New York. "What's the rush?" said Dr. Jeffrey. "You didn't come all the way out here just for an hour meeting?" He offered to show me around the area, and I agreed.

We drove through the country roads, and he took me to a gunpowder-making plant, which was surprisingly interesting. Then he insisted on taking me to dinner—his treat. Did he give all his prospective clients this treatment, or was I something special? At the restaurant, he ordered me clams on the half shell, with horseradish sauce—my favorite. How did he know? We had some very expensive wine, and he ordered dinner for both of us. He was taking charge, and I knew it, and liked it.

The consultation had turned into a first date. We talked and talked, on into the night. He was naturally interested in my family, but he wasn't starstruck—having dealt with many celebrities himself, he took all that fame nonsense with a grain of salt, which I found appealing.

Jeffrey wouldn't hear of my heading back to Chicago that night. He brought me to a picturesque country inn, and insisted on paying for my room. Given the circumstances, I felt obliged to invite him up, but he stayed only a few minutes. He kissed me on the cheek and wished me good night. "I'll see you for breakfast."

Alone, I sat on the bed and tried to figure out what was happening. I'd come to Chicago for a boob job, and suddenly I was in the middle of a Harlequin romance: the dashing country doctor, the clams on the half shell, the four-poster bed, all the ingredients for a hot, steamy bodice ripper. I crawled into bed, my head swimming, intoxicated with the possibilities. What would tomorrow bring?

I didn't have to wait that long. At about two in the morning,

I heard the key turn in the lock, and suddenly the door was opening. There was a man in the doorway.

I sat up, instantly terrified. "Hello . . . ?" I said groggily, trying to get my bearings, fighting through the fog of too much wine.

"Shhh . . . ," the man said gently. He shut the door behind him and locked it. My heart was pounding in my chest. Who was he? How did he get in? What did he want?

I got the answer to the third question first. Without a word, the man lifted the sheets at the bottom of the bed and slipped underneath them. I watched as his head bobbed under the sheets, moving slowly and steadily north until it nestled between my legs. Then I felt his fingers prying my thighs apart, and his tongue lapping at the fringes of my vulva.

It was Jeffrey, of course. He had taken another room in the inn, let himself into my room with his own key, and now was putting his compendious knowledge of female anatomy to work. We had gone way past Harlequin: this was like every *Penthouse* magazine–*My Secret Garden*–Erica Jong fantasy come true.

The good doctor knew what he was doing down there. This was a man with professional chops in every sense. He carefully peeled back the various folds of my vagina, opening it up like a flower—much as Eguchi-san would skillfully summon forth the blossom of a clementine—and probing gently, gently, with his erudite tongue, like a hummingbird searching for nectar.

I should have stopped him right away. The man had broken into my room, he was taking enormous liberties, he needed to account for his outrageous behavior—but it felt so good, I wanted it to go on . . . No, I should stop him . . . Well, I could always stop him in a few minutes . . . No, this is wrong, wrong . . .

Then the first orgasm washed over me, and that settled the debate. In for a penny, in for a pound. The orgasms kept coming, one after the other, and I just lay back and kept riding the waves. If this was a dream, it ranked right up there in my top five.

Then it was over. His appetite sated, he slowly withdrew from the bed and, without a word, left the room.

In the morning, Jeffrey was waiting for me downstairs. "Sleep well?" he asked, betraying not a hint of what had happened the night before. Had it been a dream then, after all? No, there'd been too many orgasms; I would have woken up by the third one.

Over breakfast, Jeffrey excitedly discussed his plans for my breasts. He definitely saw room for improvement, and he was eager to get his hands on them. He knew I was pressed for cash at the moment, but we could definitely work something out.

This put me off a little. I know I'd gone to Dr. Dietrich specifically to have my breasts done, but after yesterday, and especially after last night, I assumed he would want to preserve my assets just as they were. He was obviously attracted to me, so why should he want me to change?

He also mentioned that it would be beneficial for me to get implants in my buttocks, too, just to plump them up a bit. Right now they were a little on the flat side.

Oh really? Now there was something wrong with my ass, too? It was good enough for the boys at the noodle shop!

This sudden insensitivity, coupled with the nocturnal visit, made me back off from making any rash decisions. "Let me go home and think about it," I said—and by "home," I meant Paris.

Back in my tiny studio on the Left Bank, I tried to forget Dr. Jeffrey, but it wasn't easy. Within a week, I got a letter from him. I was afraid it might be a bill for the consultation, but no, it was a love letter. A very courteous, discreet love letter, but a love letter nonetheless. He missed me; we had such a great time together; when would he see me again?

I was thrilled. I realized that I missed him, too. I still had those misgivings, though, so I wrote back a friendly, noncommittal reply.

That was the beginning of a six-month correspondence. It began politely, with respectful expressions of admiration and regard, but very quickly blossomed into a full-blown epistolary *affaire d'amour.* He wrote about his passion for me, his ardent love, his desire to be with me always and forever. I told him how I spent my days walking along the Seine, or wandering the Louvre or the Tuileries, and thinking only of him, him, him. (Not entirely true, but I was trying to be as romantic as possible.) We didn't get steamy and sexual in our letters, but we didn't have to: we both knew what had happened back at that country inn, and that there was plenty more where that came from.

Pretty soon I had convinced myself that I was hopelessly in love with him. I built him up in my mind as the ideal lover: wise, experienced, mature, adventurous. Together with me, the impulsive, impetuous naïf, we made the perfect match.

Anastasia Gratsos thought so, too; she was constantly trying to push us together. She called me every now and then—"Do you like him? Do you think there's something there? When are you coming back to the States?" she kept asking.

Frankly, I was just waiting for a good excuse, and finally Jeffrey gave me one: he was building a huge mansion for himself on his property near San Diego, and he wanted me to see it. That was good enough for me.

Jeffrey was waiting when I landed in Los Angeles. He looked even more handsome than I remembered him. We drove down to San Diego and checked into a motel near the construction site. It was going to be a fun weekend.

Things immediately turned strange.

As soon as we got to the motel room, Jeffrey wanted to make love—right away. Yet I needed just a few minutes to unwind; I was hoping to freshen up a little and maybe unpack first . . .

No! He wanted me now. Now! He threw me on the bed, and before I knew it, he was on top of me, pulling off my clothes and pushing my legs apart, foreplay be damned! He was going to have me, goddamn it!

It was fast, frenetic, exciting, and exhausting. I had never made love with anyone who was so aggressive and unstoppable. I hardly had time to gasp between thrusts. When he was finished, I was so out of breath I couldn't talk.

"That was fantastic!" I managed to get out.

"Okay," Jeffrey said. "Roll over."

Roll over? I looked down and saw that he was ready for action again. Already?

I guess I didn't move fast enough for him, because he grabbed me and spun me over, and we were off again—and again, and again.

I don't know how to explain it, but in the space of a two-hour ride down the 405, Jeffrey had morphed from a courtly, polished doctor into a voracious sex machine. He was putting me in all kinds of positions: against the wall, over the vanity, upside down . . . coming at me in every direction. I was spinning around like a pinwheel.

There was no emotion behind it, though. None. Not a trace of that ardent, caring lover I'd read so much about in his letters. It was all about sex, nothing more—and his sex, not mine. Whether I was getting any pleasure out of it didn't seem to matter at all to him. I was just a rag doll he was throwing around the room.

I guess one often fantasizes about being swept away in a riot of sexual ecstasy, but this wasn't ecstatic at all. It was cold and animalistic. The sex was almost brutal in its forcefulness—and relentless. He never got fatigued. I couldn't understand what kept him going. This was long before Viagra, but since he was a doctor, maybe he had access to medicines that mere mortals didn't.

When he did take a break, it was to perform oral sex on me—which was thoughtful, I guess, but it came with a little quirk: he asked me if I had any perfume. I didn't; I never used perfume. So he took out his own perfume—curious that he would be carrying women's perfume around with him, but that was the least of his oddities—and insisted I spritz it around my crotch. He refused to go down on me unless I had a sweet-smelling vagina. (He was no Pierre.)

I should have told him to go to hell, but I really needed the rest, so I dabbed the perfume on my inner thighs, and when I was sufficiently fragrant, he went to work. I tried to enjoy it, but I was too exhausted.

Then back to the grind. This went on for hours, all through the night. I think we may have stopped for dinner, but it was only the briefest of respites. Finally I begged him to stop. I was too sore; I couldn't take it anymore.

Jeffrey shrugged, and rolled over in bed. "Tomorrow I'll show you the mansion," he said, and fell asleep.

Actually there was no mansion; there was a spot where the mansion would be. The next morning, we took a tour of the site. He owned a huge piece of property in the hills, and judging from the view and the blueprints, you could see it would be magnificent when it was completed.

Right now, however, there was nothing. The foundation was being poured, and there were lots of construction workers milling about. Otherwise, it was just a lot of sagebrush. *This was worth flying from Paris to see?*

While we walked about, I started feeling a pain in my groin. After all that crazy sex, maybe I'd pulled a muscle, or something was torn. I'd have to take it easy today.

When we got back to the motel, though, I barely had time to get an aspirin down my throat before Jeffrey pushed me back on the bed. Time to earn my keep.

The moment he entered me, I felt a searing pain. "Stop, stop!" I cried.

He didn't stop.

"No, it hurts!"

"Oh, it doesn't hurt that much," he insisted. Oh, but it did. I struggled away from him and went into the bathroom.

I discovered to my horror that there was blood in my urine. In fact, my urine *was* blood

Jeffrey looked down into the toilet bowl, unimpressed. With an impatient sigh, he inspected me. "Hmm," he murmured, "it looks like cystitis."

"Cystitis? What's that?"

"It's an infection. It happens. I'll write you a prescription."

He scribbled a prescription for an antibiotic. I started for the door.

"Wait a minute," he said, grabbing my arm. "Not yet." He threw me back on the bed.

It took about a day for the antibiotics to kick in. Until then, the pain was excruciating—which didn't matter to Jeffrey. He kept screwing me. That's why I was there. He was furious that I'd gotten this infection, but he wasn't going to let it cramp his style.

I found out later, by the way, that traumatic cystitis results from a bruising of the bladder, which can be caused by unusually forceful intercourse. So I was definitely fucked into this condition.

It was at about this point that I began to realize that Jeffrey was not merely weird but probably a monomaniacal sociopath. He had that depraved indifference to human life that you hear so much about on crime shows. Somehow I hadn't picked up on this. I guess I'm just not very good at reading men.

Now I was genuinely frightened of him, and I didn't know what my next move would be. Jeffrey had shown flashes of his temper already, and I could well imagine the kind of violence he might be capable of. No one, not even Luke at his most out of control, terrified me as much as Jeffrey.

So, on the third day, when he asked me to marry him, I immediately said yes. I didn't want to marry him, God knows, but I didn't think I had a choice. I couldn't say no. He was already bouncing me off the walls for fun; what would he do to me if I actually crossed him?

I called Mom in Malibu, ostensibly to break the news, but I think secretly in the hope that she would save me.

"What?" she rasped. "*Who?*"

"Dr. Jeffrey Dietrich," I said.

"Doctor? How did you meet *him*?" Already she was skeptical.

"He's a plastic surgeon. I wanted to get my breasts enhanced."

"Well, you *could* use some help there," she conceded. "That doesn't mean you have to marry the guy. Are you in love with him?"

I paused a moment. "Yes. I guess."

Mom heard the panic in my voice. "I'm coming down there," she said tersely. "Right now."

Two hours later she was pulling up to the motel. I was nervous about Jeffrey—would he be angry that my mother was coming to visit without his permission? Already, in the space of three days, he had so taken control of my mind and my nervous system that I was petrified at the thought of upsetting him.

To my relief, it was the charming Jeffrey who emerged to greet Mom. He was delighted to see her, he really admired her film work, she was even more beautiful in person—he could not have been more cordial or gentlemanly.

Mom wasn't fooled. She was in show business; she knew when she was being bullshitted. He was too old for me, and there was something about him that she just didn't like.

She never said as much, but when she wouldn't stay for dinner and wanted to head back home right away, I knew she was less than enchanted with him. She wanted me to go back to Malibu with her. "You don't mind, Jeffrey, if she visits with her mother for a few days, do you?" she asked. He probably *did* mind, but she had so artfully phrased the request that it would have been churlish to deny her.

I was planning to be gone for only a few days, but things played out much differently after Mom realized she'd forgotten her reading glasses.

We were sitting in the car outside the motel, and Mom was trying to figure out how to get back on the freeway. She had a map spread out in her lap, but couldn't figure it out without her glasses. I was hopeless at reading maps, so Jeffrey was leaning into the car window, trying very patiently to explain it to her:

"You have to follow this road here, and where it forks, you bear to the left . . ."

"Wait, wait, you're talking too fast!"

Jeffrey smiled tightly, and spoke slower: "When the road forks, you bear to the left . . ."

"There's a left here?" she said testily. "Where? I don't see it."

Of course she didn't see it; she didn't have her glasses. When Mom got frustrated with something, she often found comfort in snapping at everyone else.

Unfortunately, Jeffrey was not one to be snapped at. He was an important doctor, accustomed to being listened to, and his mood could turn on a dime, as it did now. His patience instantly evaporated, and he snatched the map from Mom's hands, crumpled it up into a ball, and tossed it through the window at me in the passenger seat. "Here, you'll find it," he said, and he walked back into the motel.

Mom looked at the crumpled map in disbelief, and then at me. "Let's get the hell out of here," she suggested. She floored the gas pedal, and we shot off like two bats out of hell.

She didn't say too much until we found the freeway, but after that she gave free rein to her opinion. "He's an asshole! A pompous, self-important asshole! And an *old* asshole! You're not marrying that middle-aged prick, no fucking way!"

Now, I have to say, I was raised in Japan to be proper and soft-spoken, to strive always to swallow my emotions. I never swore, and whenever my mother let loose with a barrage of colorful epithets, I was always a bit shocked and embarrassed for her. How could she say such intemperate things? Didn't she realize how poorly it reflected on her? However, in this case, I found myself in full agreement with her.

"You're not going back there," she decided. "You're staying with me."

As I heard this, I felt a calming joy come over me. *I'm staying with Mom.* I realized that this was what I had always wanted: to be with her.

So Jeffrey turned out to be a good thing after all.

Nevertheless, Mom hired a private detective to look into the background of Dr. Jeffrey Dietrich. Over her many years in the business, she'd had occasion to use private detectives, and now it was a habit with her. She was sure there was something fishy about my former fiancé, and she was going to find out what it was.

This is what she told me she discovered: Dr. Jeffrey was a successful, highly respected plastic surgeon in the Chicago area—but he had a secret side business that was in many ways even more lucrative.

It seems that Jeffrey would often attract clients (usually young women) who coveted his services but couldn't afford his gold-standard prices. Rather than turn them away, Jeffrey would offer them a sort of barter system: he would fly the women down to Colombia, where he had a business colleague who would perform breast surgery for free. Instead of putting in silicone implants, though, the Colombian surgeon would fill the women's breasts with bags of cocaine. The women would then fly back to Chicago, and Jeffrey would remove the cocaine and put in the proper implants. Tit for tat, you might say.

So Jeffrey, among his many other distinctions, was an international drug trader.

This is why Mom did nothing with the information. She thought it more prudent to keep it strictly between us. "Look, we could go after this asshole and get him arrested, but . . ."

"We might get our necks broken," I said.

"Exactly."

Looking back, I'm surprised he never suggested any such drug swap with me. Then again, I was with him for only four days total—just enough time for him to propose.

That was something I never quite figured out. Why would he want to marry me on such short notice, especially given his tastes and background? That question led me back to Dad.

When Dad found out that I had broken up with Jeffrey, he was really angry with me. "I'm very disappointed," he told me over the phone, in his gravest voice. Why? True, I had never told him how Jeffrey treated me at the motel, or what Mom's private detective had uncovered, so maybe my split with Jeffrey might have seemed capricious. Still, why should it have mattered to Dad? He didn't even know the guy.

Or did he? It was Miki's friend Anastasia who had hooked me up with Jeffrey in the first place, and she had pushed for the romance. Was it all at Dad's direction? Was he promoting the match behind the scenes, just the way he had tried to bring Luke and me together? And if so, why? Was he involved in this drug business, too? Is that where he got all his money? I flashed back again to all those puzzling scenes from Dad's life: the loose diamonds, the dead man in his office, the misleading phone calls, the orgies in his hotel room. *Who am I? I can't keep this up anymore.* Secrets built upon more secrets.

Yet there was another secret waiting for me in Malibu, in a box of yellowed telegrams in an old brown safe: a revelation that would blow all the other ones right out of the water.

CHAPTER 11

MAN IN SPACE

It was while we were driving back up the coast that I decided to ask the question. So many things were whirling through my head—Dad, Jeffrey, my life so far, from Japan to Europe to Australia, everything that appeared at once utterly random and yet somehow connected. If I could only find that vital missing piece, the common thread that would pull the vagrant strands together and give me that long-desired "Eureka!" moment.

I suspected that Mom held the answer. She had rescued me from the sociopath, she was bringing me home, I was going to be a part of her life from now on. All roads led to her, and with this bright future stretching ahead of us, it seemed like the right moment to make some sense of the past.

"Mom, is there something going on that I don't know about?" I was referring to her and Dad, and their unconventional marriage, and where I fit in.

She was evasive at first, but finally she said: "I'll tell you when we get home."

NOW let me say a word or two about Mom. She's a born storyteller. It's in her Scotch-Irish genes. She loves to entertain, and she despises the unforgivable sin of being boring—and I have to say, she's never been more inspired or inventive than when she's recounting the story of her own life.

She's written about a dozen books now, recounting her many worldly and otherworldly experiences, and all of them have been quite successful. Many critics have commented on her natural gift for storytelling. Dramatic confrontations and juicy dialogue abound.

I wasn't there when most of these stories were supposed to have happened, so I can't pass judgment on their veracity. Some of them are probably true, but even given the make-believe dynamics of Hollywood, there are a few tales that strain credulity. Just one example: Mom tells of being on the set of *Some Came Running* with Frank Sinatra when a harried production assistant complained that they were two weeks behind on the shooting schedule. Sinatra supposedly took the script from the production assistant's hands, ripped twenty pages out of it, and handed it back. "There, pal, now we're on schedule." According to Mom, Sinatra commanded such respect and fear that they never put those pages back in.

It's a good story, but if you're familiar with film history, you know that a similar anecdote was told about John Ford years before. And if you're familiar with film production, you know that it's virtually impossible to cut a random twenty-page chunk out of a script, especially one based on a bestselling novel, without causing all kinds of mayhem with continuity and character development.

Still, it's a good story, and that's what counts.

I've witnessed a few of Mom's adventures firsthand, and I've noticed a little bit of embellishing here and there. Not wholesale fabrication, exactly, but artful stretches of the truth. With her, a simple trip to the supermarket becomes a search for spiritual enlightenment. My minor bout with endometriosis turns into a hospital scene out of *Terms of Endearment*, with a frantic last-minute dash to the airport thrown in for good measure.

For the most part, so what? It's a showbiz axiom that you never let the truth get in the way of a good yarn. There are exceptions, though. The true reason for my childhood move to Japan is one of them. That's a story that was never clear to me from the start, and as the years went by, it grew only murkier and more convoluted. Still, since it was clearly the most influential decision bearing on my life, it was important for me to find out what had actually happened, and why.

There was an accepted explanation at the time: my mother's career in Los Angeles was taking off like a rocket, my father had important business concerns in Tokyo, and it made sense for me to be raised in the more stable of the two environments. Children, after all, need consistency, and in Japan I would receive structure, a sense of traditional values, and one parent's full and loving attention—more or less.

If you read my Mom's various memoirs, however, you'll find that this story has been tweaked and contradicted more than once. In her first book, *Don't Fall Off the Mountain*, I was sent to Japan because my father was stricken with hepatitis and languishing in a Tokyo hospital, far from home and all alone. (Mom didn't know about Miki at the time.) For some reason, Mom felt that my presence at Dad's bedside would go a long way toward raising his spirits. So, the story went, she put me on a plane and shipped me across the Pacific to work my two-year-old magic, a miniature

Florence Nightingale. I turned out to be such a tonic for Dad that he recovered in record time—and although I was supposed to return to L.A. after that, he decided to keep me with him, as a lucky charm, perhaps.

According to Mom in that first book, now *she* was the one who was lonely. She missed us so desperately that at one point she joined us in Tokyo, shucking her career to become a modest Japanese-style housewife. (I don't remember this at all, but I was only two, so who knows?) For six months we led an idyllic life—we were a complete family again—but eventually Mom started to feel restless stirrings. Performing was in her blood; it was what she needed to do—but how could she abandon us again? She was torn between the dictates of conscience and career: a wrenching dilemma.

It was only when I, little precocious Sachi, sensed her growing discontent and told her that she needed to follow her dream—"Why don't you go back to work, Mommy?"—that she returned to the States to resume her movie career and become the great star she is today. Yes, it was all thanks to me.

That was just one story. If you check out her later book, *Dance While You Can*, you'll see that I'm sent away for the more mundane reason that Hollywood is an awful place to raise a child, and I'd have a much better chance of growing up normal in a different, more becalmed setting. Here's the strange thing, though: in this version, I move to Japan when I'm six years old, not two. What happened to those four years? And what happened to her long months of living in Tokyo, and my words of wisdom that sent her back to America? Did any of that happen? Again, who knows?

In an even later book, *My Lucky Stars: A Hollywood Journey*, the Mob story emerges: Mom gets the word from an associate that the syndicate is thinking of kidnapping me. It seems the goons want to muscle in on Mom's career and get her under their exclusive control (which is a twist on the older story, which held that the Mob was angry with Sinatra). She has no intention of playing ball with them, so Dad insists, for safety's sake, that I leave the country. (I don't know if I'm six or two in this story; it's not clear.)

The dialogue in this beach scene is especially rich: Mom gets off a few of her choice expletives ("those cocksuckers!") and has one visionary outburst in which she declares she's not going to knuckle under ("and you can tell them to shove their horses' heads up their asses!"). Since this scene takes place a good ten years before *The Godfather* was published, I don't know where she pulled this iconic image from, unless her gift for channeling had granted her access to the future as well as the past.

They're all good stories, I have to admit: solid, motivated, reasonably credible. Still, they can't all be true.

In fact, none of them is. The inside, exclusive story, the one Mom revealed to me when we arrived in Malibu, is the least believable of them all, but it's the one that actually happened—or so she swears.

WE arrived at her beach house. I followed Mom into her bedroom, where she pulled an old brown safe out of her closet. She carried it into the living room and fiddled with the combination. The safe popped open and she removed a tin box containing a stack of old telegrams. "Read," she said. "This will explain everything."

The telegrams gave me an ominous twinge. More letters from Miki, perhaps?

I sat on the living room couch, picked out the first telegram, which was dated April 1956. It read something like this:

*My darling Shirley, I miss you so much. Can't wait to
see you again. Love and kisses. Paul.*

Huh.

It was highly unilluminating. Someone named Paul. Obviously a romance. Was it an affair? Had she been cheating on Dad?
Did it matter? They were both proud of the fact that they had a
modern, open marriage, so a little dalliance on the side was no big
deal. Was this something deeper, though? Was Paul the true love
of her life?

I looked at Mom, bewildered. She gave an existential shrug.
"Keep reading."

So I read another telegram, dated a few years later:

*Looking down and thinking of you. I hope Steve is
taking good care of Sachi. Please give her my love.
Yours always, Paul.*

So this Paul character knew my dad and me, and one could
almost sense a bonhomie between them. But why would he have
been concerned about my welfare? Why would he even have
thought that Dad might *not* be taking good care of me? What
business was it of his? And why had he been sending *me* his love?

I ran the name through my head, trying to make a connection. Paul, Paul . . . Did I know any Pauls? It wasn't Paul New-
man, was it? Mom had made one movie with him, *What a Way to
Go!*, but he was already married to Joanne Woodward at that time,
and they were a famously faithful couple . . . No, it wasn't very
likely. And I was pretty sure it wasn't Paul Lynde. What did "looking down" mean, anyway? Looking down from where?

There were many more telegrams to get through. I read them
one by one, trying to piece together the secret.

Still missing you terribly.

It's cold up here.

Up where?

Can't wait to be back on earth.

Back on earth? What the hell does *that* mean?

I waded through dozens of messages, trying to make sense of these cryptic pre-Twitter fragments. Finally I gave up and tossed the telegrams aside. "I'm not getting it, Mom."

"Keep reading."

"I don't want to keep reading. Why don't you just tell me? Who's Paul?"

Mom took a deep, dramatic pause. It was the moment of the big reveal, and she was milking it.

"Paul . . ." She ran her hand across her mouth anxiously, and had to take yet another moment. Finally: "All right, I'll just say it: Paul is your real father."

There's a curious sense of dislocation you get when you receive news that's completely at odds with everything you've ever known and understood about your life. It's like when you arrive at the trick ending of a movie such as *The Sixth Sense* or *The Usual Suspects*, and you discover that everything's the opposite of what you thought, and all those baffling twists of logic resolve into a crystal-clear picture. Except in this case there was no sudden clarity, no "Eureka!" moment at all, just ever-deepening confusion.

"My real father? Paul is my real father? How come I've never heard of him? Where is he?"

"Right now, he's in outer space." Mom said this with disarming matter-of-factness and a quiet sense of pride.

"He's in *outer space?*"

Mom made an equivocating gesture. "He's on a mission for the government."

"A mission? What kind of mission?"

She gave me a patient smile. "A *secret* mission, sweetheart. All I know is, he's in the Pleiades. The Seven Sisters." She pointed heavenward.

I looked blankly up at the ceiling. Mom explained that the Pleiades is a star cluster in outer space. There are seven stars altogether, seven, which is a very significant number in Christianity, Buddhism, practically all religions or mythologies: the Seven Days of Creation, the Seven Stages of Enlightenment, the Seven Seals of the Apocalypse. . . . She went on and on. I just nodded slowly. I had to abandon the Pleiades for the moment anyway, because there was a more pressing issue to confront.

"So, if my real father is in outer space, then . . . who's Dad?"

"You mean Steve?"

"Steve, my dad."

"Steve is not your dad. *Paul's* your dad."

I pressed on. "Okay, then, who's Steve?"

"Well, Steve is no one, technically."

"What does that mean?"

Mom took another long, measured pause. "Steve—how do I say this? Steve was created by the government."

Now *I* had to pause. "*Created?* What do you mean 'created'?"

"He's a clone," Mom said.

I stared at her a moment. "Dad's a clone?"

"*Steve's* a clone. Dad's in outer space."

I studied Mom's face carefully for traces of a telltale smile, or any sign that she was holding in her laughter. She had to be joking, right? She *had* to be.

"I don't understand. Dad, *my* dad, the guy I grew up with—

he's a clone?" Plummeting helplessly down the rabbit hole, I tried to put on the brakes. "Mom, are you serious?"

She seemed affronted. "Of course I'm serious. You don't believe me?"

There was a hint of prickliness in her voice, and I realized I would have to dial back my incredulity a little or else she would shut down and I'd never get the rest of the story out of her. So I proceeded with a cautious reasonableness. "I believe you, Mom. I'm just trying to understand . . . You think the government cloned Dad?"

"They do it all the time, sweetheart. You see, Paul's space missions are so top secret, even *I* don't know what he's up to. So the government had to create a second Paul, to avoid suspicion. In case the Russians found out."

"Found out what?"

"It's a *secret*. A very important government project—that's all I know. With global implications. And I'm helping to support it. I send money every month. It's my way of serving my country."

I just stared at her. I didn't know what to say.

Mom sighed. "I knew you would have a hard time with this. That's why I've tried to keep it from you all these years. But look, the facts are all right there. He's been sending me these telegrams all along." She ran her fingers through the telegrams as if she were Jimmy Stewart on the Senate floor in *Mr. Smith Goes to Washington.*

It was true; the telegrams were right there. They genuinely existed. *Someone* must have sent them.

"Okay, if Paul is my real father, how come I've never met him?"

"You *have* met him. He comes down from space every now and then to visit. But we didn't tell you because we didn't want to upset you. They look so much alike, you just never noticed the difference. Sometimes it was Steve; sometimes it was Paul."

"Can *you* tell them apart?"

Mom gave a small, secretive smile. "Well . . ." Choosing not to elaborate, she tried to reassure me: "Look, Sach, I know what you're thinking. I've been skeptical at times, too. But I know for certain that Paul is Paul, and Steve is Steve. I know it."

How did she know it?

She told me the Caesar story.

Caesar was the family dog, a boxer with the sweetest temperament. He was the pride of the household, and Mom and Dad both doted on him, Dad especially.

When poor Caesar finally died of natural causes, Mom was crushed. She had a bigger concern, though: How would her husband handle the news? "You know how much Paul loved that dog," she reminded me.

"I know how much Steve did."

"That wasn't Steve. That was Paul."

Every time I interrupted her, I got more confused, so I just let her go on with the story.

"When Caesar died," she continued, "I had to break the news to Paul. But he was in space, so I called Steve in Tokyo and I told him, 'Caesar died.' And he took the news very matter-of-factly. 'Uh-huh, uh-huh. I see.' Didn't faze him at all—which proved to me right away that Steve wasn't Paul.

"So we discussed whether he should relay the news to Paul right away, or whether we should wait till the next time Paul came home and I'd tell him myself. Steve felt I should be the one to tell him, and I agreed.

"So it was a couple of months later now, and Paul was between missions. I had to pick him up at the airport, and we drove back to

Malibu. I didn't say a word; I pretended that everything was fine. Then we pulled into the driveway, and finally I had to tell him that Caesar wasn't going to be there waiting for him; he was gone. And when Paul heard that—when he heard that Caesar was dead—he just fell apart. He was crying, he fell to his knees in the driveway, banging his fists on the ground, tears streaming down his cheeks—this was real pain. He was in anguish. No faking. I'm an actress; I know acting. And he would have had to be the greatest actor in the world to fake that.

"So, obviously, Paul was Paul, and Steve wasn't. Steve didn't care at all about Caesar. It didn't matter to him. Because, you see, you can't clone a soul."

I couldn't argue with that.

I was still having trouble wrapping my head around the initial premise. "I'm sorry, Mom, I'm sure it's all true, but I still find it hard to believe. I mean, if the government really wanted to keep something secret, is that really the best solution they could come up with? A clone?"

Mom fixed me with a benevolently patronizing look. "Sachi, you're very young, and you're very naïve; you don't know how the world works. The government does all kinds of crazy things. Do you realize they have surveillance satellites up there in space that can listen in on any conversation we have on earth? Wherever you are, if you're out on a nature hike, or on a boat, anywhere—they're *listening*."

Mom suddenly looked toward the ceiling, raising a finger. In a hushed whisper: "They're listening right now."

She started yelling at the ceiling, defying those Orwellian transmitters: "I know you're listening, but I'm telling her anyway! Because she's my daughter!"

She waited a moment, as if expecting a response, and then

turned back to me with a resigned shrug. "I'm probably in trouble now—but whatever. You deserved to know the truth."

By this time I must have looked completely shell-shocked, because Mom placed a comforting hand on my wrist, patting it gently. "I know. You're confused; you're disoriented. It's totally understandable. But I checked out Steve very carefully, and I knew he would take good care of you. Was it an ideal situation, being raised in another country by a clone? Of course not. But there's always a struggle between public duty and personal need, and I think, all things considered, we managed to find the right balance."

I needed a little time to sit with this information. In a way, I wasn't completely surprised. It would be another year before Mom came out with her most talked-about and influential book, *Out on a Limb*, in which she made public her belief in reincarnation and the astral plane. She'd been developing these interests in private for years, so I was familiar with her unique perspective on the cosmos, and generally prepared for anything.

This, however, was beyond me. Mom, for all her eccentric notions, was still a fiercely intelligent woman, capable of cold, clear-eyed logic when the situation demanded it. How could she have come to believe that Dad was a clone? Where could she have gotten such a story? It was insane.

Yet . . . the telegrams were right there. They were real. Mom couldn't have sent them to herself. They sat there in their box, mockingly real. They were saying, *Rationalize all you want, sister, but we're here and we're not going anywhere.*

When I considered their concrete reality in tandem with Mom's unshakable faith, I found my own conviction wavering. It *is* a strange, secretive world out there, after all. Crazier things have happened, I guess. So maybe, I thought . . . it's true?

Then a casual phrase dropped earlier came drifting back, and I grabbed at it as if it were a lone, spindly branch overhanging a waterfall.

"Okay, so wait a minute, Mom. You send *money* to the *government* for this? How much money?"

"Sixty thousand dollars."

My jaw dropped. Sixty thousand dollars? Shipped into space? Oh, what I could have done with sixty thousand dollars! Gone to college, for one thing. "Sixty thousand dollars a year?"

She looked at me as if I had two heads. "A year? No, a month."

I gasped. "Sixty thousand a *month*?"

"Of course. Space travel is very expensive."

I had to get this on the record. "All right, since 1958, you've been giving the government sixty thousand a month?"

"No, it was a lot less back then, but as the years went by, we had to adjust for inflation."

"Where do you send this money? NASA? Washington?"

Mom was being very patient now. "I send it to Steve, the clone. That's the whole point. He's supposed to be my husband, so it doesn't look suspicious if it goes to him. And then he forwards it through the proper channels."

Now the fog was starting to lift.

"He forwards it? Sixty thousand a month? That's, what, seven hundred and twenty thousand a year?"

Mom was untroubled by this expenditure. She usually hated parting with money, but this was a special case. "It's a lot of money, yes, but it's for a worthy cause. We all have to make sacrifices for the general good."

"Steve doesn't have to make any sacrifices," I observed. "Steve has a very comfortable lifestyle for a clone."

Mom shrugged. "He has to keep up appearances." She could

see that I was getting at something unpleasant, and whatever it was, she was instinctively mounting a defense.

"He appears to be as rich as Croesus," I told her. "You know, he goes to expensive restaurants every night? Every single night. He has a yacht in the Mediterranean, and his own private island in the Pacific. He drinks Dom Perignon for breakfast. Every breakfast! He has potatoes shipped to Tokyo from Idaho! Then he scoops out the insides and fills the potato skins with Beluga caviar. That's his midnight snack."

There was a pause as Mom processed this information.

"So, what are you saying?"

"I'm saying he has an awful lot of spare change. About sixty thousand a month's worth."

Mom was genuinely shocked. "You think Steve's been taking your father's money?"

"He *is* my father!" I exploded. "He's not a clone! Steve Parker and Paul are the same person! The whole story is a fake. He made it up to trick you into sending him a check every month. Mom, he conned you! Dad's a con man!"

The moment I said it was the very moment I realized it myself: Dad's a con man.

This was something I had never allowed myself to consider, but as soon as it came out of my mouth, I knew it was absolutely the truth. I'd never quite understood what Dad's business was, but now I knew: he was an operator, a flim-flam artist, a jet set Harold Hill. His job was to enjoy his own life at everyone else's expense. And his biggest pigeon had been his own wife.

A Dweller on Two Planets—the epic story of Phylo the Tibetan, who lived in the lost city of Atlantis—that's how it began. Dad gave Mom that book on the set of her very first movie, *The Trouble with Harry*. Mom had responded positively to its message and came to embrace the possibilities of reincarnation, telepathic communication, and other forms of expanded consciousness. Just as Dad had hoped.

Having laid the foundation, he was now in the position to convince Mom that he was two people: he was a space traveler cruising the Pleiades, and he was a clone of that space traveler. And one of the reasons he had to relocate to Japan was to keep anyone from detecting his clonehood. Once there, he needed Mom to finance his playboy lifestyle, so he appealed to her sense of patriotism and got her to bankroll the "space mission."

It was an incredibly bold plan. The risks were obvious. If Mom hadn't gone for it, their marriage would have been over in a New York minute.

Yet he knew that she would go for it. Like any great salesman, he could read his mark like a book.

He also had a masterstroke up his sleeve, and that was in bringing his daughter to Japan. It was a classic application of reverse logic: everyone (i.e., the Russians and various foreign spies) knew that a responsible mother would never send her child overseas to live with a clone, so Mom *had* to send me—it made the ruse complete.

This was also why Dad never spent any money on me; he *couldn't*, because all that money was supposed to be going to the "government." If Mom saw him buying me new clothes or taking me on trips or paying for my college education, she might get suspicious. So, for the sake of the scheme, I went without. At the same time, by raising me Japanese—docile, submissive—he could guarantee that I would accept any outlandish situation without question. He really was a brilliant man.

Of course, the success of such a campaign was predicated on the unlikely scenario that Mom and I would never discuss the arrangement. Ever. Now we had discussed it, though, and the cat was out of the bag: Dad was exposed as a humbug, the man behind the curtain.

Now Mom was the one whose world had been turned upside down. Open marriage aside, Dad was her great lifetime love. She respected him, she adored him, she took comfort in the fact that he was her true soul mate and they would always be there for each other.

But he wasn't there. Maybe he had never been. Maybe their entire relationship had been one elaborate con. "Paul" was my mother's fantasy, and Steve—charming, enigmatic, high-living—was a con man.

At first I had felt a sense of triumph in disclosing the extent of Dad's machinations to Mom. For once, I was the one who had the answers instead of the questions. I was the one who was in the know.

This quickly changed to deep sympathy for her. I knew what she was suddenly facing—profound betrayal, the loss of love—and my heart broke for her.

She stood with her arms folded, staring toward the floor, stoically weathering the emotional assault. I waited for her reaction.

Finally, she shook her head. "Ridiculous," she said.

"It's not ridiculous," I insisted. "He *is* a con man. You know he is! He's certainly not in the Pleiades. Do you know how far away that is?"

"Forty-three light years," she said with fading defiance. "So what? You never heard of hyperspace?" She wasn't giving up. She was holding on to the dream, come what may.

"Oh, Mom . . . How did you ever fall for this?"

Mom snapped. "I didn't fall for anything! Your father is in space, and Steve is a clone! And that's the end of it." She grabbed the box of telegrams. "I knew I shouldn't have told you. You just don't have the maturity." She stomped back into the bedroom.

. . .

SHE needed time. Dad, whether he was Paul or Steve, was the love of her life, and she had invested everything in that relationship. To accept now that he had manipulated her in this spectacular fashion, deceived her and played her for a fool, would have been too devastating to bear.

But she was also a very smart woman, and she knew she couldn't keep deluding herself. After taking a few days to absorb the story, she knew she had to confront Dad.

I remember we were sitting in the kitchen in Malibu, enjoying a very tasty Chilean red wine—at only five bucks a bottle—when Mom jumped up and said, "I'm going to call him."

I felt a twinge of alarm. "Are you sure you want to?" I knew that once they spoke of this, there would be no going back. I felt terribly guilty, too, because, unknowingly or not, I had brought about this situation. I was the messenger of doom.

Mom got Dad on the phone, and immediately started firing questions at him. "What's this about a chalet? You have a *chalet?*" "I didn't know you had a yacht!" "You have a helicopter business? Since when? What is this?"

I couldn't hear what was going on on the other end, of course, but I could see from Mom's face that Dad was doing his best to spin the story to his advantage.

Mom wasn't falling for it. For the first time, she could see right through his diversions. Then she said the words that made my stomach leap: "I want a divorce."

I was shocked. I didn't realize she was ready to take that extreme step—and maybe she wasn't, until she heard Dad's voice and the charming lies he was casually spinning. I was glad I had the wine to calm my nerves.

Even more shocking was the look on Mom's face when she

heard his reply. She was clearly stunned, and deeply unsettled. She slowly put the phone down, as Dad had already hung up on her.

"What did he say, Mom?"

Mom took a breath, and then answered, "He said, 'You're out! OUT!'" She mimicked his voice, harsh and ugly.

"Out of what?" I asked.

She shrugged. "Out of his life," she surmised. She sat down to finish her wine, but I could see that she was rattled. It wasn't easy to get to Mom, but that violent outburst had really gotten her. I could read the deep hurt and shock and abandonment on her face; she was suddenly a little girl, orphaned and cast away from the only mooring in her life. I felt so sorry for her at that moment that I wanted to wrap my arms around her and hold her, give her comfort.

Mom then hired a private investigator to check into my story.

The investigator confirmed that Dad was living a lavish life-style, with no visible source of income except my mother's monthly stipend. He wasn't in outer space; he was cruising the Aegean with Aristotle Onassis. The investigator also discovered that much of Dad's official past history had been fabricated: he never lived in Japan with his father, he never served in the armed forces, he never met a little Japanese orphan in Hiroshima named Sachiko. There was no indication that he had had any connection at all with NASA or the U.S. government.

There was, however, some kind of government file with Dad's name on it, labeled "top secret." Since it was top secret, we never found out what it contained. It could have dealt with his years in space, or it could have been surveillance accounts of his various dealings with influential foreigners. He was, after all, good friends with Prince Sihanouk of Cambodia (or so he claimed).

The investigator also told Mom that Dad was hiding his money in Miki's accounts. That one really threw her for a loop. She knew that Miki existed, but she thought of her as a minor character—in fact, that she was Steve the clone's girlfriend. She didn't realize until now that Miki was her real husband's lover, and living off her money.

So, in 1982, after twenty-eight years of marriage, Mom filed for divorce.

IT was a great relief to me when Mom finally accepted the clone story as false. *Oh, thank God*, I thought, *I'm not the one who's crazy.* We actually had some sardonic fun going over the whole story of Dad's con, the scope of his deception, the obsessive attention to detail that had made it all work: *The Dweller on Two Planets*, the telegrams, the government satellites.

"You know," Mom reflected, "I would fly all over the world to meet him, all these secret meetings when he was supposed to be Paul. And I used to wonder in the back of my head if he was Paul or Steve. So I would come up with little tests to see how he responded. Things that only Paul would know. He always passed, but still, I was never quite sure. But then he pulled that Caesar routine, crying in the driveway, and that's when he really hooked me. He was that good. He's a great actor."

Her admiration was steeped in scorn. She had loved my father, and now she detested him. Part of that was my doing, and I felt some guilt about it. So I would always try to balance the equation with stories of the good times I had spent with him in my childhood. I told her about the places we went, the experiences we had: ice-fishing in the Japan Alps; driving around Hawaii; cruising the Greek isles on his yacht, *Happy Pappy*.

She didn't want to hear it. She was not interested in my good times. She was far too wounded. I think nothing hurt her in life as much as that betrayal. I don't know what disappointed her more—the fact that her husband had cheated on and lied to her, or the fact that there was no actual Paul in outer space. The great romantic notion of her life had been crushed, and the world had become depressingly ordinary. How could you not be bitter about that?

Mom talks about her divorce in one of her books, but she has a slightly different version of the events leading up to it. She claims that she discovered my dad's treachery—the lies, the money swindled, Miki—through a channeler, someone who was letting a disembodied spirit speak through him. She would regularly go to spiritual channeling sessions for enlightenment, and on this occasion she got more enlightened than she'd bargained for: the channeler told her that Dad was a fake who had squandered much of her fortune and transferred the rest into Miki's account. A private investigator later confirmed everything the channeler said.

It's pretty close to my version, except that there's no mention of clones. She totally buried the lead role.

About six months after the clone situation imploded, I was called to give a deposition in Mom and Dad's divorce. It was a difficult situation for me. Much as I had been stunned by the revelation of my father's betrayal, I didn't want to testify against him.

By this time he had stopped talking to me altogether. He'd really grown fond of that regular check coming in every month, and he was not appreciative of my well-intentioned meddling. "Idiot!" What else could I do, though? Did he want me to lie? Obviously, yes.

The morning of the deposition, I woke up with a raging fever. It was 103 and climbing. I felt terrible. I needed to go back to bed. I called the lawyer and asked if we could get a postponement.

My father refused. He didn't care if I had a fever. He wanted me deposed, now.

By the time of the deposition, my temperature was at 105 degrees, and I was practically delirious. It was a surreal situation: the lawyer was bombarding me with questions, but I can't remember what they were. I can't even remember if I answered coherently. The whole day was a fog.

I do remember Dad and Miki sitting across from me at the conference table. I'm not sure why Miki was even there, but this was probably the first time Mom had met her as a rival. (They may have seen each other in Japan, but it had no significance then.) I remember the coldness coming from the other side of the table. From Miki, I expected no less, but while I had experienced Dad's icy anger before, I'd never felt the full brutal force of it as I did now. There was not an ounce of love coming from him, not a glint of warmth or charm. When the deposition was over, he got up and left, without saying goodbye. We didn't speak again for many years.

Mom and I never discussed the clone story again after that. It retreated back into the closet, back into the tin box, back into the old brown safe. She never got any of her money back, and she and my dad never reconciled. She does say in one of her books that she will always love him, and when she meets him again in the next world, with all their human foibles and frailties fallen away, that love will burn even brighter than ever. I hope so.

CHAPTER 12

THE ACTING BUG

I t took me a long time to get used to living in Los Angeles. I'd spent many a summer with Mom as a child, but back then, I was just a visitor passing through, and didn't feel the need to immerse myself in the idiosyncrasies of American culture. Now I was here to stay, living in Mom's Malibu home, and I had to figure out how to make sense of this crazy world.

Starting with Mom. She was a mercurial, perplexing creature; I already knew that. Living with her day after day, though, adjusting my slow Japanese rhythms to her hard-driving American energy—that was the challenge. And it was my challenge, not hers. She was a star; she wasn't changing. It was up to me to negotiate the hairpin turns of her personality and keep our relationship on an even keel.

Not that it was ever hard to read her moods. She was very up-front with her feelings: if she was bored with you, or contemptuous, or pissed off, you knew it. The trick was anticipating when the weather was going to turn, because she could shift from a warming breeze to an ice storm in a millisecond.

In general, I discovered that she was always happy to see me, or anyone, for about four hours. For four hours, she loved you. Then, suddenly and without warning, you became an intolerable burden. The iron door came down. You could set your watch by it. One minute she was Miss Hospitality, the next minute "When the fuck are you leaving?"

Since I wasn't leaving, this was something we had to work out—and I would *make* it work out, because she was all I had left. Dad wasn't speaking to me, my personal history was an apocalyptic wasteland of Lukes and Jeffreys, and my life compass was spinning in all directions. I needed a rock, something to cling to. That was going to be Mom, whether she liked it or not.

Of course there were so many demands on her attention, I knew I needed a hook to make myself a part of her world. But what? What could I bring to the table?

Well, I was a pretty good cook, from my days in France. "Fine," Mom said, "you can do all the cooking." Not *all* the cooking—she had a chef for that—but whenever she had guests, she wanted me to show off my skills, so she could brag about me.

She would spring these parties on me at the last minute.

"Sach, I'm having a dinner party tonight!"

"For whom?"

"Just a few people. Maybe twenty. Robert Redford's coming. Faye Dunaway. Sydney Pollack."

Okay, I may have been out of the loop, but I knew who *those* people were.

"We need food. Here, go out and get something." She handed me ten dollars. "And save the receipt. We can write this off."

I looked down at the lone bill in my palm and gave an incredulous chuckle. "Mom, I can't get food with this."

"Why not?" she asked. "What's the problem?"

"Ten dollars?"

"Yessss . . . ?" She drew the word out, still not getting the point.

"For twenty people? What can I buy with this, a box of pasta and a pound of butter?"

Mom stopped now and gave me the Look. I've mentioned the Look: sharp, piercing, basilisk-like. "So you're saying you need more money?"

"Yes."

This did not sit well with her. Her eyes narrowed, as she tried to search out the truth in my dissembling eyes. Then she folded her arms and took a combative stance. "Are you on drugs? Is that what you need the money for?"

I was dumbfounded. "Drugs? What are you talking about?"

"Listen, Sachi, I've seen this happen to other kids in Hollywood. Their parents indulge them, let them have whatever they want, and the next thing you know, they're smoking pot, shooting heroin, killing people . . . Ever heard of Charles Manson? Squeaky Fromme?" (Actually I'd never heard of Squeaky Fromme, but I gathered that she wasn't a very reputable character.) "Do you want to be a cult murderer, is that what you want?"

"I just want to make dinner."

She grudgingly gave me more food money, but it didn't leave her pocket willingly. Mom was always pretty tight with a buck; there's no way around that. It wasn't long after I moved in with her that she brought up something that had obviously been bugging her for some time: "Say, when are you gonna pay me back for that car?"

"What car?"

"The five-hundred-dollar piece-of-shit car you bought in Australia."

"The Vauxhall?"

"Whatever. Do you still have it?"

"That was five years ago. It's probably in a junkyard somewhere."

She nodded knowingly. "I told you it was a waste of money." Then she waited, as if expecting me to produce the cash right there.

"Sorry, I forgot, but I'll pay you back . . ."

"When? The interest is mounting up."

"Interest?"

She widened her eyes, as if to say, "We had a deal, remember?"

"Okay," I began, "so, tell me how much I owe, and . . ."

"Eight hundred and forty-five dollars," she shot back without hesitation. I don't know if she pulled this figure out of thin air, but I was in no position to question it.

"Oh. Okay."

Mom watched me for a moment, and then sensed perhaps that she may have been a little too harsh. "I mean, take your time. Get a job first. Just don't forget."

Her fear of my drug susceptibility, by the way, was completely baseless. I'd smoked pot three times in my life, and puked three times. I was not an enthusiast.

Mom was even less drug-savvy than I was. You'd think somebody with her reputation for experimentation would have been sampling all kinds of hallucinogens, and have had platters of mushrooms and peyote on the dining room table for general consumption. But no, she preferred "natural highs."

Once, we went to a dinner party where Mom was the only celebrity, and therefore the de facto guest of honor. Everybody made a big fuss over her and treated her like royalty, which she graciously accepted as her due. After dinner, the host brought out a "special sugar" with dessert. It was a bowl full of cocaine. Mom, being the honored guest, was offered the first dip. So of course she poured two heaped spoonfuls—and I don't know how many thousands of dollars—into her coffee. The collective gasp that followed almost sucked the remaining oxygen out of the room.

"How the hell was I supposed to know it was coke?" Mom said afterward, shrugging. "What am I, a drug mule?"

It always amused me that Mom would watch her money like a hawk but never seemed to know what things actually cost. She'd haggle over pennies, and then spend a king's ransom on a new pair of shoes.

I remember being in the kitchen one time, making whipped cream, when she came back from one of her shopping jaunts on Rodeo Drive. "What do you think of this blouse?" she asked.

"It's beautiful."

"Two thousand dollars."

I gulped. "Wow. That's a lot of money."

She shrugged as if to say, "So what, I deserve it." She looked over my shoulder. "What are you making here, whipped cream?" She stuck her finger in the bowl and tasted it. Then a mischievous impulse seized her and she dipped her finger in again and stuck a dollop on the tip of my nose.

This could not go unanswered. I took a slightly bigger scoop of cream and stuck it on *her* nose. Not content to give me the last word, she grabbed a handful and smooshed it right into my face. I returned fire, slathering her face, and the next thing I knew we were throwing great gobs at each other, slipping and sliding as we chased each other around the kitchen, and then fell to the floor, rolling in whipped cream and laughing.

She totally ruined her two-thousand-dollar blouse in the process. She didn't care. She was having fun.

That's one thing I can say definitively about Mom: she loved to have fun. She could be inspiredly silly without a trace of self-consciousness, and she had a healthy sense of humor about herself and the world. I think that's why she managed, in all her talk of astral planes and extraterrestrials, to maintain the public's affection. She didn't seem to take herself seriously, even when she was taking herself very seriously.

We still had our walks on the beach, and she would still pick up sea urchins and react with delight when they closed on her finger. There would be stops at Wil Wright's for ice cream, and days on the couch where we ate popcorn and watched movie after movie; and when thunderstorms rolled in, we'd cuddle up in bed, although I was a little old now for the tale of Princess Lightning. In some ways she was younger than me, a wide-eyed six-year-old who loved to start trouble and then throw back her head and laugh. Those giddy moods of hers didn't last long, but while they did, we laughed and laughed.

ANOTHER memorable event took place in our kitchen a few months later. Mom and I were making pies together—I don't remember why—and as we rolled out the dough side by side, I had what you might call an epiphany. For the first time, I was actually baking with my mother; the way they did in commercials and old black-and-white TV shows. After twenty-seven years, we were finally performing a classic domestic ritual.

I didn't point this out to her, because I didn't want her feeling guilty about it. It wasn't her fault that she hadn't been there for me growing up. Okay, maybe it *was* her fault, but now wasn't the time to make an issue of it. So I just sighed. "Wow, Mom. Life is so strange."

I kept rolling out the dough, until I felt Mom's eyes on me. She was staring at me, and turning something over in her mind. "What?" I asked.

"Say that again," she said. "The same way."

I was a little confused. "What? Life is so strange?" She gave me a coaxing nod, so I tried to replicate the way I'd said it, complete with sigh. "*Life is so strange . . .*"

Mom pondered this slowly. "Hmm."

What was this about? Was she upset? Had I offended her some-how? I wasn't calling *her* strange, after all. She was getting me all nervous.

"Let's play a game," she suggested now. A game? "I want you to go outside and pretend that someone was just hit by a car, and you have to run in and tell me about it."

I tried to get this straight. "You want me to go outside . . . ?"

"Go! Now!" she barked. "Don't think! Just do it!"

So I did. I hurried out the door. What was I supposed to do? Oh, right, someone just got hit by a car, and . . .

I rushed back into the kitchen. "Oh my God! Mom! Help me! My friend . . . this car came out of nowhere and ran him down . . . He's bleeding . . . he's dying . . . ! You have to come right away! Right away!" I was breathless and hysterical, and to my surprise, tears sprang into my eyes.

Mom was watching me keenly. I could see she was impressed. I could also see that now was not the time to break character. I had to push further.

"I'm not kidding, Mom! This is serious! This is not a game! My friend is dying! You have to hurry! Come on!" I started pulling on her arm, dragging her toward the door. I finally stopped when we reached the doorway, and I found myself out of breath, but a little exhilarated. It seemed like a pretty good performance.

Mom was still in nodding mode. "Okay, do it again."

"Again?"

She pointed me out the door.

So I ran out, went down the stairs, rushed back up the stairs, burst into the kitchen, and went through the whole routine again. "Oh my God! Mom! Help me . . . !" I went even bigger this time, hitting all the notes, letting my emotions pour out, but controlling them at the same time—in other words, acting.

Mom took it all in, and then made her pronouncement, which was all the more effective for its quiet restraint: "You're very talented."

I was stunned. "Really? You think so?" Nobody had told me I was talented since 1962, with *To Kill a Mockingbird*.

She crooked a finger at me. "Let's take a walk."

I dutifully followed her out of the house, and we started down the road. After a respectful passage of time, I finally asked, "Where are we going?" but Mom wasn't saying. She liked controlling the situation.

We stopped finally at a cottage. Mom knocked at the door. A kindly middle-aged woman answered it.

"Peggy," Mom said, "I want you to meet my daughter, Sachi. She's an actress."

I felt a thrill go through me. Mom had just told a complete stranger that I was an actress!

As we entered the woman's house, Mom explained to me, "Peggy is an acting teacher." Indeed she was. Peggy Feury was one of the most revered acting teachers on the West Coast. She and her husband ran the Loft Studio in downtown L.A., and she was a charter member of the famous Actors Studio. She had all kinds of young, exciting actors in her stable, and they all loved her.

I didn't know all this at the time. If I had, I would have been a basket case, because Mom insisted that I audition for Peggy, right then and there.

"Now?" It was all too sudden. I was still in a pie-making frame of mind. "Can't we do it tomorrow?"

"Peggy's a very busy woman. So am I. This is your chance." In other words, now or never. "You have nothing to be scared of."

What was I supposed to audition with? I had nothing prepared. Did she want me to do my hysterical car crash routine again? Even I knew that bit probably wouldn't travel well.

Mom and Peggy found me something to read. I don't remember what it was now—one of those boilerplate monologues you find in acting books. I was reading it cold, but I gave it my best shot.

Peggy was a wonderful audience. She smiled, shook her head in delight, leaned forward, gave a little "go for it" shake of her fists. She was totally present, very supportive. Mom stayed in the background, arms folded, not cheerleading but completely confident that I would deliver.

When I was finished, Peggy leaned back and smiled warmly. "Would you like to join my acting class, Sachi?"

It's funny how the direction of one's life can spin around and find its true course in an instant. Did I want to join her class? Of course I did. I was an actress, wasn't I?

I walked back to Mom's house on a cloud. I was so excited. "Can you believe it? Peggy Feury wants me in her acting class!" There was only one problem, and Mom was happy to articulate it: "How are you gonna pay for it?"

She didn't need to add the disclaimer "Don't look at me."

I couldn't afford to pay for the lessons. I'd already taken a job teaching English to Japanese children, but that money went toward the household and paying off the Vauxhall. Still, Peggy Feury wanted me to succeed as much as I did, so I worked things out with her. Peggy suffered from narcolepsy; she couldn't drive a car because of the concern that she might drift off to sleep behind the wheel. So I became her personal driver. I drove her to the studio and back home, and anywhere else she needed to go. I also swept the stage, emptied the garbage, ushered on scene nights, and cleaned the toilets. I was there all the time—and I loved it.

I'd never had the experience of being a part of the theater before. Yes, I'd been backstage at Mom's shows in Las Vegas, and on movie sets, and at opening night premieres—I knew about all the flash and the glitz—but I'd never acted in a high school show or a neighborhood theater; I'd never known the excitement and creative joy of working at my craft, bringing a scene to life, being part of an artistic community.

And I'd never fallen under the spell of a truly gifted teacher. Peggy was the kind of acting mentor who inspired you not through excoriating rants and humiliation, but by creating a safe place where you could fail and soar, take risks, be fearless. She demanded a lot, but she did so in a spirit of trust and respect. As a result, you would do anything for her. There were many wonderful young actors at the Loft—Angelica Huston, Charlie Sheen, Crispin Glover, Michelle Pfeiffer, Sean Penn—and they all revered Peggy. She was a true gift to the acting world.

Peggy wanted us to put the truth on the stage, stressing the real and the natural over Acting 101 basics. The first person I ever saw do an entire scene with his back to the audience was Crispin Glover. He never once turned around to acknowledge our presence, and it added such power to the scene that it changed my perception about stage acting. One time Sean Penn was playing a homeless person in a show, and he refused to bathe. He would come to class in ragged clothes and greasy hair, stinking to high heaven. Of course, he didn't care. That was Sean; he didn't give a shit what anybody thought. I can still smell him. Pierre would have approved.

In my case, Peggy gave me enormous confidence just by acknowledging that I had talent. At the same time, she recognized that there was something inside me that was blocking me from being completely expressive. "You're too Japanese, Sachi. You're holding back as an actress when you should be letting go."

I understood what she meant, and I tried to let go, but I couldn't undo a lifetime of social engineering. Japanese women were expected to behave in a certain way in public. Giving full vent to your emotions simply wasn't appropriate or even conceivable. I was torn between two mentors: I wanted to please Peggy, but what would Eguchi-san have thought?

The situation came to a head one day when I was performing a scene in class with another actor. I know it would make the story more interesting if I said it was Sean Penn, but I honestly don't remember who it was—or what the scene was—but I know it was supposed to be romantic. We were kissing and touching and getting physical and—I couldn't open my legs. They were shut tight. No matter how passionate the scene grew, I wouldn't let myself go.

Peggy called me on this. "Sachi, why are your legs closed? You're attracted to this man, you're feeling sexual, your body should be inviting him. Instead you're locked up like a bank vault. Come on, spread your legs a little, enjoy the moment."

I couldn't. In spite of Peggy, in spite of all my classmates staring at me as if I were from another planet, in spite of my mom's long shadow, I couldn't. Now, you know my history; you can't say that I was prudish. I wanted to do what Peggy asked: I wanted to spread my legs wide, I wanted to show that I could surmount my hang-ups and be true to the dramatic situation.

But I couldn't.

Peggy was not going to let this pass. She came up onstage and faced the audience. "See, we have a Japanese woman here," she explained. "She looks Irish, but she's Japanese. And she can't spread her legs. So I'm going to help her. I'm going to pry those legs open if I have to use a crowbar."

Peggy grabbed my knees and forced them apart, straining like Samson at the pillars of Gaza. I was shocked, and I actually felt myself fighting against it, but Peggy prevailed, spreading my legs wide open and holding them there. "Now say the line," she commanded.

And I said the line—whatever it was—and it worked. It flowed. Everything in the scene made sense, and in that instant, for the first time, I understood acting. Peggy had unlocked something deep within me, she'd exorcised some demon I didn't even know I had, and it would never haunt me again. I remember Angelica Huston coming up to me afterward and raving about my instant metamorphosis. "You just opened up like a flower. It was like night and day. You were a different person."

And I was. I have to say, from that moment on, I was extremely sexual onstage. I had no qualms about expressing myself physically or emotionally. If the script said we were grabbing each other's crotches, then that's what we were doing. Even if I had to go topless (as I did a few years later, in *The Lulu Plays*), I didn't bat an eyelash—even with my two fried eggs.

Peggy was such a remarkable teacher. Not the least of her talents was an ability to fall into a narcoleptic nap in class, to completely sleep through an acting scene, and still, afterward, give a perfect moment-by-moment critique. She appeared to be fully asleep, but somehow she heard every word, beat, and inflection. It was scary.

Like so many other aspects of show business, an acting class becomes like a family. You trust your partners with your deepest emotions, and wind up knowing all kinds of intimate things about one another. You work together in intense dramatic situations, and then you go out to drink and unwind and laugh at one another's jokes. There are romances, breakups, and long confessionals at the local bar. You borrow money from each other; you get on each other's nerves. Once, Michelle Pfeiffer loaned me a green dress for an acting scene. I didn't return it for a long time, and I think she's still pissed off at me.

Of all the talented actors in Peggy's class, there was one who caught my newly liberated eye. His name was David Weininger, and he was a young but seasoned actor who understood his craft and was a thorough professional. He was also very sweet, and we hit it off immediately. I would say we were just like brother and sister, except that eventually we found ourselves involved in a relationship. Don't worry: there was no bait and switch here; he wasn't a Luke or a Jeffrey. He was a genuine nice guy through and through.

David was my true bridge from Japan to America. He spent hours and hours explaining American culture to me. It was through him that I came to understand how my native country worked.

It didn't happen overnight. One time he took me to see Richard Pryor in concert. I was appalled: here was this man onstage, using the foulest language imaginable, and everyone around me was hysterical with laughter, rolling in the aisles. It incensed me; I was personally insulted. I thought, *This is the rudest person in the world, and these people around me are just as rude.* The whole spectacle filled me with disgust.

This amused David to no end, of course. He explained to me that this was just the raw energy of American humor. The offensiveness was what made it funny.

I didn't get it. Saying mean things and making people uncomfortable didn't seem very funny at all —at least, not the way I was brought up.

"But you're not where you were brought up anymore, Sachi," David said. "You're in America."

It took me a while to reconcile myself to this reality. Surely I could hold on to the precepts and values I grew up with—humility, acceptance, self-effacement—and still find success in Los Angeles. Right?

The first crack in my Japanese edifice was a tiny one, but it was the tremor that presaged a major plate shift. I was talking to David on the phone one day, and he was waxing a bit pompous about a new experimental play he was performing in, and how it might finally put him on the map. Just from the sound of it, I could tell the play was a turkey. "Oh, yeah," I said sarcastically. "The studios are going to be burning up your phone line."

David gasped. "What did you say?" he asked. "Are you being sarcastic?" I giggled nervously, hoping I hadn't offended him, but he was thrilled. "Oh my God, listen to you—you've become an American. That's so cool!"

"Really?" I asked timidly. "You think that was good?"

"That was great!" He laughed. "Sachi the wiseass! We have to celebrate!" He was genuinely delighted for me. I'd had a breakthrough! Maybe I could make it in this country after all.

I had another breakthrough when I was driving home in my

beat-up car on the Santa Monica Freeway. I needed to change lanes and exit, but no one would let me in, no one would slow down, no one would give me the courtesy wave. I was boiling with rage, even though I knew this was par for the course on the freeway—it's every girl for herself, and the only way to change lanes is to barrel in, and fuck everybody else—and that's exactly how it erupted from my mouth: "*Fuck you!*" I started screaming. "Get the *fuck* out of my way so I can get in there, you *asshole!*" It's the only way to drive in L.A., and it felt *so* good. I understood how cathartic and empowering a well-placed obscenity could be.

So now I was cursing and being sarcastic. Mom would have been so proud.

I wasn't seeing Mom all that often, because a few months after I started Peggy Feury's class, I moved in with David. I soon discovered that, although he was eager to instruct me in American mores, he really enjoyed having a faux-Japanese girlfriend. I was always cooking for him, cleaning up after him, deferring to him. It was never his turn to do the dishes. He loved it. David was a wonderful guy, mind you, but he was still an actor, and he enjoyed being taken care of.

In all fairness, though, he took care of me, too. He was very sensitive to my emotional needs, appreciative of my budding talent, and ever trying to build up my self-esteem. He knew when to laugh with me, and when to give me a constructive kick in the behind. He was my best friend, and still is.

I would guess he got his nurturing instincts from his father, Dr. Benjamin Weininger, a revolutionary therapist and a very brilliant man. Dr. Weininger had offices in L.A., and he was legendary for his ability to reach through to subjects who seemed mentally and emotionally beyond hope. He was something of a miracle worker.

I saw the wondrous results of his therapeutic techniques first-hand when my mom came to David with a problem: a friend of hers, a very famous film director, had a daughter with severe emotional problems. She was acting out in bizarre ways, walking backward, pulling hunks of hair from her head. They'd been trying for years, since her childhood, to find some kind of treatment for her, but nothing had worked—and now she was a young woman, with a bleak, unpromising life ahead of her. Mom had heard of David's father and his seemingly miraculous cures: Could he help?

Dr. Weininger asked them to meet him at his office at the Southern California Counseling Center, which was down on Pico Boulevard. David and I were waiting on the sidewalk when Mom and the director pulled up in a town car. I could see from the looks on both their faces as they stepped out and surveyed the crumbling neighborhood that they were sure they'd made a wrong turn somewhere. Then out came Dr. Weininger, dressed like an old bohemian hippie, with jeans and long hair and bare feet. He didn't look like a world-renowned therapist, but then again, he had survived Auschwitz, and he didn't care what he looked like.

The director's daughter got out of the car now, and walked into the clinic backward. Dr. Weininger made no comment as he accompanied her. I could see the hope fading in the film director's eyes. This would be another cruel disappointment, he was sure.

Five hours later, the daughter emerged from the office, completely changed in aspect: no bizarre behavior, no walking backward, no hair pulling. She seemed like a normal, healthy girl. And the cure lasted: today, thirty-five years later, she's still doing fine. It seemed like nothing short of a miracle.

Mom was astounded. "What did you do?" she asked Dr. Weininger. She had to know.

"I went to her level," he said.

Tellingly, he didn't say he went *down* to her level. He didn't make value judgments. He showed her the respect of meeting her where she was, and seeing what she saw.

Perhaps that's how David managed to handle me so well. He went to my level. He looked at the world through my eyes, and comprehended it the way I did. That made all the difference. Many years ago I'd scored high on my Qantas test for my ability to empathize. Now, for the first time, someone was empathizing with me, and I realized how important that was, and how much I'd needed it.

A terrible postscript to the days I spent studying with Peggy Feury: in November 1985, she was driving home to Malibu from the studio when she fell asleep at the wheel and crashed into oncoming traffic. The car exploded into flames. Her body was so charred that they could identify her only through her dental records. No one knew why she was driving in the first place. She was supposed to have a personal driver. That used to be my job.

Chapter 13

· ═══════════════════ ·

"That's George McFly?"

Nineteen eighty three was a true annus mirabilis for Mom. Not one but two life-changing projects came down the pike, *Terms of Endearment* and *Out on a Limb:* her Academy Award–winning movie, and her most controversial book. She'd been famous for twenty-five years; now she was going to become an icon. I'm not sure if that's what she wanted, but that's what she was going to get.

Terms was filmed in Lincoln, Nebraska. David and I flew out to visit Mom on the set. The first thing we noticed when we got there was the tension. It was not the happiest place on earth. There was a great deal of emotional weight in the script that the actors were working through, and a lot of that turbulence bled into their personal relationships. Everyone was in a bad mood—except for Jack Nicholson, who refused as a matter of principle ever to be in a bad mood. He seemed dedicated to the proposition of enjoying himself at all times.

Debra Winger was playing Mom's daughter in the film, and it's no secret that the two of them didn't get along swimmingly. Some claim that they detested each other, but I don't know if I'd put it quite that strongly. She and Mom just had different ways of working, and their styles didn't always mesh. Mom was from the old school of "hit your mark and say your lines." Debra was more instinctive and "go with the moment." Both wound up giving spectacular performances, and their scenes together were marvelously alive and filled with emotional truth. Yet none of it came easy.

At one point Debra dug so deeply into her role as a cancer-stricken mother that she landed in the hospital. I felt bad for her. "We should go visit Debra," I suggested.

Mom waved her hand dismissively. "Ah, don't worry about her. She's just doing it for attention. She's nuts."

I couldn't understand that. Maybe Debra was nuts—I didn't know her; I couldn't say—but if she was in the hospital, something was obviously wrong with her, and it seemed only right that someone should visit her. So I decided to go by myself. The thing is, I needed flowers. It's unthinkable in Japan to visit anyone in the hospital without bringing flowers. Since I didn't have any money for flowers, I asked Mom. "She doesn't *need* flowers," Mom insisted. "Just leave her the fuck *alone!*"

So I left Debra alone—which I regret, because maybe she and I would have become friends. We had a lot in common: we were almost the same age (Debra was twenty-eight, just a year older than I); we were actresses; and for the time being, we had the same mother.

It didn't happen. In all fairness, it probably never would have happened anyway. I don't think Debra wanted to be friends with me. She was generally aloof with me, never really gave me the time of day. I couldn't tell if it was because I was a nobody, unworthy of her attention, or because I was Mom's real daughter and she was envious of me. Or maybe it was just part of her process: she may have been so consumed by her role that she didn't even know I was there.

I didn't feel any envy toward her at the time, but it was admittedly disconcerting when the movie became a hit and all the magazine articles came out dissecting Mom and Debra's special mother-daughter connection. Interviewers would often ask, "Does this film mirror your relationship with your real daughter?" "No, not really," Mom was always honest enough to point out. She wasn't the obsessive, suffocatingly attentive type who would climb right into her baby daughter's crib to soothe her. "I never would have given up my work to stay home," she told *People* magazine in 1984. "My philosophy was always to just let her grow up and to be there if she needed me."

Mom was also on combative terms with director James Brooks. Some of this was just part of the creative process—they were both fighting for their own visions, a laudable and necessary thing in the service of art—but some of it was also frustration. This was Brooks's first feature film, and his slow, reflective approach was sometimes maddening. He would shoot scenes over and over, and then decide to rewrite them, or drop them altogether. As much as Mom may have disliked Debra, she hated the way Brooks treated Winger. She found him abusive and manipulative in his handling of the younger actress. "He wouldn't try that shit with me," she declared. Actually he tried other shit on Mom, and what really irked her was that his strategies worked so well.

I was on the set one morning when they were doing an outside shoot. Everything was on hold while the cameras were being set up, and Jim Brooks was lying in the grass, relaxing, hands behind his head, staring up at the sky.

Mom waved me over. She had a mischievous glint in her eye, which was usually cause for concern. She pointed to Brooks. "Go stand over him and smile, and say, 'It's all I can do not to step on your face.'"

"Why?" I asked. I knew it was supposed to be funny, but I didn't get it.

"Just do it."

I didn't want to. To my mind, there was no way you could interpret the gesture as anything other than hostile, and why would I want to be hostile to James Brooks? He was not only a film director but a major TV producer. How was this going to help my career?

"Oh, what's the big deal?" Mom said. "It's a joke. Just do it." Implicit in her goading was the suggestion that if I didn't do it, I wasn't cool.

But I wanted to be cool in her eyes. I admit, I was her puppet: if she asked me to do anything, I would do it. I needed her approval, just as I'd needed Dad's.

So I did it. I walked up to Mr. Brooks and stood over him, straddling his head. He looked at me with surprise, and I delivered my line: "It's all I can do not to step on your face."

He was startled, and then he broke into a smile. I looked over at my mother. She was laughing hysterically, as were some other actors and crew members.

So it was evidently funny. I still didn't get it.

I discovered much later, reading Mom's book *My Lucky Stars*, that the line came from a scene that was cut from the film. Jack Nicholson's character stumbles over his garbage cans and lies drunk in his driveway, and Mom stands over him and says, "It's all I can do not to step on your face." So it was an inside joke that everybody on the set got. Except me.

But James Brooks seemed to like me after that. He always said hello and gave me a friendly smile. Maybe he respected my gumption. On the other hand, he's never cast me in anything, so maybe not.

After about a week of hanging around the set of this soon-to-be-classic film, David and I had had enough. Movie sets are terminally boring as a rule, but there's another dynamic in play that isn't often commented on, and that's the sense, if you're a visitor, of being at a country club that you don't belong to. The set of a feature film is the biggest high school clique in the world. Everybody working on it is an insider, one of the chosen elect, and consequently assumes a sense of privilege and entitlement far beyond any reasonable expectation. This elitist mind-set starts with the above-the-line talent (the stars with their trailers, the big-name directors, the cameramen and designers), everyone who is clearly indispensable and beyond brilliant, and it filters down to every anonymous gofer and day player. They all think they walk on water, because they're working on a movie and you're not.

I can't condemn them, because I've worked on a number of movies myself, and I know the seductiveness of that insular, clubby feeling all too well. It's like living in a gated community: if you happen to be inside the gate, it's wonderful, with the perks and the inside jokes and the soothing waves of self-importance. If you're not, if you're not a member of the club, then you're nobody, plain and simple, and you're either invisible or treated with condescension and rudeness. There's not much reason to hang around, unless you enjoy watching people being bratty and obnoxious.

Surprisingly, the one person who seemed to rise above this

fraternity mentality was Jack Nicholson. You would expect him on reputation to be the brattiest of them all, but he was so confident and comfortable in his own skin that he didn't need to be fawned over. Whenever I saw him, he was unfailingly nice and gentlemanly—and devilishly charming, of course. It was no wonder he was getting laid all the time. He knew a secret all too many movie stars never quite grasp: just because you're famous, it doesn't mean you have to be an asshole.

In between the shooting of *Terms of Endearment* and its December release, Mom's book *Out on a Limb* was published. This event, more than anything else, redefined Mom's persona to the world. With one bold stride, she stepped out of the shadows and became the New Age standard-bearer for her generation.

Out on a Limb was her third autobiographical book, but the first that discussed in depth her belief in mediums, UFOs, and, most prominently, reincarnation. You probably know all the stories about her past lives: She was an Indian princess; a geisha; a man from Atlantis. She slept with Charlemagne in a past life. She also slept with the Swedish prime minister Olof Palme in this life, and he used to be Charlemagne in a past life, so she nailed him twice, a millennium apart.

I was not exempt from the metaphysical carousel. Mom was convinced that mine was an ancient spirit that went back thousands of years. In one incarnation, in fact, it seems that we switched roles and I was *her* mother. I hope I treated her well.

None of this was revelatory to me, of course: I knew all about her spiritual interests, her extraterrestrial visits, and so forth. I was a little surprised that she was going public with it all, though. I figured that, after the clone episode, Mom might back off on her astral enthusiasms. Instead, she was doubling down.

She quickly became a lightning rod for believers and skeptics.

Spiritualists venerated her; late-night comics ridiculed her. And what, people wanted to know, was my reaction? What did I think about my mother's cosmic disclosures? Did I consider her a visionary or a crackpot?

Publicly I supported her: "She's my mom, and she's wonderful." Privately, I remember wishing she would just shut up—but not because I didn't share her beliefs. It was just that, for me, reincarnation wasn't a big deal. In Japan, everybody comes back. Everything that dies will be reborn. It's an accepted belief in the culture, but not something you talk about. It's all internalized, part of your moral DNA. While you are always aware of karma, and you try to lead an exemplary life, there's no dwelling on it. It's ingrained, totally reflexive, and private.

So I couldn't understand why Mom was talking about it in public, and why everyone was listening. The hoopla, the seminars, the talk show appearances—it seemed so over the top, and I had no patience for it. I never told her so, because I didn't want to hurt her feelings, but to my mind, none of this was New Age. It was totally Old.

Having said that, there was something beautifully endearing about the fervor of her beliefs. She really wanted to fill her soul with something meaningful. I think show business in particular excels in creating a certain kind of personal emptiness: you work on a play or a movie and it becomes your whole existence, and then it ends, and suddenly there's a vacuum where your life used to be, and you have to figure out how to fill it. You can jump into another movie right away, and keep that cycle going—one movie after another, until you die—or you can find something more enriching and sustainable to base your life on.

Mom discovered something better, something that worked for her. Whether anyone else embraced it was beside the point. Like any convert, she enjoyed sharing her epiphanies with the world, but she wasn't all that concerned if anyone followed her. She was a searcher, on her own spiritual journey, and the journey would never end.

MOM'S performance as Aurora Greenway in *Terms of Endearment* won her all kinds of acting awards, but the Oscar was the one she desperately wanted. She'd been denied it for *Some Came Running*, *The Apartment, Irma La Douce*, and *The Turning Point*, and now, as the age of fifty loomed, she knew that this could be her last best chance.

I went to the awards ceremony as her date. I was so excited to be there with her on perhaps the greatest night of her life.

Rock Hudson and Liza Minnelli were the presenters of the Best Actress award. When they read out the list of nominees, I suddenly felt a moment of panic. What if she didn't win? She was going against Meryl Streep in *Silkwood*, Jane Alexander in *Testament*, Julie Walters in *Educating Rita*, and her own costar, Debra Winger. They'd all given brilliant performances. Holy shit, she could lose!

Then Liza announced Mom's name. I'll never forget that moment. A great emotional cheer exploded from the audience, and Mom turned and gave me a kiss. I could see on her face that this was her defining moment: her life now made complete sense.

She went up onstage and made a lovely, gracious speech. She looked so beautiful and radiant up there, and I felt so proud and happy for her. It's a great gift to see someone you love getting her fondest wish come true.

Mom finished her speech with an inspirational thought: "God bless that potential that we all have for making anything possible if we think we deserve it." Then she looked at her Oscar and said matter-of-factly, "I deserve this. Thank you," and walked off. I have to be honest: I cringed a little with embarrassment. I thought to myself, *Oh, Mom, you overdid it.*

No one else seemed to think so. It was her night, and she could do no wrong. We hit all the celebrations afterward—the Governor's Ball, Spago—and we partied into the morning. Everyone was getting progressively drunker and sloppier, except for Mom. She was always very disciplined about alcohol, and I had great respect for the way she kept control, even on this night of all nights, when she had every excuse to go wild. The rest of Hollywood could act like fools, but Mom was pure class, all the way.

THAT same year, I got pregnant. This should have been more happy news, because I really wanted to be a mother. (In a *People* article about my mother, just before the Oscars, I'm quoted as saying, "I want to marry eventually and have a home and children and do all those things wives do." Honestly. This is the same article where Mom declares, "I don't think there's any more important profession in the world than being a mom.")

David wanted to be a father, but we had no money. We were two penniless actors trying to get our careers started. Having a baby now, at this stage, seemed a totally impractical thing to do. Unless we had help . . .

I went to Mom and asked if she could give us a hand financially. I knew this went against her long-standing mantra of "you're on your own," but on the heels of her book and her TV appearances, where she spoke out so passionately for self-actualization and karma and getting out of life what you put into it, I thought perhaps she had evolved a more generous worldview and would be in a giving state of mind.

She said no. The whole idea, to her mind, was ridiculous. "You can't have a baby. How old are you?"

"I'm twenty-seven."

"Oh. Well, even so, you don't have the time to take care of it. You and David live in that tiny place. There's barely room for the two of you, and you want to bring a baby in there? What's that going to do to your relationship?"

"Make it stronger?" I weakly suggested.

Mom scoffed. "Yeah, right. And I thought you wanted to be an actress. How are you going to have any kind of career with a baby? Are you insane?"

That was perhaps the crux of it. She'd had a baby, too, but she'd also had a wealthy husband (or a clone of one) who could take care of it, so she could continue her career. Even so, that hadn't worked out, since his wealth turned out to be her wealth. Was she saying that having me had been a mistake, too?

After sounding all her arguments, Mom shrugged with resignation. "Well, it's your choice." Still, it wasn't much of a choice if she wasn't going to help us—and she wasn't.

David's dad, Ben, said he would try to come up with some money, but he didn't have much. He did have a philosophy to share, though: "Commit, Sachi. You have to commit. When you commit to it, whatever 'it' is—a baby, a job, whatever—commit to that thing a hundred percent, and it will set you free."

I needed money more than inspirational motivation at that point, but I should have listened to him, because I know now he was dead right. If I'd had the baby, it would have been tough, but it would have worked out somehow.

I didn't listen, though. I couldn't see any way out. I didn't want to have an abortion, but what else could I do? Bring the baby to term and then give it away? That would have destroyed me.

Right up to the day of the procedure, I kept asking Mom for help, but she'd said her say, and now she wouldn't even engage in a conversation about it.

I had the abortion at St. John's Hospital in Santa Monica, the same hospital where I was born. To compound the dreadful irony, the same doctor who delivered me as a baby was performing the procedure. I felt ashamed and mortified—and guilty.

As much as I wanted to blame Mom, I know it was my decision to terminate, and it haunts me even now. I sometimes lie awake thinking about that child who never was. I sometimes dream of that lost soul. He or she would have been almost thirty now.

My regret grew even more acute when, years later, I conceived my daughter, Arin. That night is vivid in my memory: my husband and I had made love around midnight, and now it was around 4:30 in the morning. I was in a half-awake, half-asleep state, when quite suddenly a beautiful, indescribable feeling of love, happiness, and peace washed over me. Some kind of being, a female being—an angel, perhaps—had entered my body, and I felt transformed and transfigured, and suffused with great serenity.

About three weeks later I found out that I was exactly three weeks pregnant. That night, a new soul, Arin's soul, had entered me. She became my angel, my protector, my love, and everything I'd ever yearned for. I'd never had such an amazing, powerful feeling before—or since.

It took me back to that first conception, and I wondered who that soul had been, who had entered my body and lived there, and who I'd destroyed. Could it be that Arin was that same soul coming back? Was there life after death, and had my lost child rechosen me?

Maybe God or nature or the universe makes things right, no

matter how much we try to screw them up. Although I strongly believe in a woman's choice, I know in my heart that, in my case, I made the wrong one. It was a terrible mistake, and I'll always live with the guilt and the regret.

MY career, such as it was, continued on its bumpy struggling-actress way. I went to plenty of auditions and met with a parade of agents and casting directors, but nothing was happening.

It was Burt Reynolds who finally gave me my first film role, in *Stick*, which he was directing. The movie was based on an Elmore Leonard book and was shot down in Fort Lauderdale. I was playing Bobbi, the bartender, and I had three scenes with Burt himself, who was one of the nicest guys to work with.

I was nervous and excited, and the night before my first scene, I came down with a 104 fever. I couldn't believe it. My first big break, and I was deathly ill. What was I going to do? I called David back in Hollywood, in a panic. "I won't be able to act tomorrow. I'm too sick. They'll fire me. They'll make the film without me!"

David attacked the problem patiently and thoughtfully. "You know you're not really sick, Sachi. This is all in your head. You're making this fever happen."

He was right, and I knew it. The only time I ever got a fever, it was related to my acting career—before either an audition or a big scene in class. My own body was sabotaging me.

David went to my level, so he understood this. He talked to me for about twenty minutes, and the fever magically receded. I went to bed feeling ready for the next day.

The next morning, I woke up to another fever. It was higher now: 105. I called David. "I'm really sick this time! I'm not imagining it!" David, who was three hours behind me, sleepily talked me back to health. "You're not imagining the fever, Sach. You're imagining the reason for it." Twenty minutes later, I felt fine.

So I went off to the set, but by the time I arrived, I had a fever again. I called David back. And so it went the rest of the day. He talked me down from the ledge over and over until the shoot was done.

I tried to analyze why I would do this to myself. Was I afraid to fail? Or afraid to succeed? Was I worried that I might be infringing on my mother's territory? What if I get this job or that role? Maybe she won't like me anymore!

I remembered the fever I'd had at the deposition for my parents' divorce. Had that been psychosomatic, too? Triggered by a fear of stressful, unpleasant situations? Was this going to plague me my entire career? Was I going to *have* a career?

The actual shooting of *Stick* was delightful. Burt was a terrific director, nontemperamental and very easy to work with. Candice Bergen, who had the female lead, was a sweetheart. She was totally genuine, nothing actressy about her—and she was very friendly to me. Once, she asked me to have dinner with her, but for some foolish reason I said no. I really wanted to go, but she was already a big star, and I didn't think I was important enough to hang out with her. I didn't feel worthy. I was still a nobody, and I didn't want to pretend I was a somebody. Hollywood can really fuck up your thinking.

BACK in L.A., I auditioned for *Cocoon*, the Ron Howard movie about aliens and old people in Florida. I was going out for the role of Kitty, the alien who appears as a young woman. I auditioned maybe seven times, and every time I felt the approval growing. Steve Guttenberg, who would have played my love interest, worked with me in the later auditions, and our chemistry was really good. After the last audition, at which I wore a short dress to show off my legs, I could tell that I basically had the role. I felt that it wasn't so much my acting ability as the entirety of who I was: the girl-next-door type, pretty but not gorgeous, a good fit with Steve. The fact that my mother was on speaking terms with inter-planetary life forms surely didn't hurt.

Ironically, the premise of the film is that a race of aliens called Antareans came to Earth thousands of years before and founded the mythical city of Atlantis. They were returning now to re-trieve some of the Antareans left behind in cocoons. (I don't know why they weren't Pleiadians; maybe there was a copyright problem.)

So it all seemed meant to be. Everyone loved the screen test. All systems were go.

Then I got the call from Mort Viner, Mom's agent. "Sorry, but they went with Tahnee Welch." Who? Tahnee Welch, Raquel Welch's daughter, an exotic beauty who was as far removed from the hometown sweetheart type as could be. Apparently they had two clear choices, and they went with the sexy bombshell.

I was devastated. I thought I'd scored my first big part, and my career was off and running. Not so. Mom was philosophical. "You never know what they're looking for. You just have to do your best and hope it works out."

"But you said we could make anything possible if we thought we deserved it," I said, referencing her Oscar speech. "I think I deserved this."

Mom shrugged. "I guess you were wrong."

I went to the premiere screening of the movie with Mom and Mort. It was very difficult to sit through that film and watch my role being played by somebody else, but I called upon my Japanese stoicism and pretended to enjoy it. I understood why they'd cast

Tahnee—she was gorgeous—but I also felt that by giving the character such otherworldly beauty, a dimension was missing in the romance. Steve and I would have been so cute together.

I went up to Ron Howard after the screening to congratulate him. A very sweet, decent guy, he looked a little regretful. "I should have gone with you," he said. I smiled graciously, but all I could think was, *Why didn't you?*

Anyway, I kept auditioning, and other, smaller parts followed.

I only had two lines in *Back to the Future*, but everyone seems to remember them. They occur in the scene in the parking lot outside the prom. George McFly, played by my old acting partner Crispin Glover, is being beaten up by his eternal nemesis Biff. Suddenly George makes his hand into a fist and punches Biff, knocking him flat. I rush up with a group of gawking teenagers and ask, "Who is that?" and when I'm told, I exclaim in disbelief, "That's George McFly?"

It's a great moment.

I had two scenes in *About Last Night . . .* , the adaptation of David Mamet's play *Sexual Perversity in Chicago*, with Demi Moore, Rob Lowe, and Elizabeth Perkins. I played a girlfriend. The actors were in their Brat Pack heyday, and they were all very hip and with it. I tried to fit in, but I wasn't cool enough to run with them and I knew it.

Then I landed a small part in *Peggy Sue Got Married*, as one of Peggy Sue's high school girlfriends. I'd already played a girlfriend, and I'd already been in a time-travel movie, and now I was playing a girlfriend in a time-travel movie. I was starting to run out of options.

So I went to Ireland. A young director, Ronan O'Leary, offered me a role in *Riders to the Sea*, his adaptation of the John Millington Synge play. I don't know how he knew about me, but he'd seen me in something and liked my look. He thought I seemed very Irish.

Ronan himself was like a little leprechaun, full of beans; he loved to talk, and he was passionate about film, which really appealed to me. I was perfect, he said, for the part of the young daughter Nora, who waits desperately for her brother to come back from a storm at sea. "The camera loves you. And you're so right for this part. I have to have you."

It would be a short film, less than an hour long, but I jumped at the chance. My mother and sister in the film were to be played by Geraldine Page and Amanda Plummer. This was the kind of opportunity I'd been waiting for.

Before the shoot, we spent about four days rehearsing in Paris, in Geraldine's apartment on the Left Bank. I loved being back in Paris. I showed Geraldine and Amanda all the little cafés and bistros I used to haunt, and since I spoke French, I could proudly serve as their tour guide. We stopped at the place where I used to work, and I was warmed by the fuss the staff made over me. You'd have thought I was the big celebrity.

Most of the film was shot on the Aran Islands, off the west coast of Ireland. As the play itself was set on the middle island of Inishmaan, we filmed in some of the actual locations. Inishmaan is a spectacularly wild place, with magnificent views of the Atlantic, and rocky outcroppings everywhere.

I would wake up every morning well before call and walk around the island in the early fog. It was so beautiful in its desolation and loneliness. Just about every morning, I would visit the stone seat *Cathaoir Synge* ("Synge's Chair"), which overlooks the Atlantic, where the playwright Synge would sit and be inspired. His great plays, including *Riders to the Sea* and *The Playboy of the Western World*, were supposedly written in this spot. Looking down at the surging waves, I would become Nora, and imagine my brother's *currach* (boat) smashing against the rocks, and his Aran sweater washing up onshore. It was an ideal way to set my mind for the day's work.

There were no hotels on the island, so we were all put up in different homes. I stayed in a classic Irish cottage, with stone walls and a thatched roof. The husband and wife—I've forgotten their names, but let's say Donal and Maureen—treated me like a princess, tending to my every need. Maureen refused to let me lift a finger to clean or help out. When I told her I needed a hot bath every night to relax, she insisted on drawing it herself. There was no hot water, so she would fill the bathtub with freezing cold water and then put hot coals in a little stove beside the tub, which would heat the bathwater to the desired temperature. She also made her own black bread every morning. I would come back from my walk and have a fresh warm slice; the bread was dense and heavy, almost hard, and it looked like it was made of peat turf, but I would put a big slab of butter on it and it was delicious.

The diet on Inishmaan was basic: fish, chicken, seaweed soup, brussel sprouts, and all manner of potatoes (mashed, roasted, boiled). The ground yielded nothing but stones—there was almost no soil for the crops to grow on—and whatever sprouted up was blasted down again by the wind. It was a harsh, punishing world; you could feel it in the souls of the people. Their days were full of struggle and pain, but their nights at the pub were full of joy and laughter. It's easy to sentimentalize the fortitude and spirit of the Aran Islanders. I wouldn't say they were happier than anyone else, but their lives had a spare, stark clarity. There was no bullshit there. People weren't bedeviled by choices, because they had no choices. They lived simply, and simply lived.

My hosts had a marvelously Irish relationship, full of loving contentiousness. Maureen would bark orders at Donal—"Wipe your boots! Fetch some coal!"—and he would bolt down his dinner and head for the pub, or sometimes they'd go together, and I might tag along. Every single night, they would make love. I couldn't miss hearing their old bed as it creaked rhythmically in the small, quiet house. It was a comforting sound, the sound of life going on.

I think I enjoyed the Aran Islands even more than the filming, but both were great experiences. Ronan was a wonderful director to work with, never condescending or sarcastic. There was always positive energy coming off him. I could tell that Geraldine respected him a lot, and that spoke volumes for his talent.

Geraldine Page was perhaps the finest actress I've ever worked with. She was a totally honest artist, incapable of a false moment. She was also a master of business—working with props, fiddling with her clothing, bringing the scene alive by simulating the naturalness of real life. "Most actors don't know how to do business and talk at the same time," she told me. "But in life, that's what you do. You don't stop to deliver a line and then go back to washing dishes, and then stop to deliver another line. It's all of a piece, and you have to make it seem that way. Whether you're setting a table or adjusting your sleeve, you have to keep it natural."

She also taught me to get my lines down as soon as possible. "You don't ever want to think about your lines. They should be part of you, under your skin." If you have to think about the script, you're not dealing with the emotions underneath. Her advice for learning lines: "Fold your own laundry." If you run your lines as you fold, you'll find out how well you know them. If you can't fold the laundry correctly, then you have more work to do.

Geraldine was an amazingly generous colleague on the set. Whenever we did our close-ups, Ronan would offer, as customary, to have the stand-in read Geraldine's lines off camera. Most actors would have been happy with that arrangement, but Geraldine wouldn't hear of it. She'd say her own lines, thank you, and what's more, she'd give 100 percent of her acting ability in every take. None of this would show up on-screen, except in the performances of her fellow actors, and that's what mattered to her. She cared deeply about the whole piece, and if there was anything she could do to make it better, she would.

I absorbed her lessons like a sponge, and took them with me. I always try to be off camera for another actor's close-up. Folding laundry during rehearsal is now a cherished ritual. I remember doing a play a few years later: there was a scene at a restaurant table, and I worked up some business about cleaning the outside of the salt and pepper shakers with my napkin, because it seemed in tune with my character. This wasn't something the director wanted; it just occurred to me naturally, a way of informing a small moment onstage. When the play was reviewed in the L.A. papers, a critic made admiring mention of my business with the salt and pepper shakers. *That wasn't me*, I thought; *that was Geraldine*.

We finished shooting on Inishmaan, and I said a sad goodbye to Maureen and Donal. By now I was no longer a guest in the cottage. I'd become a part of the family, and Maureen was barking orders at me, making me do my own wash and heat my own bathwater. She gave me an Aran sweater as a parting gift—she would have knitted it herself, but she didn't have time. It was warm and comforting, like their home, and like the sweater from Hildy in New Zealand, sticky with lanolin oil.

We moved on to Dublin to shoot some interiors. Even though *Riders* was a relatively low-budget film, it was big news in Dublin, where everyone knew Synge's work by heart. One of the many visitors to the set was Kevin McClory, my mom's old friend. I had

stayed with Yuki at his mansion in Connemara so many years before, on our break from Charters Towers. It was so great to see
him again!

He took me to dinner at our hotel restaurant, and was full of
compliments and enthusiasm. How grand was this?—he had
known me since I was a baby, and here I was, acting in his town,
a movie star! He was so proud of me. He knew *Riders to the Sea* as
well as any Irishman, and he thought the character of Nora the
perfect role for me.

I listened intently, eating it all up. I knew this boded well for
my career. Kevin was a big producer, and he was saying just what
I would have wanted to hear: that I was an actress of consequence,
and he wanted to work with me.

After we said good night, I went upstairs feeling fairly intoxicated by my run of good fortune, and decided to order myself a
massage. Geraldine and Amanda had had massages on the company; why not me? The desk clerk asked me if I wanted a man or
a woman. Either, I didn't care. Back in Japan, it didn't matter
about the sex of people who gave massages, because, as a rule, they
were blind—not out of prudishness, but because their sense of
touch was far more acute.

About an hour and a half later there was a knock on the door.
"Who is it?" I asked. A male voice answered. "It's me."

Oh, it's the massage therapist, I thought, and opened the door.

It was Kevin McClory. I was confused. We'd said good night
two hours ago. "Kevin? What are you doing here?"

He smiled. "I want to come inside."

He wanted to come inside? "Why?" I asked, but as I looked at
him, I knew exactly why.

Now, Kevin was a very handsome man, tall and dapper (not to
mention rich as Croesus). There was much to recommend him as

a one-night stand. But he was my dad's age. He'd known me since I was a baby. And let's not forget, he was my godfather.

I was so shocked, I really didn't know what to do. I didn't have the feminine wherewithal to say no, or to josh him out of it—"Oh, Kevin, you know that's not a good idea. Do you want me to get you a hooker?"—or to even voice my puritanical outrage. So I slammed the door in his face instead. It was all I could think of.

He called me later from the lobby, but I wouldn't answer. I had no idea what to say. And that was that. I never heard from him again. I probably sabotaged my career big-time with that move, and I'm sure there was a savvier way to handle the situation.

On the other hand, he was my fucking godfather!

I was extremely proud of my work in *Riders to the Sea*. I felt it really marked my arrival as an actress. Back in Malibu, I got a tape of it, and we had a little private screening, just Mom and a few friends. I really wanted to see Mom's reaction. I knew she was going to be bowled over. I couldn't wait.

Before we started, she was bubbling over with a sort of calculated, actressy enthusiasm. "This is so exciting. I can't wait to see this. Everybody get in your seats, the movie is about to start!"

It was very cute, and a little annoying. In her own way, she was grabbing a little bit of the spotlight. I didn't care, as long as she was being supportive.

The movie started. I looked over at Mom. She was leaning forward, gazing at the screen, her chin in her hands, like a child waiting for a special treat. *Oh, Mom, you are so gonna love this!*

It was about fifteen minutes into the movie when I looked over at Mom again and—something had changed: she was sitting back now, and she had a tight, analytical look on her face. The pure joy of moviegoing had vanished. Then she abruptly stood up and went into the kitchen.

Was something wrong? I waited for her to come back. She never did. I could hear her rattling around in there.

"Mom! You're missing the movie!"

"I can see it from here!" she called from the kitchen.

I could see *her* too, and what she was doing was digging into a pint of ice cream. She stood just behind the kitchen door, and kept sneaking furtive glances from around the corner at the TV while she ate. You could tell that she was trying not to watch, but she couldn't resist.

When the movie was over, everybody gathered around to congratulate me. Mom kept her distance, watching with a small, pained smile. Finally, after the guests were gone and we were alone, I got to ask her: "So? What did you think?"

She busied herself cleaning the cups and chips off the side tables. "It was fine," she said with a shrug.

Fine—the word landed on my heart with a thud. I may have been naïve, but I knew a backhanded compliment when I heard one. "What does that mean—'fine'?"

"Well, you know . . . I'm used to professionals."

Another slam, and that one got my hackles up. "*Professionals*? Geraldine Page isn't a professional? Amanda Plummer isn't a professional?"

"*They* were very good," Mom conceded. So now her point was clearer: the movie was good, the other actors were good. I sucked.

"You see, what it is, Sach . . ." She paused as she pretended to search for the words, although I knew damn well she had them already loaded in her gun. "There was too much crying," she finally declared. "When you do all that emoting and weeping, there's nothing left for the audience to feel. *I* didn't feel anything. Just remember that the next time you try to act: don't cry so much."

"What do you mean '*try* to act'? I can *act*, Mom. Don't tell me I can't act!"

She rolled her eyes wearily, as if I were intent on misunderstanding her. "Of course you can act. You're my daughter; you had to inherit *something*, but that doesn't mean you *have* to act. Because you know what?" She looked at me intensely now, as though she were just hatching an idea. "You know *what*? You're a wonderful cook."

What was I supposed to do with that comment?

"So?"

"So, you should be cooking. Making use of your real talents." She clapped her hand to her forehead, a why-didn't-I-think-of-this-before gesture: "You should do a cooking show!"

"A cooking show?"

"On TV. You can cook different meals, like the *Galloping Gourmet*. That would be marvelous. I would watch *that*."

I couldn't begin to follow her logic. "Anyone can cook!"

"Not like you. You're special. When you're special at something, do it. When you're not . . ." She spread her hands wide to suggest the futility of such a quest. She was telling me my acting career was a quixotic, foolish dream.

Seeing the dejection in my face, she took this as a cue to elaborate even further. "Look, I was *meant* to be a star. So I am. That's how it works. Karma. You're how old now, thirty-one? Face the facts: if you haven't made it yet, it wasn't meant to be."

She had one last thought to leave me with: "But a cooking show . . ."

. . .

ABOUT a year earlier, Mom had been approached by Pepsi to do a commercial. It was for Diet Pepsi, a drink they were marketing to the younger generation. Their idea was to pair Shirley Mac-Laine, Oscar-winning actress and New Age guru, with her own daughter, who was apparently trying to get into acting herself. It would cross all demographic lines.

Mom wasn't interested. "Why do I want to do a commercial? It's not like I need the money. I don't even drink fucking Pepsi." But it was a great opportunity for me—a major commercial, with national exposure. "Come on, Mom, it'll be fun!"

"All right, I'll do it for you," she said grudgingly.

I'm standing in a garden. EXTREME CLOSE-UP as I take a swig from a can of Diet Pepsi. WIDER NOW as Mom approaches:

MOM: "Sweetheart, what's the matter?"

SACHI: "I'm drowning my sorrows."

MOM: "You are depressing the scenery."

SACHI: "Oh, Mom, I really wanted that job."

MOM: "I know. But listen, when one door closes, another door opens. I always learned more from my failures than I did from my success."

SACHI: "You mean I can learn from failure?"

MOM: "Yes. You don't want to get a PhD in it, but you can learn."

SACHI: (giggling softly) "I'll drink to that."

As we walk through the garden, arms affectionately circled around each other's waists, Martin Sheen's voice-over ties it all up: "There's one soft drink that fits the spirit of today. Diet Pepsi—the one-calorie choice of a new generation."

Mom was paid a cool million for that spot. I got scale.

CHAPTER 14

FAMILY FEELING

Mom was a tad schizophrenic about my career. She was always encouraging, giving me advice, wishing me the very best, but then, whenever I actually *did* something, she would not-so-artfully suggest that I was wasting my time. I could never figure out what she wanted for me, or expected from me. If only I could talk to someone who understood her better than I did, someone who really knew her, someone like . . .

Well, Uncle Warren. He'd grown up with her, he'd followed her escape route out of the alcoholic Baptist world of their parents, and he'd experienced the same kind of dizzying success. He of all people could probably shed some light on her paradoxical thought processes.

Except that Warren was not a part of my life. I wanted him to be, but there had always been a cool distance between us, and the gulf had widened considerably over the years. I was too young to command his attention when he was coming into his own, and by the time I got back from Australia and France, he was a superstar, with *Bonnie and Clyde*, *The Parallax View*, *Shampoo*, *Heaven Can Wait*, and *Reds* under his belt. For the latter two, he received Academy Award nominations for Best Picture, Best Director, Best Actor, and Best Screenplay, the only person to achieve that distinction twice. (The only other person to do it even once was Orson Welles, for *Citizen Kane*.) He won the Best Director Award for *Reds*.

Warren Beatty was a major Hollywood player in his own right, so much so that people often tended to forget that he and Mom were brother and sister. They seemed so distinct and original, each in his or her own way. They never acted together, and they approached performing from completely different directions: Warren was a serious actor who could do comedy; Mom was an entertainer who could do drama. Warren never did a musical, thank God, and Mom never did an epic movie or a gangster flick. They didn't even look that much alike.

Only in attitude—in their drive, their ambition, their laser-like focus on success—did they display a genetic similarity. Warren was, if anything, more driven than Mom, more ruthless in his determination. He still had that "don't come too close" aura, and it was now even more pronounced. You couldn't get near him: he had the isolated, impenetrable façade of the very powerful.

Around this time, I was working on a play in class with a dark-haired beauty named, I think, Laura. We'd go out for drinks afterward, she and David and I, and in the course of a conversation she casually let drop that she was Uncle Warren's girlfriend. Here was a happy coincidence! Admittedly, Warren had dozens of girlfriends, so it wasn't unlikely that you'd run into one sooner or later. Still, the fact that Laura and I had become buddies prior to the disclosure made it much easier to cultivate her friendship without inviting suspicion.

"How is my uncle doing?" I asked innocently. "I haven't seen him in such a long time."

"You should come over for dinner," Laura said.

"That would be fun," I said, trying not to sound overeager. "When?"

"How about right now? Come on!"

We got in the car and drove over to Mulholland Drive. I was a little nervous that Warren wouldn't be happy to see us there. He had very definite boundaries set up around his life, and you crossed them at your own peril. Yet, as it turned out, he was surprisingly gracious. He welcomed us in, and made us feel entirely at home.

There was no dinner ready, but Warren had a cook on call, who was happy to whip up a delicious meal for us. The kitchen had a row of refrigerators filled with food, so we could basically pick our own menu. And since Warren loved ice cream, too—he had that in common with his sister—every possible flavor was stocked in the freezer.

Warren was a wonderful host to us, and made us feel completely at home. I hadn't seen him in several years, but he acted as if it hadn't been more than a couple of days. At the same time, he gave little outward acknowledgment that we were closely related. We didn't discuss family matters at all—he didn't ask about Mom, and I had enough sense of diplomacy not to bring her up. (They had such a volatile off-and-on relationship, you were never quite sure which way the wind was blowing; better not to set sail into that changeable sea.)

He invited us both back again, and David and I visited several times after that. Even after he broke up with Laura—which was inevitable; the girlfriends came and went—Warren still invited us over. He really liked David. They immediately clicked. They were like two college buddies who had that guys way of talking in shorthand, making unfinished observations and understanding each other perfectly. David would have a scotch, and Warren would have maybe a club soda—I never saw him drink anything stronger—and they would sit around on the couch shooting the shit. I would sit off to the side, listening. Warren never gave any indication that he noticed I was there or not, but I didn't care. It was gratifying just to be there with him, closing the family circle.

I think Warren liked David so much because it was obvious that David didn't want anything from him. David was neither starstruck nor ambitious. To him, Warren was just another guy. They could hang out, joke around, talk about cars or baseball or anything, and it never went any further than that. As for Warren, who was constantly surrounded by climbers and hangers-on, he found in David that rare thing: a person whom he could trust.

IF you're an ordinary noncelebrity, you will seldom feel more vestigial and out of place than when you're walking down the red carpet at a big Hollywood premiere. I walked down a number of them with Mom, including the Academy Awards, and I knew the routine cold—she would swan ahead, escorted by her latest boyfriend or her agent, and I would trail a step behind, basking in the residual glamour but keeping a low profile. Every few feet, Mom would stop to give an interview, and then I would have to stand behind her and smile and look interested. It was a true acting job, because I knew I was on camera, but there was nothing for me to do. Nobody wanted to talk to me; nobody cared about my opinions. If I had been really gorgeous, at least there'd have been a reason for me to be there, a fetching piece of scenery. Yet I was just a cute girl in a nice dress. I wasn't even blonde.

One time, we went to some kind of flashy benefit in Century City, and there was the red carpet waiting for us again. As usual, Mom stopped to hold court with her fans, being very gracious and bubbly—"Hi! . . . Hello! . . . How nice! . . . You're too kind!" Then that moment came when her eyes glazed over and she'd had enough. "All right, we're done"—and she left them flat and headed into the theater.

I started to follow meekly behind, as my role demanded, when suddenly I heard someone yell from the crowd:

"It's Sachi Parker! Sachi Parker! Tracy from *Capitol*!"

At that time, I was in the soap opera *Capitol*. I played Tracy Harris, a young mom who used to be on drugs and whose daughter was taken away from her. Tracy struggles to pull her life together and get her daughter back, but she often finds herself in locked battle with the unsympathetic social worker. I remember at one point my character loses it and screams at her nemesis, in the grand soap opera tradition, "Get out! Get out! *Get out!*"

Mine wasn't a major character, but soap opera fans are devoted to the point of obsession. They know every character, every actor, every twisted plotline. So when Mom moved on and I momentarily emerged from her shadow, they spotted me, and they went crazy. "Sachi Parker!"—they knew who I was! I was instantly mobbed by adoring fans. It was surreal and disconcerting—I was nobody; what were they getting so excited about?—but at the same time, I loved it. For the first time in my life, I was signing autographs and posing for pictures!

"Miss Parker, Miss Parker! Over here! Smile, Miss Parker!"

I was finally having a moment in the sun! It was really cool.

In the midst of this ego-stroking orgy, I looked over at my

mom, eager for some recognition, some maternal pride—but she was livid. Her eyes were these narrow slits shooting out beams of concentrated fury. She was actually being made to stand around and wait—on the red carpet!—while people made a fuss over insignificant *me*!

Sensing the inappropriateness of my celebrity, I tried to sign my name faster. I should have just broken away and moved on with her, but so many people wanted to talk to me, and I was having so much fun! Finally, Mom gathered herself up with an imperious shrug, turned to her agent, and rasped, "Let's go," and she stormed into the theater without me.

That was my last red carpet for a long time.

DAVID and I ended our relationship in 1988. It was an amicable breakup, probably the most civilized I'd ever had. Everything about David was and still is civilized.

I met Mitch Garvey at a party in Venice. He was tall and handsome, and had a sort of midwestern casual cool. I thought he was a big producer, which was just the type of guy I was prowling for at a party like that. I knew I looked hot—I was wearing a clingy spandex-type dress and my trusty push-up bra—so I went up to him and flirted, turned on the charm, used all the old tricks.

It turned out it he was just an assistant director, but by the time I found this out, I was already hooked. He took me out for sushi, and in the midst of our dinner, I mentioned who my mother was. "Who?" Mitch said. "I've never heard of her." It was fairly unlikely that someone working in Hollywood didn't know who Shirley MacLaine was, but I wanted to believe him. How cool— he was interested in me just for me!

It wasn't too long after that—a couple of months—that we got engaged. I know I seem to be getting engaged every time I turn around, but I think I always felt a loneliness and insecurity at my core, and I hoped that marriage would solve that problem.

For some reason, Mitch thought I should contact my dad and tell him about the impending wedding. Maybe it was because Mitch was a proper midwestern type of guy, and he wanted things done correctly. Or maybe it was because he thought Dad had money. Either way, Dad and I hadn't spoken since the deposition. I didn't know if he would even pick up the phone.

I called our home number in Shibuya, Tokyo, and waited nervously for Dad to answer. He didn't. The new owners answered. I didn't know the house had been sold.

I shrugged off my disorientation and asked the new owners, "Do you know where my father is?" They didn't, but they gave me a phone number. It was an American exchange, and when I looked at the area code I discovered that it was in the Boston area. So I called the number.

Yuki answered.

I was baffled. I recognized the voice immediately, but what in the world was she doing in Massachusetts?

"Yuki?"

"Yes?" she said warily.

"It's Sachi."

"Hello."

"Is this your house?"

"Yes." She was being very frugal with her information.

"Is my dad there?"

"Well, I don't know."

What did that mean? "You don't know if he's there? Because I really want to get in contact with him."

"Yes, well, I really can't say right now." And it was crystal clear, from her inflection, that she couldn't say because Dad was right there in the room with her.

I wasted no time. I found out the address from the phone number—it was in Hingham, Massachusetts—and Mitch and I grabbed the next flight from LAX. We had to get out there before my father moved somewhere else.

We landed at Logan Airport the next morning in the freezing cold—which was unfortunate for us, because we were still dressed for Santa Monica. We rented a car and found the house. We didn't call ahead—this would be an ambush, pure and simple. When we pulled into the driveway, we saw two little girls watching from the window. They were Yuki's children, Audrey and Emily.

I knocked on the door, and little Audrey answered. "Hello!" she said brightly. Then suddenly Yuki was at the door.

"Yuki," I said, "is Dad here?"

Then Dad walked up behind her.

We went to lunch together at a seafood restaurant on the water, Dad and Yuki and Mitch and me. It was an odd, awkward meeting at first. Dad pretended that nothing was amiss, that we were all on great terms. He was in his charming mode. "Sach the Pach!" he said, shaking his head with a grin. He was happy about my engagement to Mitch, and gave us his blessing, and then we launched into a lot of inconsequential talk. Yet, there came a point when I felt it necessary to acknowledge the elephant in the room.

"Dad, I'm glad that we're talking again."

Dad smiled tightly, and rattled the ice in his scotch. "Sure."

"It's been very tough being apart from you, because I love you."

I could see him withdrawing now, putting up the force field. So I forged ahead.

"I just want you to know, whatever's happened between us, I forgive you."

Dad was startled, and turned red with anger. "What do you mean? You forgive me for what? I should be forgiving *you*! You're the one who opened your big mouth!"

I looked over at Yuki; she gave me a sympathetic look. She knew what I was feeling. Then an interesting thing happened—I reached out and took Yuki's hand, and her hand tightened over mine. I felt a strong, pure current of love coursing between us. I don't know where it came from, and I don't know where it went, but for an extraordinary moment, we were soul mates. It was such a powerful, sweeping feeling that everything else at the table, including Dad, became incidental. Tears sprang to my eyes, and to Yuki's, too, and we both started sobbing uncontrollably, in a silent way, trying hard to be composed and stoic as the tears streamed down our faces.

Then, quite suddenly, the moment was gone. Our hands broke off, we pulled ourselves together, and the rest of the meal passed in awkward silence.

When we returned to the house, Yuki gave me a tour of the upstairs and downstairs, but she didn't want me going into the basement. So naturally I *had* to go into the basement. I managed to sneak down there while Mitch kept them distracted.

What I found was a rambling living space, completely furnished. There was a huge kitchen, a fireplace, and a bedroom with a king-size bed. In the kitchen, I found special Japanese cooking utensils. I'd heard that Yuki's mom would sometimes visit, so maybe this was her room? Yet, I knew it wasn't. Traces of Dad were everywhere: in the refrigerator were his special mustards and his Dom Perignon. In the cupboard, I found his elegant bone china teacups, and his Darjeeling tea. And in the bedroom closet: Miki's clothes. Clearly she was living here, too.

I looked around the bedroom. On the bed-side table was a

photo of Dad and Miki on their wedding day. So they had gotten married! Miki was now officially my stepmother! There were also photos of Yuki and her kids, and Yuki's mom. And a picture of Dad walking Yuki down the aisle on *her* wedding day. It was now one big happy family.

I flew back to L.A. feeling both fulfilled and confused. I tried to put the pieces of the puzzle together. Dad had clearly fallen on tough times since Mom cut him off, although he still possessed that confident swagger, the sense that prosperity was well within his grasp (and he still possessed that chalet, that yacht, and that private island, so times weren't that tough).

Yuki, for her part, probably felt that she owed him for her education and support, so she provided him with a place to stay, as any good Japanese daughter would. But why didn't anyone tell me what was going on? Why didn't Dad tell me that he was married to Miki, and living with Yuki and her family? Why was I purposely kept in the dark?

Maybe the bigger question was, why didn't I just ask? Why didn't I confront Dad about his secrets? Why didn't I ask Yuki, especially after our epiphany? Because I couldn't. Because it wasn't good form. Because I still couldn't shake off that stubborn Japanese insistence on decorum at all costs.

MOM had a house in Seattle, Washington, with a view of Mount Rainier. We would often fly up there, she and I, and spend a weekend. I was the resident cook. There was a pool and a hot tub, and Mom would sit out there reading scripts while I went for hikes in the nearby forest.

We had some beautiful moments up there, but one day stood out for me, and not in a happy way. Mom and I were in the hot tub relaxing. We were talking about various things, and I don't know how the conversation turned in this direction, but for some reason, out of the blue, Mom announced, "Sachi, there's something I want you to know. I'm not leaving you any money."

"What?"

"In my will."

"You're not leaving me any money?" I was bewildered on two fronts: why was she bringing this up now, and why was she not leaving me any money?

"I'm giving it all to the Kronhausens," she said.

The Kronhausens? Those freeloaders who had coaxed me into losing my virginity? Those characters who had already talked Mom into buying them a farm in Costa Rica? *Those* Kronhausens? They get the jackpot?

She was also planning to leave some money to a Spiritual Awareness Center somewhere in California, or was it New Mexico? The plans sounded a little vague, but the main point she wanted to get across was that I was getting nothing.

"Okay," I said quietly. I didn't argue with her, or ask her why. It was her money; she could do what she wanted with it.

Still, at that moment, I felt utterly abandoned. I don't know why: she'd never given me any money before, cutting me off when I was eighteen, and she'd even made me pay her back for that broken-down car. There was no reason for me to expect her to take care of me in her will. Still, I held out the hope that, because she was my mom, she cared about me.

There was always this twisted, tangled confusion of love and money in our family. Mom used to tell me, "Your trouble is, you need money to feel love." It was an odd contention, because I never had either. I think it was Mom and Dad who had created this love-money equation, in the way they doled it out or withheld it. I came to understand that, in their world, material gifts equaled affection—and I was clearly undeserving of both.

To give her her due, maybe Mom was afraid of spoiling me. So many Hollywood parents tried to buy their kids' love, lavishing money and sports cars on them, and it almost always turned out disastrously. Mom wanted to avoid that for me, so she went to the other extreme. Her intentions were good—she was protecting me—but in the process, she made me feel unloved.

Mom laid her head back on the edge of the tub and closed her eyes, as the water churned around her. She had made her statement and had moved on. There was nothing more to discuss.

This really ruined hot tubs for me. Seattle lost a lot of its charm, too.

NOT surprisingly, I started seeing a therapist. Jean was a heavyset white-haired lady in her fifties with a quality of softness and kind-liness about her. She had twinkly eyes and a very round, maternal shape. I told her about the growing conflict with my mother, and she suggested that maybe I should bring her in for a joint session and see what we could work out. It could really be helpful and could bring us together—or (more likely) it could blow up in our faces. Jean was right, though: one way or another, the issues had to be addressed.

"Mom, I think we should go into therapy."

"You and Mitch?"

"No, you and me."

She laughed. She thought that was ridiculous. For all her cutting-edge enlightenment, Mom didn't think much of thera-pists. She considered them manipulative charlatans who preyed on weak-minded wimps—like me—and she did not suffer them gladly.

Still, I worked on her and managed to get her to a counseling session in Jean's office. Jean welcomed us warmly, and kicked things off in a soothing voice: "Okay, what would you like to talk about?"

Mom shrugged. This wasn't her idea, and she wasn't going to give it the validation of an opening remark. She passed to me.

"Well," I started, "I've been trying very hard to get my career going, and I feel that my mother could be of some help, but it seems that sometimes she's just not on my side. It's a very tough business, you know, and you need all the support you can get."

"It *is* a tough business," Mom countered, "and that's why you have to be tough to survive in it. People don't help you? So what? Help yourself. Hey, I could make a phone call and get you a role like that"—she snapped her fingers—"but is that what you want? Do you really want to get a job that way?"

"Yes," I admitted.

"People don't like nepotism in this business," Mom said. (This was one of her favorite maxims, although I didn't see much evidence for it in Hollywood.) "You have to make it on your own. I did."

"Yeah, well, you had Charlemagne and E.T. helping you." I was being sarcastic again, but I didn't think she would hit me in front of Jean.

She glared at me evenly. "All right, I'm going to put this as gently as I can: everybody in creation knows that you're my daughter, but you still can't buy a job. What does that tell you? Maybe you're just not very good." A hit, a palpable hit.

"Okay, let's take a step back," Jean said. "Sachi, talk a little about your childhood."

"Well—"

Before I could get started, though, Mom was back in there with a preemptive strike: "She had a wonderful childhood. She traveled all over the world. I spent *my* entire childhood in Virginia. *That* was a treat."

Jean asked, "Was it a wonderful childhood, Sachi?"

"I was raised by my father in Japan. I saw Mom only once in a while."

"I was a working mother," Mom explained.

"And do you feel that she abandoned you?" Jean asked me.

"Abandoned her?" Mom answered. "I saved her! The Mob was after her. They wanted to kidnap her. I saved my daughter from the Mafia."

Jean kept focusing on me. "Sachi?"

"I wouldn't say she abandoned me, but I did feel there was something missing from my childhood."

"Oh, really? What was missing?" my mother said. "I gave you everything you needed. Got you clothes every summer. Bought you that stupid car. Name one thing I didn't give you."

"I wanted to go to college . . ."

Mom exploded. "You have some fucking nerve! I sent you to the best boarding schools in Europe. It cost me a fortune! You wanted me to spring for college, too?"

"And I wanted a baby."

Mom turned to Jean for support. "A baby, at her age!"

"I was twenty-seven!"

"You didn't have the maturity."

"You were twenty-two when you had me!"

"And look what happened to you!" This was like one of those courtroom moments when the defendant inadvertently blurts out a damaging admission, and then is stunned by the self-realization that maybe she is guilty after all. Except Mom didn't look guilty. She just looked more pissed off.

I waited for Jean to step in, but she was watching quietly, waiting to see where this would lead. So I took the initiative, trying to sound as reasonable as possible. "Look, Mom, you didn't have to spend a dime on me. I didn't want your money. I wanted *you*. I wanted you to take care of me, tuck me in bed, make sandwiches for me. I wanted you to make those peanut butter and jelly sandwiches for me every day. That's what I wanted."

Jean turned to Mom. "How do you feel about that?"

Mom had had enough, and pushed herself out of her chair. "How do I feel about it? I feel that this is a big goddamn load of nonsense! I feel like I'm swimming in bullshit!" She turned on Jean. "And *you're* bullshit! And I'm not staying to listen to another word!"

Mom was heading for the door when she had one more thought to share. She stormed back at Jean. "You know what happens when you break down *therapist*? It's '*the rapist!*' How do *you* feel about *that*?"

Having nailed Jean with that sally, Mom steamed out the door, confident in her sanity.

CHAPTER 15

DOMESTICATION

n 1988, I auditioned for a TV show based in New York City
called *Manhattan Express*. It was a live morning news show, but
it shot at six in the evening, because the TV audience was in
Japan. *Manhattan Express* was produced by Fuji Television, and it
was like a *Today* show for Japanese viewers. The news would deal
with U.S. and world topics, much like any morning show, and the
anchors would be typical photogenic all-American types, except
that they would be speaking Japanese.

By the time I auditioned, they had already done an exhaustive
search for a Japanese-speaking Jane Pauley. It was desirable that she
shouldn't be too pretty, but have camera experience and speak flu-
ent Japanese and English. Now, there are different levels of the
Japanese language, and I had stalled at the twelve-year-old level—
I spoke children's Japanese. I thought this might be a drawback,

but it actually boosted my standing, because I came off as child-like, which is what the Japanese audience wants in a female an-chor. They don't care for women who come on too strong. So I was hired.

My male counterpart was Christopher Field, who had gone to Harvard and spoke high-level Japanese, which suited his role as the hard-core news anchor. I was the fluff, offsetting him with light-weight puff pieces, anything to do with society, entertainment, celebrities, or human interest. The job paid $1,300 a day, so I wasn't complaining.

It was very difficult at times to project the image they wanted. I remember in particular the Pan Am Lockerbie bombing in De-cember of 1988. Chris was going to report the tragic story, and they wanted me to sit beside him and smile during the broadcast. Smile? Smile at what? Two hundred and sixty people had just got-ten blown out of the sky! I couldn't believe it. *You want me to be charming and smiley while Chris is delivering this awful news? He's not smiling, why should I? I'll look like an idiot!* Still, they insisted that my disconnected grin would be calming and reassuring to the Japa-nese audience—and I mean, they *insisted*. So I did it. Remember, $1,300 a day.

I was on *Manhattan Express* for six months or so. It was seen only in Japan, but I got to appear in PR spots on *Good Morning America* and *Entertainment Tonight*. It was a great gig—until it abruptly ended. Without asking me, my agent, Denny, demanded more money. This, of course, was the American way: to angle for a raise at the first opportunity. The Japanese way, however, was to be loyal and patient; making salary demands was considered the height of rudeness. So they fired me.

Not too long after that, I broke up with Mitch. He'd turned out to be a less-than-perfect fiancé. He had a violent temper, and he crossed the line more than once. Years earlier I would have put up with it, or tried to run away, but I was a grown woman now, more independent and confident, so I just told him, "It's over."

Mitch didn't take this well. He yelled at me, threatened me. He slashed my tires. Somebody peed on the kitchen floor of my condo in Marina Del Rey. I could never prove it was Mitch, but it had to be *somebody*. True, an animal might have gotten in—but man, there was a lot of pee. No raccoon could have produced it. Maybe a coyote.

Mitch also wanted half my earnings from the TV show, citing our "common-law marriage." When I laughed off that absurd notion, he told me: if I didn't give over half, he would go to the tabloids with the clone story.

I called his bluff on that one. Who would ever believe it?

After we broke up, Mitch got involved in a new relationship with a mystery woman. I confess, even though I'd initiated the breakup, I got really jealous. "Who is it? Who?" I had to know. He wouldn't tell me.

Then one night I had a dream. In it, Mitch was kissing another woman. She turned, and I saw her face. Oh my God.

When I awoke, I immediately called him up. "It's Debra Winger, isn't it?"

He was surprised. "How did you know?"

I had some extra time on my hands, so I finally got my breasts done.

I was going to do a play called *Independence*, by Lee Blessing, in North Hollywood. In the play, my character had a scene where she appears topless. I wasn't really self-conscious about my natural breasts, but when the production was postponed for a year, it seemed like the perfect opportunity to finish what I'd planned with the sinister Jeffrey so many years before. I had the money saved from the morning news show, so I went ahead and did it.

They were fabulous; I loved them. If I didn't get more work in Hollywood with these babies, then the system was definitely broken.

WHEN we eventually did *Independence*, I was in the dressing room backstage with the other actresses and I took off my shirt. There was a collective gasp of admiration. "Did you get your boobs done?" They were volubly impressed. I have to tell you, it may sound shallow and regressive, but there's something very gratifying about being told that you have an attractive body. It reminded me of being back at the noodle shop, with the waitresses marveling at my American assets. Plus, it gave me such confidence onstage: when the topless scene came along, I was proud to take the girls out.

Next up: *The Lulu Plays*, an adaptation of Frank Wedekind's German plays *Earth Spirit* and *Pandora's Box*. I played Lulu, the girl who goes from street girl to dancer to wealthy man's lover to prostitute, and winds up getting killed by Jack the Ripper. It was a great character arc, and I spent a good deal of the play topless again—which I relished: I'd developed a kind of fearlessness onstage that I could never approach in real life.

Lulu was a pitch-black variation on the whore with the heart of gold—the kind of role my mother had patented. I got some excellent reviews, but the one that mattered most would be Mom's. So I was especially nervous the night she came to see it.

After the show, we went to a local Denny's—not exactly Sardi's, but commensurate with the stature that live theater commands in Los Angeles. Mom had offered me the usual generic compliments, but she hadn't told me yet what she really thought, and I knew it was coming. I watched her eat her omelet in silence, and finally I had to ask the fateful question: "So, Mom, what did you really think of my performance?"

She solemnly put down her fork, waited until the moment was dramatically right, and then, without a hint of sarcasm, with an almost passionate earnestness, she said, "Sweetheart, I'm only going to say this once, and you will never hear me say it again. Tonight you gave one of the most remarkable performances I ever saw. It was truly transcendent. I was touched, and I was shattered. And when I am on my deathbed, and they ask me what was the greatest single performance I ever saw in my lifetime, I will say that it was you, in this play. And then I will die. And that's all I have to say, and I will never say it again."

Then she went back to her omelet.

She never did say it again, but she didn't have to. I was overwhelmed. Tears welled up in my eyes. This was so beyond anything I might have expected her to say. It was the best thing I'd ever heard from her—from anyone—in my life. It was as if she were passing the torch to me, and giving me her professional blessing. I had never felt as connected with her as I did on that night twenty years ago.

My performance as Lulu won me a Drama-Logue Award for Best Actress in a Play. In a wonderful coincidence, Mom won a Drama-Logue Award the same year, for her one-woman show, so we went to the awards ceremony together.

I suspect that if I hadn't won, Mom wouldn't have gone at all. The Drama-Logues weren't the Oscars or the Golden Globes; there was nothing formal or ritualistic about the ceremony, and the crowd was entirely different, struggling actors and theater folk, most wearing jeans rather than tuxedoes. There was a lot of clapping and cheering. Everybody knew each other from auditions and scene classes, and they would yell at you from across the room—"Hi, Sachi!"—and shout congratulations.

When Mom showed up, they made a huge fuss over her. She was easily the biggest star there. I realized then what a big deal it was for her to come to this function; I knew it was her way of showing support for my career.

It was a very special night, and I got all teary when I went up to accept my award. I thanked the director, the producer, my fellow cast members, and then I turned to Mom. "I especially want to thank my mom, who's here with me tonight." A nice warm round of applause followed.

"I so appreciate her," I went on. "She's taught me everything about acting. She's my role model. And it means so much to me that she's here to share this moment with me." I held up the award. "This is for you, Mom. Thanks for everything. I love you!" As the applause swelled, I went back to my seat and gave her a big hug.

About a half hour later, Mom received her award. The applause was tumultuous as she stepped up onstage. She made her thank-yous, and then said a few heartfelt words about the magic of theater. "It all starts with you actors. You are the torchbearers. You make it happen. I salute you all."

Then I saw her glance toward me. *Here it comes*, I thought. *She's saving me for the end.*

"Of course, what makes this award extra-special is that my daughter is with me, getting her own richly deserved award for her performance in *The Lulu Plays*. She's worked so hard to get to this point, and as much as I cherish this award, I cherish even more the opportunity to be here with her on her special night, and watch her following in my footsteps. I could not be prouder of her. Sachi, I love you!"

That's what I was waiting for her to say.

What she *actually* said was "Thank you," then left the stage.

I don't know why I expected more—it was her speech, she could say what she wanted—but it truly hurt my feelings. Just when I thought I'd raised myself to a certain level of respect in Mom's eyes, I was made to realize once again that, to her, in an elemental way, I didn't exist. It would have been a small thing for her to acknowledge me in front of my peers, but that was just the point. Mom didn't do small things.

I had my new breasts for three years. Then my husband made me take them out because he didn't like them.

Frank Murray was a Wall Street broker from Greenwich, Connecticut, who dabbled in producing. I met Frank in North Hollywood, when he produced *Independence*. He certainly had no objections to my breasts then, but once we got married, his more conservative instincts took over.

I met Frank during the last week of rehearsals, when he came out to check on the progress of the show. I walked onstage wearing a fishnet top that was meant to fit over a T-shirt, but I wasn't wearing a T-shirt. It was cold in the theater, and my nipples poked out right through the fishnet. This may have been what caught his attention. After rehearsal, he asked me out, and I said no. I had no interest in investment bankers who thought just because I was walking around with erect tits I'd be an easy lay.

That evening, the whole cast went out together for a late dinner, and Frank came along. I was dating a writer from *Star Trek: The Next Generation* at the time, but I was still very much on the market, so I dressed sexy, in a skimpy, tight-fitting outfit. It was a cold night in L.A., and I was freezing. Frank took off his jacket and put it over my shoulders. It was a very romantic, chivalrous gesture. I thought to myself, *Uh-oh, I'm falling.*

At dinner, Frank couldn't have been more gentlemanly. He was polite and attentive, and he talked charmingly about his travels around the world. He reminded me of my father.

When he sent me roses the next day, that sealed the deal. I was head over heels.

To my surprise, Mom really seemed to like Frank, in her contrarian way. She didn't care for his Republican-ness at all, and he didn't care for her Democratic bent, but they enjoyed sparring with each other. They would get into impassioned arguments, and at the end of a bloody fight would regard each other with a grudging admiration.

So when, three years later, Frank proposed to me in St. Thomas, I couldn't wait to spread the good news. "Mom, I'm engaged!"

She took the news in stride. In fact, she sounded highly underwhelmed about the whole thing. "Uh-huh. Okay. All right."

She seemed to be making a judgment on my level of excitement. I couldn't understand why she wasn't excited along with me. Was she afraid she was going to lose me? I know that sounds a stretch, but I'd been living near her for the past ten years, and now I was planning to move to the East Coast, and Connecticut. Maybe she'd gotten used to me, and hated to let me go.

Maybe that's why she called Frank on the phone one day, unbeknownst to me, and gave him some interesting advice, which he shared with me afterward:

"Frank, I have to be honest. It breaks my heart to tell you this, because Sachi is my only daughter, and I love her dearly, but just be aware that you can't count on her. She's completely unreliable. Probably because she's so self-absorbed; it's hard for her to think of anyone but herself. And she's a liar. You can never trust her. Don't believe a word she says about me. I don't think she can help it. It's pathological." (I guess she was still hung up on Charters Towers and those missing airplane tickets.) Then she delivered the coup de grace: "It's probably not a good idea to marry her."

Mom always had to be different. Instead of telling me that Frank wasn't good enough for me, as most moms would have, she told Frank that I was the lemon. A novel strategy.

Frank, cleaving to his Republican roots, ignored the Democrat, and we started planning our wedding. It was originally going to be a small ceremony—I wanted to get married under a tree in a California canyon, with just our friends in attendance, and I would be barefoot with flowers in my hair. Very hippy-dippy. Frank came from wealthy stock, though—his great-grandfather was the Hardart of Horn & Hardart, the famous automat food-service company—so his family turned the wedding into a lavish affair in Greenwich: a High Mass in a Catholic church, and the reception at a country club. I didn't want any of this formal frippery, but Frank did. He wanted a big wedding, and he got it. It was almost as if he were the bride.

Inevitably, the wedding plans grew bigger and bigger—more food, more music, more obscure relatives—and with that came the vital question: Who's going to pay for all this?

Tradition dictated the bride's side of the family. I didn't want to go to Mom; I knew that would be a diamond-hard nut to crack. So I turned to my father. Clearly he wasn't riding as high as in those glory days when Mom was supporting his playboy image, but I assumed he must have had some kind of nest egg squirreled away.

Dad was affable enough on the phone. "How much do you need, Sach?"

"Not that much, really. Twelve thousand dollars."

Silence.

"That's pretty reasonable for a wedding in Greenwich," I pointed out.

More silence.

"Dad?"

"I'll see what I can do," he finally replied.

A few days later, I received a check from Dad for three hundred dollars. I bought my wedding dress with it.

Next stop—Mom. I knew I'd never get anywhere with her over the phone, so I drove over to Malibu and confronted her face-to-face.

"*What?* Twelve thousand? Is that what you said?" She was giving me the Look.

"It's not really a lot."

"Not a lot? Twelve thousand? I see."

As she paced around the house, mulling it over, I followed after her and explained the expenses of the wedding ceremony and the reception in great detail. She needed to know where every penny was going. I didn't want her to think I would be using the cash to support my thriving crack habit.

She truly didn't want to give me the money, but I think I shamed her into it. ("If you don't help us out, what are people going to think?") There was a downside to her largesse, though. Now that she was springing for the wedding, she figured it was her own private party, and she started inviting all her Hollywood friends. Then Frank's family invited *their* friends, to balance things out, and the next thing you know, we had doubled the price tag.

I called Mom up in Australia, where she was shooting a film. "Mom, it's going to cost a little more . . ."

"No, that's it! That's it!"

She wouldn't bend on this. Frank and I had to pay for the rest of the wedding ourselves. Mostly Frank, since I was broke. To his credit, Frank didn't have a problem with this. He knew that my mother was pretty tight-fisted, and I think he felt a certain pride in handling the freight on his own wedding without any help from the famous Shirley MacLaine.

Still, the situation left me feeling embarrassed and depressed. It would have been one thing if Mom had been a woman of modest means, or if we'd been estranged, or if she were devoted to charitable causes. But she was a rich woman, and she lived in a rich manner—a house in Malibu, a ranch in Santa Fe, a house in Seattle, an apartment in New York—and she'd had no problem sending sixty thousand dollars a month into space and subsidizing a clone.

Mom flew in to Connecticut for the wedding, and stayed at the upscale Homestead Inn in Greenwich. We had dinner at the inn the night before the ceremony, just the two of us. After a few drinks, I felt my emotions taking over. I knew I should have escaped to the ladies room, but I couldn't. I just sat there and started crying.

Mom looked at me with puzzlement. "What's the matter with you?"

"I don't know, I just—I feel like you don't love me."

"Of course I love you."

"I just don't understand," I said. "I'm your only daughter—why is it so difficult for you to help me out?"

Mom had no answer for me. She went back to her dinner. The rest of the meal was *real* quiet. Maybe I'd hurt her feelings; I couldn't tell. Maybe she wouldn't even come to the wedding now.

But she did. The next day, she made her entrance at the reception, flouncing in like Auntie Mame, waving a check in her hand.

"I just want you to know," she announced to the crowd. "I'm going to pay for the wedding! This is my only daughter, and I'm taking care of her!"

She turned to me now, lowering her voice just enough to

make sure that anyone who wanted to listen in could hear. "Sachi, here—I'm giving you a check for twenty thousand dollars. Don't ever say I didn't do anything for you!"

I reached for the check, but she yanked it back, extracting a necessary word of tribute. "Who's the best mother in the world?"

"You are, Mom."

Mom spent the rest of the cocktail hour making sure that anybody who'd missed it heard the good news that she was paying for the wedding. After that, of course, it became *her* party. The wedding celebration was entirely secondary. At one point she stopped the band in the middle of the reception to announce that it was Bella Abzug's birthday, and they rolled out a cake for her. I was upstaged at my own wedding by Bella Abzug.

Yes, Mom did pay for it, and I took it as a sign that we were slowly building a bridge to each other. It might take time—there might be lots of setbacks—but the first bricks were in place, and someday . . .

FRANK and I set up house in Greenwich, and so began a long stretch of married life marked by a quiet, unexcited calm. After thirty-seven years of constant movement all over the world, I had found myself settling into the sedate rhythms of comfortable up-scale suburbia. It was nice, for a while.

Not that those years were completely uneventful. There was plenty of incident, but most of it was of the ordinary family variety. After three years in Greenwich, for instance, Frank left Wall Street and got a job as the CEO of Amana, the refrigerator appliance company. So we moved to Houston. I was seven months pregnant with our son, Frankie, and while we were down there I got pregnant again, two years later, and had our second child, Arin.

The details of those births were unremarkable, but the emotional effect that they had on me was seismic. I was scared during that first pregnancy, truly anxious about having children, probably because of my ambivalent relationship with my own parents. I was afraid that failure was in my genes, and I felt a great deal of pressure to be a good mother. I was pretty sure I was going to mess it up.

Yet, once I held those babies in my arms, I knew I had nothing to worry about. I was meant to be a mom. The love was immediate, instinctive, and unconditional, just as I'd hoped. I knew exactly what my job was, and I loved doing it. Without making any judgments on my own mom, I was determined to be there for my kids whenever they needed me. My acting career could go on hold for now. I had a new career.

IT was early 2001, and we had moved back to Greenwich when I got a call from Andy Banks, Yuki's husband. He thought I should know that my dad was back in Hawaii: he was ill with lung cancer, and he wasn't going to make it.

I was stunned. I hadn't seen much of Dad lately—Miki tried to keep us apart as much as possible—but I always thought of him as healthy, robust, a man in his prime. I could picture him sailing boats, hiking mountains, or wending his way elegantly through a jagged path of nightclub tables. True, always with a cigarette in one hand and a scotch in the other, but he was only seventy-nine, a charming, irresistible force of nature. He was too damn clever to die.

I flew out to Hawaii as soon as I could, and brought Frankie and Arin with me. He was four and she was two, and they had never really gotten to know their grandfather. This might be their last chance.

When we arrived at the hospital, we found Dad in the rehab

pool, working out with a big beach ball. They'd removed one of his lungs already, and you could see that he was very weak. Still, he worked out every day, throwing the beach ball back and forth, determined to get his health back. It was inspiring and moving to watch him, especially since at some level we knew his situation was hopeless.

At some point Dad left the hospital and joined us at the hotel, where he stayed for a couple of nights. He really enjoyed getting to know my Arin. He thought she was cute as a button. She was the same age I was when I joined Dad in Japan in 1959.

We talked of many things: our ice-fishing trips in the Japan Alps, the cruises on *Happy Pappy*, and Molokai, the site of the former leper colony. Since childhood, Dad had been telling me stories about this beautiful island in the middle of the Hawaiian archipelago; and about Father Damien, who tended to the lepers there; and about the high, sheer cliffs of Kaluapapa that kept the lepers exiled from the rest of society. I always wanted to visit there, and we talked about going now. "I really want to take you there, just you and me," Dad said. "I want to show you the cliffs."

He then discussed his will in detail. "You know my chalet in Italy? I want you to have it. You and the kids. And I have land back in Japan . . . the Nasu property. It's worth millions."

I didn't want to go in this direction. "No, that's yours, Dad. You'll be back there soon."

Dad laughed weakly. He knew bullshit when he heard it. "No, it's for you. It's all taken care of."

There was one more matter I needed to discuss with him, just to get it straight in my head:

"So, Dad," I said at one point, leaning forward and stroking his arm gently, "you really did make up that whole story about being cloned, didn't you? You know, so you could get Mom's money? And the telegrams, and the government spying on her, and the Pleiades . . . That was all you, right?"

Dad breathed heavily a few times. After a long moment of reflection, he quietly said, "Yeah."

When I finally heard it confirmed from his own lips, I was astounded. Even though I knew it was true, there had been enough of the purely incredible about it to always leave a slight doubt in my mind. I had assumed he would hide in that shadow of doubt right to the end. To admit it so easily, to finally tell me the truth— I never expected that. The effect was instantaneous: with one word, all the lies disappeared, all the cobwebs were swept away. I was finally seeing my real father.

THREE weeks later, Frank and I were back in America, building a new house in Greenwich and living in a rental nearby. One evening, Frank went over to check on the progress of the house. When he returned, his face was sheet white.

"What's the matter?" I asked.

"I saw your father in the kitchen," he said.

Over at the new house, he'd seen what he called "a shadow" of my dad standing in the unfinished kitchen. "When I walked in, he saw me and ran into the pantry, and the room became very cold. It was your dad."

"I think you're losing your marbles," I told him. "Dad's in Hawaii." An hour later came the call from Miki. My dad had passed, six hours earlier—but, apparently, he'd stopped by Greenwich on his way out to pay a visit.

We booked a flight for Honolulu the next day, but before I left, I had to go over to the new house to check out the ghostly emanation. I made Frank go with me, and together we wandered through the house. We visited the kitchen—a fitting place for my dad, a gourmet enthusiast, to frequent—but there were no manifestations, no cold spots. Then we went into the living room area. I was sitting on a coffee table, Frank was in a chair opposite me, and as we chatted about our memories of Dad, I felt a sudden beautiful warmth, starting in my shoulder and traveling down the left side of my back. It was a flowing heat of love and forgiveness, and I just let the feeling run through me.

Frank, across from me, turned white again. "Oh my God. Sach, your dad is standing right next to you with his hand on your left shoulder. He's apologizing to you, he's saying he's sorry, and he loves you."

The funeral service was held at the Halekulani Hotel, where Dad had spent so many happy days, and where I'd served as a bus-girl and fallen under the spell of Luke Garrett. Before the service, Miki gave me a stuffed toy monkey that had belonged to Dad. She said he would have wanted me to have it. I was born in the Year of the Monkey, so it had a special resonance.

I joined Miki and Yuki at the front of the room, to represent the family. Mom wasn't there: she hadn't been invited, which was fine, because she hadn't wanted to go.

Something very odd was going on at that memorial. Everyone was coming up to Miki and Yuki to offer condolences, but no one was coming up to me. I was being shunned. Most of Dad's friends from Tokyo wouldn't give me the time of day.

I couldn't understand it. What had I done? Everyone was staring daggers at me, giving me dirty looks. When it was my turn to speak at the service, all I could see was a frieze of angry, hostile faces. These people hated me.

Yuki told me later that she'd heard of Miki spreading stories about me: what an awful daughter I was, how disloyal I had been to my dad, how I had vilely betrayed him.

To give Miki her due, she was only reacting to the skewed version of events that my dad had artfully presented to her. She knew nothing about the clone story. She thought the reason Mom divorced Dad and cut him off (thereby dramatically altering Miki's own affluent lifestyle) was because I had turned against Dad and told vicious lies about him. Yuki recalled that over the years Dad would lament that he missed me desperately, and tried to get in touch with me, but that I refused to answer his calls. In truth, the very opposite was the case; he was the one who cut me adrift. But Miki had never heard my side of the story, so she believed Dad, and consequently told everyone else that I had coldly abandoned my father and broken his heart.

I'll say this for Dad, he was consistent. Whether it was me or Mom or Miki, he didn't discriminate in deceiving the people who loved him.

THE next day, we had breakfast at the hotel before flying home. Frank and the kids went for a walk around the grounds, and I sat by myself, staring out at the ocean, in a sad, reflective mood.

Suddenly Miki was sitting next to me. I was startled. I assumed she had come to console me.

Not quite. "Sachi, your father always said that he wanted me to have the Nasu property in Japan, but he forgot to put it in the will. You don't want it; you don't even live there anymore. So would you please sign the property over to me?"

Her audacity amazed me. I couldn't discuss this now; I was still in an emotional place, and I couldn't switch gears. "I don't know, Miki. I have to think about it."

Miki didn't want me to think about it. She miraculously pulled out a contract and a pen. "All you have to do is sign right here."

Tackiness aside, she made a good point. I probably wouldn't be back in Japan again, and she obviously wanted the property more than me. Plus, I had the chalet in Italy. I might as well let her have the Japan property.

Then, suddenly, I gathered my wits about me. The Nasu property was a spectacular piece of real estate in northern Japan, surrounded by golf courses and ski resorts. It was, as Dad said, worth millions. I couldn't just give it away on a whim. "No, I can't sign anything right now. Later."

Miki wouldn't give up. She kept asking, and I kept saying no. Finally she grabbed the contract and stalked off in a huff. She refused to talk to me after that, not if I wasn't going to sign.

BACK in Connecticut, we waited patiently for the settlement of the will. After several months, when there was still no word, I asked Frank to check with the lawyers in Honolulu. He discovered that there was nothing coming. There were no provisions for me in the will.

Only the Nasu property was mine. Under Japanese law, the property had to go to a direct descendant. That's why she wanted me to sign it over to her.

STILL, per another part of Japanese law, I had a year to claim my inheritance. After that, it would revert to the spouse or nearest relative. I didn't bother to put in a claim. I allowed the year to expire.

Chapter 16

The Lord and the Ring

I t was 2002, my children were in school now, and I was getting restless. I wanted to act again.

I had joined the Theatre Artists Workshop of Westport back in the 1990s, and when we moved back from Houston, I was eager to get back into the swing of things. The workshop had been founded by a group of theater professionals who lived in the area as a safe place for actors and writers to flex their muscles and try out new stuff. Many stage and film luminaries—Keir Dullea, Lee Richardson, Theodore Bikel, Morton DaCosta, Phoebe Brand, Ring Lardner Jr., James Noble, Brett Somers—would show up at the weekly Monday night meeting to view the work and give feedback.

I loved the supportive, nurturing atmosphere there. It inspired me to take lots of new chances. I acted in all kinds of classic plays: *The Seagull, The Three Sisters, A Doll's House, Anna Christie, The Beauty Queen of Lenane, The Glass Menagerie*—parts I'd always wanted to play, when I was just at the age where I could still pull them off. I never went topless, though; those glory days were over.

My favorite was *A Moon for the Misbegotten*. Josie Hogan was such a departure for me. She was an earthy, ballsy character, with a thick, wide peasant body, where I was slight and unassuming. It took me a long time to find her, and once she took possession of me, I couldn't get rid of her. I would walk around the house burly and heavy-footed, and sit with my legs splayed wide. My kids would notice and tease me all the time. "Uh-oh, Josie's making dinner tonight!"

It felt great to be working regularly as an actress again, and my confidence was growing exponentially with each performance— so much so that, in the fall of 2005, when I was appearing in the workshop's annual one-act festival, I made the supremely coura- geous gesture of inviting Mom. She was visiting the East Coast at the time, and I persuaded her to come see the last Sunday matinee performance.

I was nervous about performing in front of her. Over the past ten years, our relationship had downshifted from a roller-coaster ride of highs and lows to a pleasant cruise on a neutral plane. I was no longer active in the entertainment world, and that removed the edge of competitiveness that had always charged the air between us. In her eyes, I was now the settled suburban mom, and she was the grandmother, "Ganny," who would drop in from time to time to bring gifts and offer homely advice. She didn't see me as an actress anymore.

Just a year earlier, she'd brought me to a party in New York at some important person's duplex apartment, and there were all these celebrities there: Mike Nichols, Diane Sawyer, Jane Seymour, and Nora Ephron. I thought, *Nora Ephron*! I loved her and had been dying to meet her.

Now, it's not all that easy to strike up a chat at one of these high-powered cocktail parties, because anyone you might want to talk to is usually busy trying to find someone else more important to talk to. So the whole night, I waited for the serendipitous moment when I could just happen to run into Nora and start a witty conversation. Finally, that moment arrived: here she was, right next to me! Before I could say a word, though, Mom popped up at my side like a malevolent genie.

"Nora, I want you to meet my daughter, Sachi." Hooray, she had given me just the introduction I needed. She could have left it at that, but no, she had to add, in a patronizing voice, "Sachi wants to be an actress. She *just* started taking acting classes. Isn't that great?"

Nora smiled indulgently, offered a few words of encouragement, and moved on. I'd been effectively torpedoed. Mom knew damn well that I'd been a professional actor for thirty years, but now, in front of this elegant, sophisticated icon, she'd made it sound as if I were some bored suburban housewife with a few spare hours on her hands.

In fact, this is probably how Mom saw me. I'd removed myself from the arena; I was no longer a gladiator. She hadn't seen me onstage in more than ten years, and when she showed up at the workshop, I don't think she was expecting me to be anything more than community-theater adequate.

So we were both caught by pleasant surprise when she wound up loving the show. She was laughing her head off in the audience, letting loose with her familiar full-throated cackle. A little too loudly, of course—I could tell she was enjoying the sound of her own voice—but I didn't care. Those laughs were for me.

Afterward, as we drove back to the house, she was gushing with superlatives: "You know, Sach, you owned that stage. You were wonderful. What can I say? You're a great actress. You really are."

I listened warily, waiting for the other shoe to drop, the deflating "But" that would send my spirits into free fall. It never came. She was actually sincere. It was a mirror of that moment at Denny's after *The Lulu Plays*, when I felt I'd finally broken through to her as a fellow artist. Was she confirming that earlier appraisal, the one that had left me sky-high with hope, or was this another false start? I wanted to believe her; I wanted to be exhilarated by the possibilities of rebooting my career with her firmly in my corner. So I did.

This developed into a golden period for us as mother and daughter. We stayed in close touch; we talked on the phone all the time. We were even going to spend Christmas together. A family Christmas with Mom! What could be better?

Well, it got better. A week before Christmas, she called me up all excited: "Honey, I have the best Christmas present for you! This is perfect! Perfect!"

Now *I* was excited. My mom was getting me the perfect Christmas present! What could it be? In the back of my mind I thought, *A script! She has a screenplay with parts for both of us. We're going to act together!*

No, I couldn't think about that. It was probably a beautiful piece of jewelry, or a first edition of a book, or something like that. Whatever it was, I would absolutely love it.

On Christmas Day, Mom was at our doorstep—and with her was a tall, thin gentleman with a goatee. "Sachi, this is Casper DeVries."

The gentleman nodded. "Hello," he said in a vaguely European voice.

"He's your Christmas present," Mom said, bursting with glee. "Merry Christmas!" She gave me a big hug.

"Merry Christmas," I replied with a little bit of confusion, then lowered my voice to ask, "He's my present?"

Mom nodded eagerly. "He's going to read you!"

I didn't get it. "What do you mean?"

A trace of exasperation flitted across her face. "*Casper DeVries.* The world-famous psychic. He has a TV show."

Mr. DeVries leaned in. "I have several TV shows."

This was quite true. Casper DeVries had a cable show called *Reaching Out*, where he reconnected people with their dead relatives, and he'd done a couple of miniseries about life on the Other Side. He was also a consultant on a network show about psychic mediums. Mom couldn't have found a more perfect soul mate if she'd robbed a grave.

I still didn't get it. I took Mom aside. "So this is the big present? He's going to read me?"

"He's going to tell you *everything.*"

I wasn't sure I wanted to be told everything, especially on Christmas Day, but when I thought about it, I decided it *was* the perfect present, coming from Mom. It was certainly personal.

We had time before dinner, so we all repaired to the living room—me, Frank, Mom, the kids—and sat in a semicircle. Mr. DeVries was in a chair with his back to the fire, which imparted to him a mystical orange aura. He started going into a trance.

His eyes were closed, his hands gripped the arms of the chair, and he made odd guttural sounds, as if speaking in tongues.

"*Aghhh . . . Ooo . . . Ogggh . . . Uuuu . . .*"

We waited patiently for a spirit to grab him. Eventually he

threw his head back and began channeling someone. His voice dropped a few octaves.

"*Uggh . . . Aaaagghh . . .*"

"Who are you?" Mom asked boldly.

"*Obadiah,*" he answered. Or somebody answered.

Ah. Mom nodded with familiarity. Obadiah was the spirit of a former slave; he had visited her many times before, with the help of various channelers.

I remember one time encountering Obadiah myself. Kevin Ryerson, another well-known psychic, used to channel him a lot. Ryerson was big on trance-channeling, and he was apparently the one who first informed Mom about her past life in Atlantis and so forth. The scene is re-created by the two of them in the movie version of *Out on a Limb.*

That episode goes back to when I was still with David. We were over at the Malibu house with Ryerson and my mom, and they were having a channeling session. Ryerson went into a trance, and "Obadiah" started speaking through him. I don't remember what came out during the channeling, but I recall that Mom had lost her gold watch with a diamond-encrusted rim and she mentioned it during the session. She had searched all over the house and just couldn't find it. She kept rubbing her wrist throughout the session, lamenting her loss.

"*That's too bad,*" Obadiah said. "*We'll have to do something about that.*" I remember thinking it funny that somebody who'd suffered through the horrors of slavery would give a hoot in hell about a missing gold watch.

After the session was over, I was in the kitchen making dinner; David was with me. Mom was out taking a walk on the beach.

Out of the corner of my eye, I saw Kevin Ryerson step into the kitchen and hover by the doorway. He reached into his pocket and very discreetly (but not discreetly enough) took out the diamond-encrusted gold watch, put it on the kitchen counter, and then stealthily withdrew before anyone could see him.

I saw him, though, and David saw him.

We both gathered over the watch and stared at it. What should we do? Should we bust Ryerson? Tell Mom the truth? Would she believe us? Probably not. She was so invested in her beliefs, and they made her so happy, that we made an agreement not to say a word. Why dash her dreams?

When Mom came back and walked into the kitchen, she screamed, "Oh my God! There it is! My watch! He found it for me! Thank you, Obadiah!"

All I could think was, *Oh, Mom. You're such a little kid sometimes.*

I was not as susceptible. I had seen the man behind the curtain too many times, and that's why I greeted Obadiah's emergence now in my living room with a healthy degree of skepticism.

DeVries was now completely in the grip of his visiting spirit. Mom, an old hand at these channeling sessions, took the reins. "Who's with you, Obadiah?"

"*Steve is here . . .*"

Mom looked at me, and mouthed "your father," which I'd already deduced. Who else but Dad would be showing up in my living room?

"Does he have a message for us?"

"*He wants you to know that he loves you, and he apologizes.*"

"Anything else?"

"*He wants to thank you for hanging his picture in the bedroom . . .*"

I was startled by that one. It was true—a photo of Dad was hanging in an upstairs bedroom. How could DeVries or Obadiah have known that? I looked over at Mom, who nodded sagely.

Mom started asking the spirit some searching questions about the nature of the universe, and her place in it:

"What is the path for me?" she asked with deep earnestness.

"*You are an explorer . . . You are a star voyager . . . Many will scorn you, but you must be strong and follow your vision wheresoever it may lead.*"

Dad's language had taken on a very biblical syntax. Or maybe it wasn't Dad anymore. Obadiah indicated that someone else was present, an elderly woman. "It must be your grandmother," Mom said.

Whoever it was, I was getting antsy. This was supposed to be *my* present. "Can I ask something, please?" Mom shrugged and, with a roll of her eyes, sat back. By this time I had completely bought in to the Other Side, and I was itching to ask my big question.

"What's going to happen with my career? Will I ever make it as an actress?"

DeVries rocked back and forth, and started shaking, as he received the message. "Mmm . . . Ahhhmmm . . . *Mustn't ride on mother's coattails, must we?*"

"Huh?"

"Mmmm . . . Ahhhh. . . . *Acting classes are in order . . .*"

Acting classes? I looked over at my mother. Now she was slumped in the corner of the couch, watching like a spider, and emanating evil energy.

But back to DeVries: he was trembling, getting excited. A great vision was coming to him: "*Yes, I see . . . Sharp objects . . . Knives! Pots! Copper pots! . . . Cooking! A COOKING SHOW!*"

A cooking show. I should be doing a cooking show. That was the message that Grandma was sending from the dead.

I couldn't look at Mom now, or anyone. I felt something very hot spreading in the pit of my stomach, then rising very quickly through my various internal organs, up, up, until it was scorching my cheeks. It was as if my head had been dipped in acid.

I was so pissed off. I realized that Mom had set this whole phony business up. Why? Maybe because she was afraid I would start acting again, and she was going to dissuade me through any means, normal or paranormal.

I also realized that if I didn't leave the room immediately, my head was going to explode. I rushed into the kitchen and promptly dissolved into a hysterical mess.

They could hear me sobbing from the living room. Frank suggested to Mom that maybe she should go in and see how I was.

Mom waved him off. "Ahh, she'll be fine."

Instead, Mr. DeVries, who had emerged from his "trance," came into the kitchen to comfort me. A mistake on his part.

"You lying son-of-a-bitch!" I screamed at him. "You know not a word of that was true! Cooking show, my ass! You're nothing but a fucking phony!"

"Sachi, listen to me, please," he said, trying to quiet me. "I really *am* a psychic—"

"Ha!"

"—and I know that you're a fine actress."

"Right."

"In fact, I see you winning an Academy Award someday."

"Really?" He was starting to win me back.

"But your mother made me tell that story."

"She *made* you?"

He shrugged. "It's what she wanted. I couldn't say no."

I discovered later that Mom and DeVries had been staying—in separate rooms—the last few days at the Homestead Inn, where she would have had plenty of time to feed him his lines, and tell him all about Dad and cooking and that fucking Obadiah.

It took me a while, but I managed to pull myself together. We still had to get through Christmas dinner, after all. I went back to the living room, full of false cheer, as merry as any elf. Mom, who'd gone to such great lengths to puncture my ego, would have none of it; she took me aside: "Look, I can tell you're upset. You should be. Mediocrity is not an easy thing to accept."

"I'm not upset," I told her. "Because he's wrong, that's all. Even the best psychics can be wrong."

"He's wrong? Oh, really? He has a TV show, and he's wrong?" Mom was furious. She couldn't stand that I wasn't buying into her bullshit. She'd really wanted to put the last nail in the coffin of my acting aspirations, and her plan had been a big fat flop.

Dinner was very forced. I wanted to feed them both and get them out of my house as soon as possible, so I pulled the meal to-gether in record time—and it was, by the way, fabulous; I really was a good cook. Grandma'd got that right. The crosscurrents of tension at the table were excruciating. I was on to Mom, and she knew I was on to her. Meanwhile, DeVries was nervous that I would tell Mom what he'd told me. We ate in nerve-racking silence. Then they left. I was never so happy to see my mother make an exit in my life.

Unfortunately, we'd made a plan to have breakfast at the house the next day, before they flew back. After the channeling fiasco, I assumed they would pass on that invitation. But no, the next morning Mom and DeVries were both at the door, waiting to be fed. I couldn't bear to look at them. "I don't have time to make breakfast this morning," I told them. "Sorry."

Mom looked a little stunned. I think it was the first time in my life I'd ever been cold to her. I didn't even want her to hug me. We said a very icy goodbye.

THE deep freeze was on for about a month. Then, one day in early 2006, out of the blue, Mom called. "Sach, I have some exciting news. Are you sitting down?"

"Yeah." I was not sitting down. I couldn't imagine what news she could have that required my sitting down for, unless she was going to tell me that Paul had finally returned from the Pleiades.

"I'm doing a new movie up in Canada. It's called *Closing the Ring*."

"Good for you," I said flatly. So nice to hear that her career was moving right along.

Mom didn't pick up on my sarcasm or chose to ignore it, because she went on brightly: "And there's a role for you! You're playing my daughter. Is that perfect casting or what?"

My ears pricked up. Wait a minute—a role for me? What was she talking about? Now I sat down. "I'm playing your daughter? You mean, I already have the part?"

Mom laughed. "Of course not. You have to audition, like anyone else. But do a good job, and I'm sure Dickie will take our long-standing friendship under consideration."

"Dickie?"

"Lord Attenborough."

My heart leapt. "I'm auditioning for Richard Attenborough?" This was developing into something serious. It had been a long time since *The Bliss of Mrs. Blossom*, and now of course Lord Attenborough was an Oscar-winning director and a major producer, but if he still remembered me as little "Poppy," there was a better-than-even chance I could get this part.

It seemed too good to be true, and that's why I became suspicious. "Why?"

"What do you mean, 'why'? Why not? You want to be an actress, don't you?" Still, even Mom could sense there was a hollowness to this argument. The question I was asking was, why *now*, after all these years?

"Look," Mom said with a sigh, "it's very simple: I want to help you out. I want to make things right. Other mothers help their daughters, why shouldn't I?" Before I could answer this, she moved on. "They're going to fly you up to Toronto this weekend to do a screen test. Can you make it?"

I was still a little befuddled. "Sure, I guess . . . I'm just . . . surprised."

"Well, don't be surprised. You're a talented actress; you deserve a break."

I started to choke up. "Mom—thank you. I promise you, I'll do whatever I can to make you look good. I'll be totally prepared. I'll give it everything I've got. You're taking a big risk, but I'm going to make it work!"

Mom tried to put it in perspective. "Well, remember, they're looking for a twenty-six-year-old, and a name, so don't get your hopes up."

I was fifty years old and no name at all, but that didn't stop me. "I don't care," I said. "Even if I don't get the part, I'm just happy that this is bringing us back together. It means so much on a personal level. This makes up for everything."

Some of this was pure actor-speak. Of course I *did* care; I desperately wanted the part. Finally, a chance to act with my mother, in a big film, with a famous director—it was a dream setup, and I couldn't let it slip away.

The script was sent to me, and it was indeed a terrific role.

Mom and I would have some great scenes together. I wanted this part, and I was going to get it. I studied and studied, and sent on my head shot and my reel. That weekend, I flew up to Toronto and met with Lord Attenborough. "Poppy!" he greeted me in his charming English voice. He was still a delightful man, and I could see that his affection for me was still strong.

My confidence was high as I did the screen test. The makeup artist did some work on my eyes to make me look young, and she had me put a scarf around my neck to hide some wrinkles—I was supposed to be twenty-six, after all.

The test went beautifully. I really nailed it. There are times when you just know. Everyone was buzzing with compliments. When I got back to Connecticut, there was a personal message on my voice mail: "Oh, Poppy, you did a marvelous job on the screen test. You'll be wonderful as Marie."

So there it was! I had the part! Now, admittedly there was one little snag to be worked out with immigration: according to Canadian work rules, the film could hire only a certain number of American actors, and it had already reached its quota; Mom was taking up the last spot. We'd have to find a way to skirt the rules before they could officially offer me the role, but that wouldn't be a problem—not with Shirley MacLaine and Lord Richard Attenborough on the case.

With the shoot coming up, I realized I'd better get my eyes done. I couldn't count on the makeup people to help me every day. I flew out to L.A. and was treated by the same doctor who'd done my breasts, Dr. Norman Leaf. Dr. Leaf was a plastic surgeon to the stars, he did great work, and he was a genuinely nice man.

After the surgery, I went to Dr. Leaf's recuperation facility. There were all kinds of well-preserved women and men milling about with small bandages on their noses, their chins, their you-name-its. Quite a few of them were celebrities: no big stars, but lots of solid middle-ground performers trying to hold the line against time.

Mom came to visit while I was there. She brought me a nice sweatsuit. I couldn't actually see it; I had to keep my eyes closed. My head was reclined, and I held ice on my eyelids as we chatted. We talked a bit about the film. I told her how excited I was.

"Tell me, Sachi," she said thoughtfully. "What if you don't get the part? What are you going to do?"

"I *am* going to get it, Mom. You know that."

"But what if you don't? What are you going to do?"

"Don't worry, Mom. The part is mine."

We talked a bit more, and then Mom asked me again, "But what if you don't get the part? What if something goes wrong? What are you going to do?" She must have asked me that five separate times. I didn't know what she was so worried about. I already had the part.

My eyes took only two weeks to heal, and I looked great. I was all set for Canada!

But not so fast. Someone was still making a stink about immigration. Too many Americans in the movie! Mom said not to worry; she was calling all her bigwig friends. Lord Attenborough even rang up Tony Blair a couple of times. The wheels were in motion.

Plus, Mom had a nuclear option up her sleeve: "I know. I'll become a Canadian citizen. My mother was Canadian. And then you can take my spot."

I didn't like that idea. "I don't want you to change your citizenship for me."

Mom accepted my objection pretty easily. "Well, don't say I didn't offer."

More time went by, and we didn't seem to be making any progress on the immigration front. So Frank got in touch with his good friend Ed Cox, the son-in-law of Richard Nixon. Ed had connections with the Canadian government, and he was happy to help out. He didn't seem to think it was a problem at all. "Don't worry," he told Frank. "This is a walk in the park, we'll get her in."

Frank called Mom to give her the good news. I was in the room with him when he called her, and I could hear Mom's animated reaction through the receiver. "How dare you go over my head?" she was shouting. "Stay the fuck out of this! Leave well enough alone! I'm handling it! It's being handled!"

Frank hung up and looked at me bewildered. What was *that* all about?

So he told Ed Cox to back off; it was being handled.

The production start date drew closer and closer, and I was still waiting in Connecticut. A marvelous cast had been assembled: Christopher Plummer, Mischa Barton, Pete Postlethwaite, Brenda Fricker, and Mom. I was champing at the bit to get started. What was taking so long?

Finally I called Jack Gilardi, Mom's agent at ICM. "Have you heard anything about *Closing the Ring*? Did they clear things up yet?"

"Oh yeah. They went with somebody else," he said matter-of-factly.

"*What?* Somebody *else*?"

"Yeah. What's her name? Neve Campbell."

"Neve Campbell? Neve Campbell is playing Marie? When did this happen?"

"About two weeks ago."

Two weeks ago? Why didn't anyone tell me? What the hell was going on? "But—what happened? I thought Mom was handling it."

"Well . . ." I could almost hear him shrugging with indifference.

"But I had the role. It was mine."

"I guess you didn't." He could not have been more dismissive. Of course, Jack was Mom's agent, not mine. I knew he didn't really give a shit about me, but he didn't need to make it so obvious.

I called Mom right away. "Did you know that I didn't get the part? They cast Neve Campbell instead?"

"Oh, yes. I heard that. She's Canadian, you know. It made things much easier."

"Why didn't you tell me?"

Mom paused. "Well, you know how it is. Nobody wants to give bad news in Hollywood."

"You're not Hollywood. You're my mom!"

"Well, look, at least you know I tried," she said defensively. "I really did." That was true, and that was the important thing, really.

"And don't worry, sweetheart," she promised, "next time we'll find a project for the two of us, in *America*, and *we'll* be in charge. Nothing will go wrong."

I also got a call from Lord Attenborough, who apologized profusely for the way things had turned out. "So sorry, Poppy. I did everything I could. It breaks my heart. *Closing the Ring* just won't be the same without you."

They made it without me anyway. It was not a great movie, and it went straight to video—but that was small consolation.

I called Mom during the shoot. I'd become so invested in the movie, I had to hear how it was going, even though I knew it would only make me feel terrible.

"Oh, it's going *so* well, sweetheart," Mom enthused. "It's wonderful being up here with Dickie. Christopher Plummer is so good. And Neve Campbell is fine. But you know," she added ruefully, "she's not you. She's not you."

Chapter 17

Don't Take It Personally

Christmas of 2006—the Christmas after Mr. DeVries graced our Greenwich home with his party tricks—Mom invited us to spend the holiday with her in Santa Fe. "Hey, Sach, why don't you come to the ranch for Christmas? The kids can go skiing. I'll stock up on food, it'll be a blast!"

I should have been wary from the get-go—her unwarranted optimism almost begged for disaster—but I was actually kind of excited. We landed in Albuquerque, full of good cheer, and piled into the rental car for the hour drive to Santa Fe. Just as we got on the highway, it started snowing—and snowing. Before long, we found ourselves in white-out conditions. Frank could barely see where he was driving. The road itself had become just a rumor. There were accidents everywhere, and countless cars had slid off the highway and into the side trenches. Five tense, white-knuckle hours later, we still hadn't reached Santa Fe. This was not a good omen.

I kept in touch with Mom on the cell phone, trying to convey the treacherousness of the driving conditions to her, but for some reason, she couldn't conceptualize our plight. She was just pissed off that we were late.

"Where *are* you?" she yelled. "What are you *doing*?"

"We're stuck on Twenty-five."

"That's ridiculous. It doesn't take more than an hour to get here. Doesn't Frank know how to *drive*?"

"It's snowing, Mom!"

"I know it's snowing! I have *eyes*. I can *see*! But the main roads are always clear."

"But they're not!"

"Well, they *should* be!"

I called her every fifteen minutes or so, and every time, she gave me grief. Now it was getting dark, and the kids were starving. I told Mom that we were going to stop at a diner.

"No, don't stop!" she shrieked. "I already made a great dinner. Just get here!"

We plowed on to Santa Fe. Once we got off the highway, the conditions got worse. We had no idea where we were going. The roads were covered, there were no street signs visible, we were going completely on instinct and my mother's long-distance imitation of an hysterical GPS:

"Take the next right turn!"

"But there is no right turn—"

"Just take it!"

To give Mom the benefit of the doubt, I knew that she was nervous and worried for us. Crankiness and impatience were her default modes when she was under stress. She was not calm in the face of adversity, especially when she was helpless to do anything about it. So this was her way of showing that she cared. Of course, that was small consolation to me when she was screaming in my ear while, all around me, the world was being sucked into a white black hole.

Finally we started down the long downhill road to her ranch. As we descended through the snow, we wondered if we would ever be able to get back up that hill again, but we didn't care. Exhausted, we staggered to the front door, where Mom was waiting with a big, incongruous smile, as if all her hyperventilating over the phone had been part of a past life: "Hi! How are you! Come inside, it's so great to see you! Hi, kids!" She was suddenly the dream grandmother.

Starving, we headed straight to the dining room, eager to dig in to the great dinner she had promised. But there was no great dinner. There was bean soup.

I took Mom aside. "Bean soup? Is that all you have?"

"I made a huge pot."

"The kids aren't going to eat bean soup," I told her. They were still in the pizza, chicken nugget, mac-and-cheese phase of their culinary development. "Do you have anything else?"

She gave me an unflinching stare. "I have bean soup."

We sat at the table, and Mom ladled a skimpy spoonful of soup into each large bowl. The tiny portion settled at the base of the bowl in a shallow puddle. Frank and I stared down at our soup in dismay, like a couple of Dickensian orphans.

"Mom, could we have a little more?"

"No," she answered peremptorily.

"No?"

"We have to ration. I heard on the news, it's going to be a bad storm."

The snow kept falling through the night, and the house was all done up for Christmas, so we relaxed into a festive holiday mood. Mom had a stack of Academy screeners, all DVDs of current-release films. We settled back on the couch and watched *Charlotte's Web* and *Happy Feet*.

The next morning, we woke up to an arctic wonderland. The snow was still falling steadily, the landscape was a pure, endless desert of white. A sense of magic filled the air.

While we didn't know it, this was the high point of our holiday. The warm, cozy family feeling was brief and evanescent. As the day wore on, and the snow kept falling, we started coming to grips with a grim truth: we were not leaving this house anytime soon.

This wouldn't have been so bad if Mom's four-hour grace period of charming hospitality hadn't long since expired. She was tired of us already, and she wasn't shy about letting us know it. She was all Mrs. Hyde from here on in, and we couldn't escape her.

Also, the rationing continued. Mom had gotten it into her head that the food would run out soon if we didn't take Draconian measures. "We're all going to have to make sacrifices if we want to survive the week. So kids, one slice of bread each. That's going to have to hold you until dinner."

It was absurd, because there was plenty of food in the house—the pantry was stocked to the ceiling—but Mom had shifted into survival mode, and she took it very, very seriously.

By the end of the day we were all starving again. To make matters worse, she had nothing in the house that children might like to eat. There was no cheese, or frozen pizza, or pasta. There wasn't even any milk. She did have ice cream, the family weakness, but even that she parceled out stingily: "One scoop!"

There was plenty of "adult" nourishment at hand, though,

particularly of the alcoholic variety. While the food was out of bounds, it was perfectly okay to dip into the liquor supply. From the first night on, Mom was mixing eggnog like a demon, with very little egg and great sloshes of rum. Little food, lots of booze—a deadly combination.

That night Mom put another one of her Academy screeners into the DVD player: Mel Gibson's *Apocalypto*. I was a little concerned. "Mom, do you think this is appropriate for children? I heard it was pretty violent." Mom was dismissive: "Oh please. It's fine."

We gathered in the living room and watched as the ancient Mayans beheaded one another, conducted human sacrifices, cut out still-beating hearts, and practiced two hours' worth of bloodthirsty mayhem. Frank and Frankie, being manly men, enjoyed all the savagery. Arin, seven years old, sat through it politely, although she buried her head in my lap most of the time. When it was over, she enthused, "That was great, Ganny!" She had terrible nightmares all night.

The next day, the snow finally stopped coming down, but we were buried under three-plus feet of it. The incredibly long driveway would be impossible to shovel. Frank wanted to call in a plow to clear it. Suppose there was an emergency, and we had to get the kids to the hospital?

Mom just laughed. "They're not going to come out here to clear our driveway. Don't you think they have better things to do? Look at him, he's so worried about the kids, he's such a big dad. Ooh, what do you think is gonna happen?" she teased, her voice dripping with sarcasm. "The kids'll be fine."

I think the combination of the lethal drinks, the lack of food, and the hopelessness of the situation was responsible for my disastrous swerve into drunken sentimentality. We had just watched a screener of *The Departed*, the kids were in bed having sweet dreams of Mob violence, and Mom and I were both staring numbly at the fire.

"You know, Mom," I said, "I wish I knew you better."

She groaned. "Don't start that again."

"It's true. I don't feel close to you. And we *should* be close. You need someone you can trust."

"I work in Los Angeles. I don't trust anyone."

"I don't blame you for keeping everybody at a distance. You've been wounded in life. I know how tough your childhood must have been . . ."

I had inadvertently tripped a land mine. Mom exploded. "You have no fucking idea about my childhood! And don't ever assume that you do! My childhood is mine. I lived through it, not you! And I don't want to hear about it ever again!"

I waited for the dust to settle before I continued. "I'm sorry. I just want to know you. You're my mom, and I don't know you at all. And you don't know me."

"You're my daughter. What else do I need to know?"

"Exactly—you think I'm nothing. You spend your whole life reaching out everywhere, into the past, into the future, into the farthest reaches of the fucking universe, but you never reach out to me. Why? Why can't we be closer? Why do you have to live so far away from us?"

"Because this is my home. I love it here. Nobody bothers me." She added pointedly: "Except on holidays."

"But think, if you moved to Greenwich, I could see you all the time, and you could be a real grandmother to the kids. You can join my workshop, and then we can go together every week and work on scenes, and act together."

"Sounds thrilling," she dead-panned.

"But wouldn't it be great?"

"No," she said, leveling a cold eye at me. "No." Discussion over.

The driveway was finally cleared, but we still had two days left before our flight home. That was two days too many for me. I got on the phone and desperately tried to find an earlier flight. My mantra was "Forget the cost; just get me out of here!" Unfortunately, everything was booked. We would have to wait it out till the bitter end.

The night before we were going home, I said to Mom, "See you in the morning." She gave me a noncommittal look and went to bed. Now, we had to leave at 6:00 A.M. to catch our flight, and I knew Mom was a late sleeper, so in a way, this was a test. If she set her alarm clock and woke up early to see us off, I'd know that she really cared about us. Everything would be back to normal; all would be well.

I waited by the door until 6:15. I stalled, pretended I'd forgotten my comb, had to use the bathroom. I gave her every opportunity. No Mom. She was sleeping in.

We piled into the rental car and drove away. It recalled to me the time Mom came down to San Diego and rescued me from Dr. Jeffrey, and how she and I roared off in a cloud of dust, leaving the horror behind and looking forward to a new life. We couldn't peel out on this icy driveway, but the mood was similar, except now I was escaping her.

We landed in Hartford, and on the drive back to Greenwich, I remember saying to Frank, with an eerie, self-possessed calm, "That's it. It's over. I will never visit her again. Never, never, never."

After a quiet moment, he asked, "Never?"

"Never."

· · ·

THE Witch of the West Is Dead has nothing to do with *The Wizard of Oz*. It's the title of a popular Japanese children's novel, written by Kaho Nashiki, a quiet, meditative tale about a teenage girl who goes off to the country one summer to live with her seventy-five-year-old grandmother. They were planning to make the film version in Japan, and the filmmakers were after my mother to play "Granny"—the British-born character who speaks Japanese—but Mom wasn't interested.

When she mentioned the part to me in December of 2006 (just before our Santa Fe Christmas), I was definitely interested. Hell, if she wasn't going to take it, I would! So I got in touch with the casting director and flew out to Los Angeles to audition for the producers and the director, Shunichi Nagasaki. Leaving nothing to chance, I walked into the room dressed as "Granny," wearing a white wig and an old dress. I did the audition, and they took me out afterward to wine and dine me.

A month later they called from Tokyo to offer me the role.

Shooting of *The Witch of the West Is Dead* started in spring of 2007, in a village called Kiyosato, high up in the Japan Alps. The company stayed at a rustic lodge located on the site of a natural hot spring. Every morning, I would wake up and bathe in the *rotenburo*, the open-air hot spring bath. The powerful rotten-egg smell of sulfur would fill the air, but the steaming water would loosen up my muscles and get me ready for the day.

The set was down the street, on the other side of a forest patch. Most of the crew would take a shuttle down to the set, but I liked to walk through the forest, wearing the grandmother's outfit; it helped me get into character, much as I had walked the length of Inishmaan to prepare for *Riders to the Sea*. The grandmother was a tough role to get a handle on at first, until one day, when I found leather laces for her boots, and that's the moment I suddenly knew who she was.

The days on the shoot were long and unrelenting. The director, I discovered, was not only king in Japan; he was dictator. Mr. Nagasaki's decisions were unilateral, and they were final. He did not have time for questions or discussions. If he didn't like a take, he would say, "One more time," but he wouldn't give a reason why.

I would ask, "What was wrong? You didn't like what I did? Should I try something else?"

He would reply, "One more time."

So I would do another take, in a totally different way, and he would say, "One more time." And so it went. Since there were no unions, we would work twelve- to fourteen-hour days in the freezing Alps. Sometimes we'd go to 3:00 A.M., and then have to get up three hours later for the next day's shoot.

After a long day on the set we would all go back to the lodge and relax in the *rotenburo*, the hot spring bath—all of us, actors, producers, crew. Drinking sake, discussing the shoot—all completely naked. For me this was just a little weird. I was used to communal bathing since childhood, and there was obviously nothing sexual going on; we were all soaking our muscles and relaxing in an atmosphere of complete professionalism. Still, to see the producers and the director, our symbols of total authority, climbing naked into the bath with us was an image difficult to reconcile with our daytime reality. Like mollusks, they had ventured out of their hard shells and exposed their soft, fleshy bodies to the night air. Tomorrow they would be armored and imperious again.

My trials on the set went on for two weeks. Then something very interesting happened: Nagasaki and I connected. I don't know how or why, but it was like telepathy; I became one with him, and I knew exactly what he was thinking. I never had to ask him what he wanted in a scene; it was already clear to me. After that, filming became a breeze: everything was done in one take, and the shooting schedule was cut in half.

Something else happened that made the shooting of *The Witch of the West Is Dead* a truly transformative experience for me. I became reacquainted with *natto*. *Natto* is a Japanese dish consisting of fermented soybeans. You eat it with steamed rice, a raw egg on top, and chopped-up seaweed and scallions. Mix it up in a bowl, bring the bowl to your mouth, and slurp it up. It's fantastic. One of my favorite foods.

I could never have eaten *natto* in Connecticut because the preparation of it would have stunk up the house for days afterward. My family would have been so nauseated, it would have made them throw up. So they refused to let me make it. It *is* a nasty smell, but I grew up with it, so I love it.

They served it three times a day on the *Witch* set. I was in heaven.

However, there were unintended consequences. My body had grown unaccustomed to a constant diet of fermented beans and I started collecting an excess of gas, and I had to get rid of it through the only avenue open to me.

Now, I should acknowledge here that as the only American in the cast, and the daughter of a famous star, there was an unspoken tension between me and the rest of the crew. The actors were naturally suspicious of me, figuring me for a spoiled Hollywood brat, and many of them gave me the cold shoulder. Plus, I knew the director and the producers had really wanted my mother for the role.

So I had something to prove. I tried to be as friendly and

down-to-earth as possible. I always ate with everyone else at the long mess hall tables, and took whatever the cook served up. The teenage actress who played my granddaughter, Mayu Takahashi, was already well known in Japan, and she had a separate dining space, surrounded by bodyguards. I think everyone expected the same of me, but I knew that this was a trap. I wanted them to think of me as one of the guys.

That's where the *natto* came in. The bean gas was constantly building up in my intestines, to the point where my stomach was hurting from the pressure, but I refused to be impolite on the set. I didn't want to be considered a truly ugly American. So I would hold myself together for one take, and then excuse myself. I'd head out into the forest, and when I was safely alone, I'd let it rip. And it was, take my word for it, thunderous. The birds would scatter. Then I'd go back to the set for another take, and more often than not, the gas well would refill—it was like my intestines were hooked up to a bicycle pump—and I'd have to excuse myself again. It was cold up in those mountains, so each time, I would have to put on my jacket and boots just to fart.

For some reason I never made the connection between the beans and the gas. I thought my gas had something to do with the altitude, or the stress of performing. Besides, I found the *natto* comforting, so I kept eating it like crazy—and kept producing incredible, otherworldly gas. It reminded me of Mr. Gerard of Charter Towers and his propulsive farting. I just couldn't stop.

Finally, I got tired of hiding it. I could barely focus on my role with my concentration divided between mind and body, so after two weeks of stealth bombing, I said, "To hell with politeness," and let go with a blast in front of everyone. "Excuse me," I said, both sheepish and defiant.

Well, talk about an icebreaker. Everyone laughed, and a sense of relaxation flooded the set. They were charmed and delighted by my evident humanity. "So that's what you've been doing all this time!" Nobody had the slightest clue of what I'd been up to in the forest.

Except the sound man. "Don't worry," he said to me quietly on the side, "I've already heard everything." It seems that whenever I went out in the woods to fart, I'd forgotten to turn off my body mike. So he had been privy to every rude combustible sound. More than that, I would usually accompany my farts with a heartfelt commentary, often groaning in English, "Fu-u-u-u-ck!" Then, after I was spent, I would say, "Oh, yeah!" The poor guy had been listening to my gastrointestinal struggles for the past two weeks. "Why didn't you tell me?" I asked him. He shrugged. Wouldn't have been polite.

Anyway, now that I was letting my wind go free, it endeared me to everyone. I was clearly no diva; you couldn't get any more down-to-earth than this. I became known on the set as "The Farting Grandmother." There was one very sweet scene I had with Mayu as the teenage girl; we were both in bed sharing a tender moment. After every take, I would lift up the bedcovers and let one go—then go back to being sweet again. I remember one of the producers thoughtfully suggesting, "Let's just get some gaffer's tape and stick it across her butthole."

In addition to providing an endless source of amusement, my indisposition gave everyone else permission to fart, too. It became a very friendly, collegial atmosphere on that set.

One day, I finally figured out that it was the *natto*. As soon as I stopped eating it, the gas receded, and I could lead a normal life again. Still, I'd made an indelible mark on my colleagues; right to the end of the shoot, I would get the same laughing refrain at mealtime: "No more *natto*!"

The Witch of the West Is Dead was a huge box-office hit in Japan, and went on to win scads of awards. Beyond that, it was a revelatory experience for me. I was deeply proud of my work on that film, and working in Japan gave me my first opportunity as an adult to explore my roots, and gain an awareness of where I'd come from. I'd never realized how deeply the Japanese culture, the syntax of humility and denial and stoic acceptance, had become a part of my DNA, and informed my every thought and action, for both good and ill. Being there again, as an adult, made me understand who I was. I had come full circle to the world of my childhood, and found myself still there.

IN the fall of 2007, Dale Olson called from L.A. He was going to be passing through New York in about a week and wanted to meet with me. Dale Olson was one of the most famous publicists in Hollywood. Before he passed away in August 2012, he represented the likes of Clint Eastwood, Steven Spielberg, Rock Hudson, Marilyn Monroe, Gene Kelly, Joan Crawford—and Shirley MacLaine. He knew where all the bodies were buried in Tinseltown, but he wasn't one for spilling confidences and spreading gossip. He was considered by all a class act.

Dale had recently had a falling-out with my mother, which was hardly unusual. Mom was not an easy friend to maintain. She was always having little snits and kerfuffles with her buddies and business partners. I assumed that Dale wanted a sympathetic ear for his side of the story.

I had known Dale since I was a kid. He always had a smiling face and a lot of positive energy. He was an amazing cook—I especially loved his cauliflower dish, which was simply the best in the world. I always felt safe around Dale, because he made me feel that I mattered. His partner, Gene, and I also had a very special relationship, so I was really looking forward to seeing them both, and I couldn't wait for them to meet my kids.

He and Gene arrived at the house in time for lunch. I made a nice meal, and we all sat out on the patio catching up on old times, with Frank and the kids joining us. I told Dale about the Japan shoot, and how great it had gone. He seemed thrilled for me.

At some point I mentioned how disappointed I was about not getting to act with Mom in *Closing the Ring*. I told him about the Canadian immigration policy, how a new law had recently been passed limiting the number of Americans in the cast, and how Mom had done everything she could short of switching her citizenship, to no avail.

Dale was quiet a moment. "Well, that's what I wanted to talk to you about," he finally said. "It wasn't Immigration."

"What?"

"It wasn't Immigration that stopped you from doing that movie. You could have gotten around that problem easily enough."

"What do you mean?" I knew what he meant the moment he said it, but I convinced myself that I didn't.

"It was your mother."

I felt the ground drop away. "What do you mean?" I repeated.

"Your mother didn't want you to do the movie," Dale replied flatly. "She sabotaged you."

"What?" I immediately shifted into denial. "That's not true."

"It is true."

"It's *not*. You don't know."

"Yes, I *do* know." And of course he did. Dale was in a position to know.

"But . . ." It was a panic moment. I raced back through my memory, trying to retrieve any bit of evidence that might disprove

Dale's accusation. "No," I countered, "that doesn't make sense. She's the one who got me the audition in the first place. It was her idea."

"She got you the audition because she never thought you would get the part." He spoke evenly, laying out the information with a dry matter-of-factness. "You were almost fifty, Sachi. Why would they have let you play her daughter?"

"But I *am* her daughter."

Dale shook his head. "Not on film. She wanted someone else."

My heart started pounding. Frankie and Arin were still sitting at the table, finishing their lunch. I told them to go inside and play.

I tried to think my way through this. What Dale claimed was certainly plausible, but I wasn't giving up just yet. There were too many instances of Mom being supportive of me. She loved my screen test. She was there when I got my eyes done. She was going to turn Canadian. She made all kinds of phone calls to important people. And when Frank offered to help, Mom stopped him because she was handling it—

Wait a minute.

If she was handling it, why had it fallen apart? Why did she stop Frank from helping? And why did she keep asking me, "What if you don't get the part?"

Dale could see that the truth was sinking in. "I felt so bad about that movie, Sachi. I knew how much it meant to you. It wasn't right what she did, but—that's your mother. That's what she does. Remember Marion Ross in *The Evening Star*?"

Marion Ross? I did remember. *The Evening Star*, from 1996, was the sequel to *Terms of Endearment*. Mom reprised her role as Aurora, and Marion Ross played her housekeeper, Rosie. The picture was not well received, but Marion, who had played Mrs. Cunningham on the TV series *Happy Days*, was nominated for a Golden Globe as Best Supporting Actress.

"She should have won the Academy Award," Dale observed. "She had a killer scene in that movie. Big dramatic moment, and she was spectacular. Stole the film. Everyone was buzzing about it in the early previews. No way she wouldn't have won an Oscar. No way."

"I don't remember that scene."

"You never saw it. It was cut."

"Cut? Why?" But I knew why.

"*Evening Star* was your mom's film," Dale said. "She didn't want anybody stealing her thunder. So she made them take the scene out."

No. I didn't believe that. There must have been some other reason. Good scenes get dropped from films all the time, because they're incidental, or they break up the rhythm, or the movie's just too damn long. Mom couldn't be that ruthless. Could she?

Dale shook his head ruefully. "That scene alone would have put Marion Ross on the map. She was a terrific actress who just needed a break."

Yes, a break. That's all anyone needs in this business. Mom got her own break in *The Pajama Game*, when Carol Haney went down with a broken ankle, so she of all people should have been generous in spirit to others with the same dream.

Yet Mom never considered that a break. That was karma. She deserved it.

And others didn't.

"So you're not the only one," Dale said. "It's part of the business."

I still couldn't accept it. I sat there in silence, my mind spinning.

"Shirley," he finally offered, "is a competitor. She didn't want you to get ahead of her. Plain and simple."

"But I'm her daughter. She's supposed to be proud of me."

"Your mother is unique."

I was out of words. I stared at the rest of my lunch. I wasn't going to eat it now.

"Look," Dale said, trying to put it in perspective, "she's a star. She's up there on a pedestal, and she doesn't want to get knocked off. By you, Marion Ross, anybody. That's how she plays ball. Don't take it personally."

My mind drifted back over my stillborn career. All those opportunities, those roles that didn't pan out—was it all because of her? Had she been working against me behind the scenes from the very beginning? Every time I had a good audition, I would call Mom to share the happy news. Did she then go out of her way to sabotage me? Was it like one of those fiendish Hitchcock films, where the kindly benefactor turns out to be the murderous spy?

That was just too awful. I couldn't go there. Dale had to be wrong. "Please be wrong," I begged him. "Please . . ."

FOR the next six months I was in a sort of limbo. I knew Dale's story was true, but at the same time I couldn't believe it. I couldn't stand the thought of it—and I couldn't confront Mom, because Dale had made me promise to keep quiet. He knew that Mom was sharp enough to ferret out a traitor.

As time passed, I began to doubt the story more and more. I would call Dale in L.A. every now and then: "Are you absolutely sure that happened?" He was always sure, absolutely.

I wrote my mother a letter. I didn't have the nerve or the debating skills to go head to head with her, and I wanted to make sure I expressed every raw sentiment I was feeling.

I told her that I'd found out in Toronto what had really happened on *Closing the Ring* (careful to leave Dale's name out of it).

"The talk was that *you* had nixed me doing the part, and that Immigration wasn't *that* big of an issue. You pretended to help me but behind the scenes you were sabotaging me . . . have long known that you never wanted me to be in the business. Acting is the life I have chosen, and I hoped that you would support and encourage that. As a mother myself, I can't understand how you would not want anything but the best for your child. What legacy will you leave? One of a self-centered controller of other people's destinies—or of a loving, supportive parent?" I ended on a note of reserved hope: "I don't know how we can get past all this, but I'm willing to try, if you are. I love you. Sachi."

This was too important a message to trust to the postal service, so I drove down to New York City myself. Mom was staying at a friend's Sutton Place apartment. I hand-delivered the letter to the doorman, and then drove away.

I waited nervously at home for Mom's response. What would she say? Would she deny it? Would she admit it? Would this be the final rupture, or the beginning of a new, stronger relationship between us?

None of the above. I never heard from her. She never responded to me.

But Frank, my husband, got a call from Mom a few days later. She was furious, and denied the Dale Olson version completely. She also had a new explanation for my not getting the part in *Closing the Ring*.

"She said the immigration story was a front, because she didn't want you to know the truth," said Frank. "It would have hurt your feelings."

"And so what was the truth?" I asked.

"The truth was, Lord Attenborough didn't think you were very good."

I scoffed. "That's ridiculous. He's the one who cast me! He's the one who wanted me in the film!"

Frank shrugged. "She said he's Lord Attenborough. If he'd wanted you in the film, you would have *been* in the film. She saw your screen test herself, and she didn't think you were very good, either."

I knew this was bullshit. Since when did Mom worry about protecting my feelings? Everything in Dale Olson's story rang true. And if her version were true, why didn't she tell me herself?

Still, she had managed to plant the one poisonous seed that was sure to take root in my battle-weary mind. Maybe I *wasn't* good in that screen test. Maybe I wasn't a good actress at all. And maybe that immigration story was just a smokescreen to keep me from knowing the truth.

A year earlier, when the saga was still unfolding, I'd called Jack Gilardi to find out what was happening. He was the first to suggest that my screen test had been a failure. "You know, they didn't like you at all. You weren't very good."

I thought he was nuts at the time. Everyone was raving about the screen test. I dismissed him as a cranky old agent. After the deal fell apart, though, those words came back to haunt me. Then, when we were stuck at Mom's in Santa Fe, I mentioned it to her. "You know, Jack Gilardi said my screen test for *Closing the Ring* wasn't very good."

"Really?" she said with surprise. "Well, *I* thought you were great. I was *very* impressed." Then she gave a little shrug. "But, you know, I'm your mother."

Exactly.

Chapter 18

Shut Up and Deal

When I was studying with Peggy Feury back in the 1980s, she told me I needed to write my story down. "You have to get this on paper; you have to write a book about your life. It will set you free."

I didn't really take her point at the time. What was so interesting about my life? Yes, my mother was a famous movie star; and I'd traveled the world, from Europe to Australia; and my father was possibly a clone—but it wasn't as if something had actually happened to me.

Now I understand what she meant. All my life I've been in the thrall of those nearest to me: my father, my mother, my lovers. I've lived my life trying to please them. My most intimate relationships have also been my most dysfunctional, and the one that I wanted most to work, the relationship with my mother, is the one that resisted every Sisyphean effort on my part to coax it into some semblance of normality. I did everything I could to bring Mom into my life. I bent over backward, left no stone unturned. The big Hollywood happy ending never happened.

And now that I've written this book, it probably never will.

But that's where my chance for liberation comes in. All this time, in the vain hope of gaining my mother's approval and her love, I've cautiously kept my secrets, my doubts, and my pain to myself. I've held back from expressing my true self, because I was afraid if I went public with my story, Mom might never talk to me again.

But she doesn't really talk to me now, so what do I have to lose? Did she lose by writing her many books, by revealing her unconventional beliefs and promoting her quests for enlighten-ment? She may have left herself open to ridicule, but she also es-tablished, for all to see, the rules by which she lived her life. She made a statement, and it was a strong, independent one.

Maybe she'll see my choice that way. Maybe she'll admire my forthrightness and my determination to own and control my own life. Maybe she'll recognize me as my mother's daughter.

I'm kidding myself, of course. It's so easy to live your life in denial, to ignore those things you know to be true. I did it for too many years, and I fully recognize my own failing there.

Even Mom, who considers herself a clear-eyed truth-teller, will fall back on her defense mechanisms when something threat-ens her sense of self.

She called me a few years ago, when we were going through one of our friendlier phases: "Hey, Sach, you know who I saw today? Steve the Clone."

"Who?"

"Steve the Clone. He was in the Valley, buying coffee."

I had to take a moment to decide if she was serious or not. I decided she was. She'd dismissed the real story about Dad's swindle and gone back to the romantic one she preferred. "Mom, you know that's not possible. Dad's dead."

"Your *father* is dead. Paul—yes. I'm talking about Steve. He was in the Valley."

"But there is no Steve. I mean, there *is* a Steve; there *was*. But there's no Paul. Remember, we talked about all this? None of it's true. None of it happened."

I could hear Mom smiling at me. "Oh, honey, you're so naïve. You don't know what's out there. You just don't know."

Maybe she's right. Case in point: the Mystery of the Missing Blood Type.

Among her other quirks, Mom is a faddist. She's always leaping on the next new trend, and treating it like the one true path to deliverance. In the 1990s she was steered into homeopathic medicine—the cleansing diets, the lemon juice and cayenne pepper, the high colonics—and that became her new religion. I understood her enthusiasm, and I believe in the virtues of homeopathy, but I also believe in medicine. Sometimes you just gotta do whatever it takes.

Mom would have none of that. She was visiting us in Houston when my two-year-old son, Frankie, was sick with roseola. I was about to give him his antibiotic medicine when Mom grabbed it from my hand. "No! No more antibiotics!" She tossed the medicine in the garbage. I had to go back to the doctor and get another prescription.

Around the same time, she became obsessed with blood-type diets. The idea was that whatever blood type you had determined the kind of food you should eat. Type O blood had been handed down over the centuries from prehistoric hunters, so anyone with type O should eat a lot of red meat. Type A-positive, on the other hand, were gatherers, and they should eat vegetables and dairy.

Mom was a type O, and Dad was a type O, which meant that I had to be a type O. Therefore, meat. She gave me one of those newfangled George Foreman grills: it would be steak and burgers for me from now on. I dutifully tried the diet, and didn't lose a pound.

It was years later when I went in for a hospital procedure and discovered that I wasn't type O at all; I was type A-positive. So that's why the diet hadn't worked.

But wait a minute. If Mom was type O and Dad was type O, how could I be type A-positive? It wasn't scientifically possible. Mom must have made a mistake. Dad had to be A-positive, too.

Or was he? I seemed to recall Dad going into surgery in Hawaii, and himself mentioning that he was type O. But he could have been mistaken, and I could be misremembering.

Still, I had gotten to the point where everything about my life was in doubt. I knew damn well that Mom was my real mother—there was no escaping that—but was Dad my real father?

This is just wild speculation on my part, and I know it. I do look like Dad—I see myself in his face—and I feel his spirit inside me, but I think I also bear a resemblance to, say, Yves Montand (or, for that matter, Alfred Hitchcock—now there's a scary thought). The point is, I'll never know for sure. And if he wasn't my father, wouldn't that explain why he was so indifferent to me, why he was so eager to use me as a pawn and sacrifice my security and sense of identity for his own gain?

Traditionally, a Japanese Zen garden, a *karesansui*, has fifteen stones, so carefully arranged that you can see only fourteen of them at a time; you can never see that fifteenth stone.

That's how it is with people and relationships. There's always that fifteenth stone you can't see, but you know it's there. And when you find it, the fifteenth stone, that secret thing that explains all, you look back and you realize that another stone has disappeared. You can never see a person, or a relationship, or a life, whole. There are too many angles.

So, no, I still don't understand my mother. Every time I find out something new about her, something else gets hidden.

It has taken me this long to realize that I don't *need* to understand her. She's on her journey, and I'm on mine. Our lives may intersect at crucial points, but there's no reason to expect them to run side by side, on parallel tracks. Mom's spirit bounces all over the universe like a jet-powered pinball, and every now and then it settles beside me for a moment before some visionary impulse shoots it off again. I'm just a stop on the road: she doesn't need me, not at all, and she isn't going to pretend for propriety's sake that she does. She's off fulfilling her destiny.

That doesn't mean I don't feel the absence of her love deeply and keenly. It's just that I understand the situation now. My mother is Shirley MacLaine: a show-business icon; a brilliant, talented, legendary performer. That's who she is, and that's how I have to deal with her. I have to forget that she's my mom, because we can never connect on those terms She never said she was going to take care of me and be there when I needed her. That's something I came up with on my own. We can't blame people for being true to themselves.

In the final scene of *The Apartment*, Jack Lemmon professes his total love for Mom's character, and she shrugs it off lightly with the famous line "Shut up and deal." That phrase may crystallize Mom's response to human relationships more than Billy Wilder or anyone could have imagined. I don't want to hear about your problems, I don't want to hear about your love, I don't want to be bothered. Just shut up and deal.

I'm trying.

People will often say to me, "Shirley MacLaine is your mother? I love her! You are so lucky!"

They're right. I am. I'm very lucky, and I say that with no heavy-handed sarcasm or postmodern irony. I'm lucky, because I'm here. I survived.

And through it all, I still have my optimism, and my basic faith in people. I really do. I haven't become jaded or bitter. No, I still see the world in a positive, hopeful light. Maybe Dad would have said that's because I'm an idiot. If so, I embrace my idiocy. Mom doesn't mind looking like a fool for the sake of her beliefs, so, hey, neither do I.

Looking back over my life, I see that it's full of providential moments, moments of serendipity and grace. Whenever things seemed desolate, whenever I was poised to capsize, something unexpected always came along to help me out.

I think of Eguchi-san, with her fox gods and her brown underwear, teaching me to be Japanese; my beloved David, teaching me to be American; Peggy Feury, teaching me to be an actress; that kindly old prostitute in Trieste; the Yugoslavian couple in the Zagreb hotel; Shigeko in Honolulu; Margo Tolmer in Sydney; the waitresses at the noodle shop—all of them, angels who alighted on my shoulder at just the right time.

And I think of my two wonderful children, the bright beacons of my future. They fill my life with light, and I cherish and love them unconditionally. What could be luckier than that?

Frankie is basically a man now—at six feet tall, he towers over me—and he's thoughtful and responsible beyond his sixteen years. From early on, he's always showed remarkable empathy for others, and more than once he's given me his strong shoulder to lean upon. Following my lead, he's in boarding school now, but I have no doubt he'll navigate those tricky, complicated waters far better than I did.

Arin and I have a glorious mother-daughter relationship—by which I mean we argue a lot. We fight over boundaries; we scream and shout at each other. I give her hell, and she slams the door in my face. I treasure those insane moments. Some mothers might get frustrated and angry with the day-to-day struggle, but I love it, because it's something I never had with my mom. I didn't get the chance to be surly with her, or annoying, or heartbroken, or any of those cool teenage things.

My little girl is fourteen years old now, and so far we still enjoy each other's company. We like to walk around town, stroll along the beach hand in hand, get ice cream. She goes for vanilla-chocolate swirl. Sometimes she asks me for advice, and sometimes I ask her. Sometimes we laugh at something silly, laugh until we cry. Sometimes we're just totally quiet together.

And every now and then, when there's a big storm coming across the river, we open the window shades and cuddle up in bed and I tell her a story:

"Once upon a time, there was a beautiful princess, who lived on top of the tallest mountain in the world. And she was known as Princess Lightning. Because when she was happy she would laugh a merry laugh, and a great flash of lightning would flood the sky . . ."

So yes, I'm pretty lucky. I am.

ACKNOWLEDGMENTS

In summing up a life, there are so many people to give thanks for. Many of the guiding lights of my life are gone now, and many others I've lost touch with over the years; but their spirits, and the spirits of all who have lifted me and given me inspiration, are always there, filling my heart with their presence and guiding me along my path.

First of all, I really should thank my mother and father for giving me my existence, for loving me as best they could, and for supplying me with so much good material.

Thanks also to my marvelous acting teacher, Peggy Feury, who so long ago told me to "write that book." She planted the seed.

My school friend Yuki was indispensable in filling in the blanks and giving context to incidents that I understood only incompletely. She was a great help in putting the puzzle together.

A special remembrance to the late Dale Olson, who showed such courage and candor in coming forward and clearing up one of the central mysteries of my life. He and his partner, Gene Harbin, were always sweet and wonderful to me, and I will never forget their kindness.

I'm eternally grateful to Linda Konner, my literary agent, who took the idea for this book and ran with it. Linda's enthusiasm, persistence, and professional savvy were a blessing to me, and I was so lucky to find her. Let me also thank Suzanne Collins and Rosemary Stimola for their help in bringing Linda and me together.

I'm indebted to the people at Gotham Books for their belief in this project and their willingness to take a chance on an unknown writer. Special thanks to my editor, Lauren Marino, and her assistant, Susan Barnes, for guiding me through the publishing process with patience and humor, and giving shape and drive to the narrative. Without them, this book wouldn't be what it is.

The writing of this book coincided with a very difficult time in my life, and I want to thank all those people who rallied around me and gave me the strength to move forward when it would have been so easy to give up. Without the emotional support of these special people, I never could have kept my focus on the positives in life and made it to the finish line.

So thanks to Don Kelly, my suave, charming Irish-Italian pal from the Bronx, who provided a third eye and a helping hand and gave me a newfound confidence whenever I was faltering. He never allowed me to wallow in defeatism, and helped me take responsibility for my own life. I owe him so much.

Thanks also to Jim Noble, my acting mentor and dear friend, who supported my ambitions and stood by me in the toughest times, and who leads always by the example of his own grace and elegance.

Thanks to my fellow actress Joanna Keylock, who provided passion and perspective and always a sense of loving acceptance; her husband, Lee, whose straight-talking common sense saved me from many a headstrong mistake; and Barbara Parker, a great friend, who has never failed to bolster my self-esteem and celebrate my female strength.

Thanks to the very talented playwright Susan Cinoman, for giving me the idea for the one-woman show *Lucky Me*, which got me started on this revelatory journey. My thanks also to the Irish Arts Center, the Great Neck Arts Center, and the Burgdorf Cultural Center in Maplewood, New Jersey, who all produced readings of the play. It was a great thrill to share my story with an audience, and to feel them connect with me. I'm especially grateful to those audience members who insisted, "You have to turn this into a book!"

The Theatre Artists Workshop in Norwalk, Connecticut, where I worked on my one-woman show, has been a haven and an invaluable resource for me and so many other actors and writers. I consider it in many ways my artistic home, and I cherish the many friendships I made there. I particularly want to thank Barbara Rhoades, who insisted in her no-nonsense way that I get my butt back onstage, and the late Brett Somers, whose salty wit and warmth made every visit to the workshop a joy. I can still hear her voice today, and it never fails to make me smile.

Jean Bernard, my therapist, has been with me for more years than I care to remember. Her insight and calm have always been a steadying rock for me to lean on. My gratitude to her knows no bounds.

About my cowriter, Fred Stroppel, I struggle to find the words. Simply put, without him there would be no book. Not only is he a brilliant, insanely talented writer who sometimes seemed to be living inside my head, but it was also his tireless devotion to this project, along with a bottomless well of patience, persistence, and belief, that made it all happen. Whenever doubt came flooding in, he created a working environment that allowed me to feel safe and free. He has become my brother.

I would also like to thank Fred's wife, Liz. Her utter trust in our partnership allowed me to stay emotionally available throughout the writing process. She is a treasure.

My final thanks go to the two people closest to my heart: my children, Arin and Frankie. They taught me what true love is.

As always I find it more natural to express my deepest feelings in Japanese, so to all of you, and to everyone who has touched my life and given it light, I offer a very humble and grateful *domo arigato.*